Black Working Wives

Black Working Wives

PIONEERS OF THE AMERICAN FAMILY REVOLUTION

BART LANDRY

UNIVERSITY OF CALIFORNIA PRESS
Berkeley   Los Angeles   London

The publisher gratefully acknowledges the generous contribution to this book provided by the George Gund Foundation.

University of California Press
Berkeley and Los Angeles, California

University of California Press, Ltd.
London, England

© 2000 by the Regents of the University of California

Library of Congress Cataloging-in-Publication Data

Landry, Bart.
    Black working wives : pioneers of the American family revolution /
Bart Landry.
        p.   cm. — (The George Gund Foundation imprint in African
American studies)
    Includes bibliographical references and index.
    ISBN 0-520-21826-4 (cloth : alk. paper)
    1. Dual-career families—United States—History.   2. Afro-
American families—United States—History.   3. Afro-American
women—Employment—United States—History.   4. Married
women—Employment—United States—History.   I. Title. II. Series.
HQ536 .L335   2000
306.85'0973—dc21

                                                            00-023856

Manufactured in the United States of America

09   08   07   06   05   04   03   02   01   00

10   9   8   7   6   5   4   3   2   1

The paper used in this publication meets the minimum requirements of
ANSI/NISO Z39.48-1992 (R 1997) (Permanence of Paper). ⊚

For Elizabeth,
For my sister Albertine,
And for Ayo once more

Contents

Illustrations

Preface

When I had completed writing my previous book, *The New Black Middle Class*, I realized that a considerable amount of data on families I had collected had not fit into a general study of the black middle class. I began planning a second book that would focus specifically on black middle-class families. I turned to this project fully intending to examine black middle-class families, but unsure how I wanted to shape this new study. My first paper on the topic, presented while a fellow at the Woodrow Wilson Center, was a demographic profile of black middle-class families. As I continued my research, however, I was surprised how, like a character in a novel, the study soon took on a life of its own. It became an investigation of family change and the roles of the ideologies of black and white womanhood in the transformation from the "traditional" family to the modern two-earner family.

I'm not quite sure how this change in focus occurred. But one day while examining statistics on the employment of wives, I noticed that the employment rates of black wives were about ten years ahead of those of white wives. This observation piqued my curiosity and turned my thoughts in a new direction. What is going on here? I wondered. I suspected that there was more to this difference than the conventional explanation of greater economic need among black families. But was my hunch correct, and how could I identify which factors were at work?

I began by contacting a number of historian friends for leads to material on the employment of black wives in the nineteenth and early twentieth centuries. The clues to the puzzle, I believed, would be found much earlier than the mid-twentieth-century period of the statistics I had been examining. Darlene Clark Hine and Sharon Harley were very helpful in my initial historical sleuthing. I began with their suggestions and also turned to general works on women's history, then on to contemporary sociological studies of women's employment. I have always been interested in history and had even once been tempted to enter that field instead of sociology. So I found the search fascinating. I was impressed by the rich historical studies I encountered and in the process "discovered" the cult of domesticity. But I also encountered Mary Church Terrell, Maggie Lena Walker, Ida B. Wells-Barnett, and many other black middle-class women who, though middle class and married, pursued active careers. At last I felt I was on to something. These women could have followed the cult of domesticity, but chose not to. Why? Eventually I came to the conclusion that they envisioned a different life for themselves, a life in which they were not only married but were also active in their communities and had careers. These were truly amazing women. Some even anticipated by half a century the practice of hyphenating their names upon marriage.

Being a sociologist, however, I could not stop there. As persuasive as the historical record appeared, I needed to test my hunch with more contemporary empirical data. So I turned to the United States census, which provided large enough samples of blacks and whites for the detailed analysis required. Using these data, I was able to go back as far as 1940 for most of my study.

Analyzing more than fifty years of census data was daunting and required endless hours of computer work. The census data had to be reformatted, and for assistance with this task I owe a large debt of gratitude to Michael Wagner, Matthew Farrelly, and David Consiglio. I am also indebted to a number of students—Lynda Chobchean, Shari Dwarkin,

Amanda Foster, and Rose Kreider—who at different times assisted me in creating dozens and dozens of graphs, most of which do not appear in the final text but were important in providing valuable insights into the data. Kishi Animashaun gave me much appreciated assistance in typing up the endnotes and bibliography.

At various stages of this work, which lasted over ten years, I received invaluable financial assistance. I should first of all acknowledge support from the Woodrow Wilson International Center for Scholars in Washington, D.C., where I began this study and spent a delightful year as a fellow. There were also two wonderfully productive years as a fellow at the Joint Center for Political and Economic Studies, founded by Eddie Williams, in downtown Washington, D.C. At different times small grants from the Ford Foundation, the Spencer Foundation, and the Smithsonian Institution also supported my study. Last, but certainly not least, I am indebted to the generous backing of the computer science center at the University of Maryland. Without access to hundreds of hours of computer time I certainly could not have written this book.

The final document has benefited from the suggestions of a number of readers. Andrew Cherlin and my colleague Stan Presser gave generously of their time in reviewing most of the manuscript and offering important suggestions. I also wish to thank my colleague Suzanne Bianchi for reading and commenting on chapter 5, and Rosalyn Terborg-Penn for reading chapter 4 and pointing me to additional historical sources. A long conversation with Phillip Morgan directed me to still other neglected sources. I am also indebted to the comments of a number of anonymous readers. And I wish to thank my daughter, Ayo, for some helpful comments on chapter 1. I am grateful for Susan Bilek's many hours of typing and editing of the notes and bibliography and for assistance in developing the index. The speed with which she executes these tasks always amazes me. Ed Dager receives special thanks for his continuous support and encouragement over the years, though he sometimes wondered why I was taking so long to complete the book. Just when I thought I was done, Sue Heinemann at the University of California Press gave the manuscript a most thorough reading and offered many suggestions that led me to tighten my argument here or improve on wording there. I am grateful for her thoroughness and insightful comments. Her knowledge of women's history helped me plug some holes that otherwise might have proven embarrassing. My thanks also to Lisa Kinney, who provided editorial comments at an early writing stage, and to John Joerschke for the final editing. Both were very helpful. Finally, I am pleased to have Stan Holwitz as my editor at the University of California Press. His interest in and support of this project has been unflagging over the many years it took to complete. In the last analysis, of course, I alone am responsible for the contents.

Introduction

This is a book about two-parent black and white families. In a time when we commonly read about single-parent families, the breakup of families through divorce, and a long litany of the ills besetting the contemporary family, a study of "intact" black and white families may at first seem anachronistic. Yet two-parent families not only remain the norm but the statistical majority among white and—until very recently—black families as well. Because two-parent nuclear families have been the normative pattern throughout United States history and remain the measuring rod for any discussion of families today, they deserve our careful attention.[1] Indeed, we need to look closely at all the past misinformation about the American family and the continuing myths—especially about black families.

This is also a book about the changes that have taken place in the two-parent family, particularly in the middle class, over the past century and a half, and it reveals the distinct roles that black and white ideologies of womanhood have had in these changes. Reading the popular press and much of the scholarly literature often leaves the impression that rising divorce rates, teenage pregnancies, and an increase in female-headed families are the principal family stories today. These are of course important developments of the late twentieth century, not so much from the fact of their existence but because of their commonplaceness today. Yet a persuasive case can be made that the real headline stories involve the transformation of the two-parent family system itself, a transformation that is nothing short of revolutionary, irrevocably altering our very way of life. If we compare the lives of men, women, and children in the 1950s and earlier with the lives of their counterparts today, we observe riveting contrasts. Lives then and lives today often appear to have little in common.

Then, men went out to work and women mostly remained at home. Today, both husbands and wives are likely to be in the workforce. Then, husbands were heads of their families and wives and children their subordinates. Today, the ideal has shifted to egalitarian relationships and the shared headship of families. Then, children could usually count on Mom's being at home with Popsicles and Kool-Aid after school. Today, many are in day care or are latchkey kids.

Commentators have mourned and even decried these changes, claiming they signal nothing less than the disappearance of the traditional American family. The traditional family, they believe, provided a kind of stability through the rigid gender roles assigned spouses. Husbands were providers and heads of their families; wives were homemakers, the keepers of the hearth. Children grew up with clear pictures of their futures. Girls and boys were socialized in gender-defined roles, nurtured by fairy tales of knights in shining armor rescuing helpless damsels. The prince had a knack of appearing just at the propitious moment to whisk some endangered maiden away to the safety and bliss of his castle. Men were strong and masterful; women soft and vulnerable. Men went out to conquer the dangers of the world; women waited for their return. Unquestioned, this all seemed right. Was there any other way to live? Hadn't it always been that way? And wasn't it best?

No, it was not always that way. The "traditional" family of the 1950s was at that time only about one hundred years old. Women were not always seen as weak and helpless; men were not always supposed to be the sole breadwinners. The traditional family was a by-product of the mid-nineteenth-century industrial revolution. By separating the workplace from the home it robbed women of the productive roles they had played in the preindustrial world. When the industrial revolution created jobs in factories and offices, away from the home, many husbands went out to work while their wives remained at home. A "cult of domesticity" transformed what was becoming a way of life for a small, white upper middle class—probably no more than 3 percent of all families in the mid-nineteenth century—into *the* ideology of family life for the entire country. In the eyes of their proponents, these new family values were sanctioned by God and nature. I suspect that they are the "family values" some long for today and underlie the myth of a tranquil time when we allegedly lived in three-generation extended families like the Waltons.

But the traditional family exploited men and oppressed women. It placed on men's shoulders the often impossible task of supporting a family with jobs ill-suited for the purpose. The inability of most men to support their families in some comfort on a working-class salary challenged their manhood and their self-esteem. Women's destiny from birth to be housewives discouraged them from developing their talents. Higher education was thought to be injurious to their mental health, and productive work careers were held beyond their social reach. Motherhood and domesticity were their lot.

Generations of working-class males struggled vainly to live up to an upper-middle-class ideal that was out of their reach, while their wives led lives of quiet desperation attempting to run a household on their husbands' meager incomes. Their own aspirations were constricted by the four walls of domestic life. The struggle of their husbands on brutal factory floors seeped into their homes and family life, rendering it sterile and often joyless. As the Lynds found in their study of Middletown (Muncie, Indiana) in the 1920s, the average marriage was "a dreary one, especially for the working class," whose conformity to the domestic ideology meant "making do" with the husbands' inadequate income and the small additions that wives earned from washing other people's clothing.[2] Working-class husbands and wives lived separate lives with little companionship or emotional support from each other as they had often done in the late nineteenth century.

While upper-class and upper-middle-class husbands gained satisfaction, status, and power from careers in the professions or in management, their wives had scant more opportunities than working-class wives to develop their talents. Their domestic labor might be lightened by servants and by the new household technology, but their world, like that of working-class wives, was constrained by the home. While society sang the paeans of motherhood and domestic bliss, the seclusion and restrictions of their roles often took an emotional toll on these white upper- and upper-middle-class women. Many developed symptoms of "the fashionable female disease," a psychological debilitation called neurasthenia.[3] Today it would probably be perceived as severe depression or anxiety neurosis. Historian Alice Kessler-Harris writes of "symptoms of hysteria" developed by some white middle-class wives.[4] As remedies, nineteenth-century physicians prescribed either "rest" in a sanatorium designed for this purpose or (ironically) increased domesticity.

Some of these women managed to escape domestic confinement and restrictions through volunteer and charitable work—under the cloak of extending their maternal role. According to historian Mary P. Ryan in *Womanhood in America*, every new venture beyond the home, from Jane Addams's settlement house work to the suffrage movement, sought legitimacy through maternal rhetoric: "the mother of the race, the guardian of its helpless infancy" must keep watch over the ballot box.[5] This in itself was testimony to the iron grip of domesticity over the lives of nineteenth- and early-twentieth-century white middle-class women.

With the benefit of hindsight, we can see that even upper-class and upper-middle-class white males paid a heavy price for their adherence to the traditional model of the family. For all the prestige, satisfaction, and even power derived from the work world, they remained "underdeveloped" as human beings and as parents. In a very real sense, in the traditional family each spouse played a role that left him or her "half a person." A division of labor is not in itself bad: division of labor in the market enhances production, and specialization can be efficient. But when specialization becomes too rigid, closing the door to further development of the person, it stultifies rather than enlarges.

THE PASSING OF THE TRADITIONAL FAMILY

Today the traditional family has all but disappeared. Spousal roles are no longer rigidly segregated, as most wives—including many with small children—share the breadwinner's role, and most husbands contribute at least a small percentage of their time to housework and child care. The employment of wives outside the family, I argue in this book, has been the major catalyst for family change, and black middle-class wives initiated this trend long before white middle-class wives embraced it.

For wives, the rewards of employment—the increased income, prestige, and power—are immediate and tangible. What husbands gain from participating more in home life is less overt, however valuable (consider the joys and frustrations of parenting, for instance), and the loss of control and dominance in the family is all too obvious. Wives have therefore led the movement toward the modern, more egalitarian family, with husbands often reluctantly following and sometimes doggedly resisting. This "new" modern family structure—though more egalitarian and nourishing of the whole person—is not without its own set of challenges, including time constraints, stress, and parenting dilemmas. Because of these hurdles, the family's future can only be glimpsed. Many changes, particularly in the workplace and in the role of husbands, must occur before the modern family is fully institutionalized.

The Role of Black and White Ideologies of Womanhood

In the making of the modern family, black and white families have played different roles at different times. As I intend to show, beginning in the late nineteenth century, black middle-class wives pioneered an egalitarian ideology of the family that contrasted sharply with the cult of domesticity so prominent among whites. Instead of following the prevailing segregation of women to the private sphere, with only men allowed entry into the public sphere, black middle-class wives championed a "three-fold commitment" to family, community, and careers. In doing so they offered a different version of "true womanhood," one white women eventually adopted in the 1960s and 1970s. I am not suggesting that white women "borrowed" feminist ideology of the 1960s and 1970s directly from black women (although they were certainly influenced by the civil rights movement). Such is the reality of race in the United States that most white women were unaware of the norms of womanhood and family in the black community. What I am contending is that black women got there first and independently. For that reason I argue that black middle-class families were the pioneers of the American family revolution, a revolution that has ushered in a new and more egalitarian era of spousal relationships.

THE STATISTICS ON FAMILIES TODAY

As I already noted, the two-parent family has been and remains the norm for American family life, in spite of the recent proliferation of single-parent families and the growth in cohabitation. Many researchers and commentators have pointed to the decline in the percentage of two-parent families or the rapidly increasing percentage of female-headed families as indicators of a deterioration in family life and family values. But these percentages do not present the complete picture; they obscure the fact that two-parent families have continued to *increase in number* among both blacks and whites, even as single-parent families have multiplied. In other words, it is not as though there existed a finite number of two-parent families and that a large percentage of them were becoming single parents. Rather, single-parent families have grown in number as two-parent families continued increasing. In 1960, for example, there were 36.2 million white and 3.1 million black two-parent families; by 1996 these had increased to 47.9 million and 3.8 million, respectively (see table A1 in appendix A for more detail).

A great deal of ink has been spilled in writings about the increase of black female-headed families. In the mid-1960s sociologist Daniel P. Moynihan made headlines with his claim that "the Negro community has been forced into a matriarchal structure," which he traced back to slavery.[6] Historians have strongly refuted this claim, showing that both during slavery and in the decades following emancipation, 75.0 percent or more of black families were headed by two parents.[7] As census data confirm, two-parent families continued to predominate among African Americans well into the twentieth century. In 1965, the year Moynihan wrote his policy paper on black families, 73.1 percent of black families were still headed by two parents.

Figures 1 and 2 portray changes in the percentages of two-parent and single-parent black and white families from 1960 to 1996.[8] As late as 1970, only 18.7 percent of black families fit the definition of a female-headed family (a female adult householder living with her own children under eighteen). Another 1.5 percent were headed by single males, and 11.8 percent were made up of related adults ("other"), but over two-thirds (68 percent) of black families were still headed by two parents. Since only 24 percent of black couple families were in the middle class in 1970, this statistic indicates that two-parent families were still very common within the working class, including those who were poor.

The growth of all single-parent families (both male- and female-headed) was rather modest before 1970, averaging 6.6 percent among blacks and 3.1 percent among whites per year in the 1960s (see table A1 in appendix A).[9] Female-headed families then increased an average of 9.7 and 7.8 percent per year, respectively, for blacks and whites in the 1970s. The sharp rise in single-parent families, especially those headed by women, therefore, dates only to the 1970s. At least for female-headed families, this growth rate declined sharply in the 1980s, to 2.6 and 2.0 percent per year among blacks and whites, respectively. This growth rate continued declining among blacks in the 1990s, but increased slightly among whites. Moreover, since 1980 the overall percentage of female-headed families has not changed significantly, although there has been a slight increase among whites.[10]

What should we make of all these statistics? Certainly, single-parent families have increased significantly since 1970, during a period that has

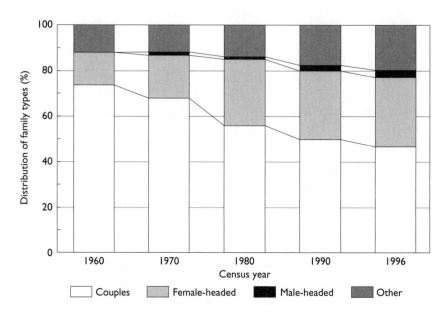

FIGURE 1.   Change in Black Family Types, 1960–1996

SOURCES: U.S. Census, P-10, no. 53; P-20–480, adapted from Table F

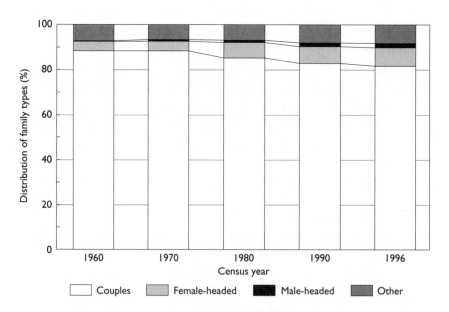

FIGURE 2.   Change in White Family Types, 1960–1996

SOURCES: U.S. Census, P-20, no. 53; P-20–480, adapted from Table F

seen rising rates of divorce and out-of-wedlock births. But we should not lose sight of how many two-parent families remain nor of the fact that their numbers continue to grow. In 1996, among whites, more than eight out of ten families had two parents. Although this ratio was much lower among blacks, almost half (48.9 percent) of black families were still headed by couples. Rather than focus on an alleged breakdown of the two-parent family among blacks or whites, then, we must conclude that a variety of factors have combined to *add* a large number of single-parent families to existing couple households. Since this development dates primarily to the 1970s we must look to external conditions at that time rather than to anything internal to the black—or white—communities or to past history. A sharp economic downturn and growing joblessness among those without college degrees—as well as a growing acceptance of divorce and premarital sex—must certainly count prominently among the contributing factors.

It seems worthwhile, therefore, to examine what is going on within the many couple families that *do* exist. Have these families remained the same in the past half-century, when so many other things have changed? Or have there been important shifts within these families that raise different policy issues for America's future? In a way, to look only at single-parent families is to see only the jar half empty. For a fuller picture, we need to also pay attention to the jar half full, to the two-parent families that are still alive and well. By understanding their dynamics and needs, we may be better able to serve their interests.

SOME COMMENTS ON CLASS

Throughout this book I point to differences between not only black and white families but also middle-class and working-class families. What is my definition of "class"? Class is a slippery concept accompanied by much confusion in the minds of both scholars and the general public. As I pointed out in *The New Black Middle Class*, the concept is frequently confused with "status."[11] In the sociological tradition of Max Weber, "status" refers to a person's subjective standing in the eyes of the community—it is an evaluation of a person's reputation, a measure of the degree of respect with which she or he is viewed. Wealth, occupation, and income contribute to a person's status, but other less tangible factors such as family background, behavior, and lifestyle have as much or even more to do with a person's status. Thus a person with considerable wealth may receive little respect because his or her lifestyle meets widespread disapproval, while a humanitarian like Mother Teresa may be held in very high esteem.

A person's class position, in contrast, is independent of the subjective views of others. It is acquired or inherited. Great wealth places one in the upper class regardless of one's behavior. Likewise one's position on the occupational ladder puts one in a particular class independently of the opinions of one's neighbors and friends. Class is therefore an objective position in an economic hierarchy, while status is a subjective position in a hierarchy of honor and reputation. Yet even with this distinction, there is some confusion over the measurement of class position. When talking to reporters who are writing about the middle class, I am repeatedly pressed to define middle class by income boundaries. "How much do you have to make to be in the middle class?" is the typical question.

Economists writing about the middle class tend to define it by income boundaries. The problem with this approach is that the upper and lower boundaries are arbitrary and without intrinsic sociological meaning—whether they are anchored around the median or some distance above the poverty line. Sociologically—again following the tradition of Max Weber—"class" refers to a person's position in the property (wealth) or labor (occupation) markets. Great wealth, such as that held by those in the Forbes 400 list, places one unambiguously in the upper class.[12] For those without great wealth, their position in the job market, their occupation, determines their economic position or living standard, and, therefore, their class.

Within this Weberian tradition, those with white-collar occupations have come to be identified as the "middle class," while those holding manual, blue-collar jobs are "working class." Consider how people at parties ask about a person's occupation as a means of determining her or his general economic standing. We have a general idea of the income attached to individual—or at least groups of—occupations, and we are also aware that some are more stable and have greater potential for mobility: a step up a ladder rather than a dead-end job. White-collar jobs tend to also have superior fringe benefits, and their occupants enjoy higher status. That white-collar occupations are no longer as secure as they were before the 1970s in no way changes their relative position in the occupational hierarchy. For every executive who receives a pink slip, many more blue-collar workers receive an unemployment check. An individual's class position, therefore, is a factor of the package of economic returns attached to an occupation: income, degree of stability, mobility opportunities, and fringe benefits.

The middle and working classes can be further divided into upper and lower, with professionals and managers forming the upper middle class and sales and clerical workers in the lower middle class.[13] Among blue-collar workers, the skilled and semiskilled fall into what I call the skilled working class and those with unskilled manual or service jobs into the unskilled working class. Each "stratum" (division within a class) can be distinguished by varying economic fortunes resulting from the average package of economic return to its members. These economic fortunes vary from the enviable living standards of top professionals and managers to the near-poverty or poverty of the unskilled. At any given moment one may be able to establish a statistical income boundary of the existing members of a particular class or stratum. But these boundaries shift constantly as new entrants begin at higher (or lower) incomes than their predecessors or as incomes rise or fall with promotions and inflation.

Defining Family Class

Traditionally a married woman's social standing in the community and her class position stemmed from those of her husband.[14] Likewise the family's status and class derived from those of the husband as head of the household. As more and more married women entered the labor force, this approach became less and less tenable. For that reason I have taken the approach that when both husband and wife are employed full time the family's class and status come from their *combined* individual class

and status positions. If both have the same class position (both professionals, both factory workers), they codetermine the family's class. When
their class positions are unequal, I have assigned to the family the class
of the spouse in the higher individual class—whether husband or wife.
An engineer husband (professional) with a secretary wife (clerical) places
his family in the upper middle class. Likewise, a wife who is a teacher
(professional) married to an assembly line worker (working class) locates
her family in the middle class. Although it is common for the husband to
determine his family's class by virtue of his own higher class, in a significant percentage of middle-class families—both white and black—the
wife determines her family's class.[15]

TRACING THE FAMILY REVOLUTION

As I have already indicated, to understand how United States families
are changing today, we must comprehend their history and, in particular, the origins of our concept of the "traditional" family. The book thus
begins by examining the emergence of the traditional family, with its cult
of domesticity, in the nineteenth century; its revival during the late 1940s
and 1950s; and its waning after 1960. As a counterpoint to the prevailing
white middle-class notions of family, in chapter 2 I discuss the black family system as it developed during slavery and following emancipation,
and I investigate how the growing urban black working class in the late
nineteenth and early twentieth centuries responded to the cult of domesticity. Then, in chapter 3, I explore in depth the competing ideology of
womanhood developed by black middle-class women starting in the late
nineteenth century. As their writings, as well as their lives, reveal, these
black women redefined womanhood and pioneered the dual-career,
modern family. Just how this modern paradigm of the family has spread
among blacks and whites since 1940, as well as how the differing ideologies of womanhood have affected this spread, is demonstrated by using
United States census data in chapter 4. A close look at data on the changing roles of wives and husbands clarifies the shift to the new paradigm
of the modern family. Dual-career couples in particular can be viewed

as the prototypes of the modern family, and as chapter 5 documents, black couples led the way. Another indicator of the move to the modern family paradigm, detailed in chapter 6, is the wife's increasing economic contribution to the family, in terms of income. Turning to the husband's contributions, chapter 7 examines the degree to which husbands have increased their share of housework and child care. Throughout the presentation of statistical findings, differences between black and white families emerge. But what do all the findings mean for families in the new millennium? In the conclusion to this book, I speculate about the future of the modern two-earner family, offering three possible scenarios and suggesting the kinds of societal changes that must occur to provide the support needed for the modern family to thrive rather than merely survive.

1 The Rise and Fall of the Traditional Family

The "traditional" American family is no more. Many of us struggling with today's complexities long for the seemingly simpler, more tranquil and satisfying family life of the past. To some this peaceful and orderly but distant past is represented by *The Waltons*, that long-running, popular 1970s television series of a three-generation midwestern rural family. For other Americans it is the entertaining television images of family life in the 1950s that conjure up the past. But as historian Stephanie Coontz notes, "Contrary to popular opinion, 'Leave it to Beaver' was not a documentary."[1] Nor for that matter was *Ozzie and Harriet* typical of family life earlier in the twentieth century or even in the 1950s. Beneath the television myths of the 1950s lay significant variations among American families. The movement of white middle-class families into the suburbs, though in full swing, included only a minority of white families at that

14

time and almost no black families. The postwar prosperity and expanding consumerism that were rapidly transforming the United States into an affluent society remained out of reach for the 25 percent of Americans who were poor.[2]

Still, the constant in the 1950s and earlier decades was the image of the family as a unit with two parents who fulfilled very different roles: breadwinning and homemaking. Underneath all the rosy images and myths of the 1950s the expectations for spousal roles were clear. A woman's place was in the home and a man's in the workplace. Never mind that many white upper-middle-class suburban housewives turned to alcohol to numb themselves from the frustrations of their limited roles and their isolation from a stimulating urban environment.[3] Or that one woman, reminiscing about her life in the 1950s, described a life of "booze, bowling, bridge, and boredom."[4] Those wives who dared to push against the boundaries of their proper domestic role were subjected to harsh criticism from the "authorities" of the day and the popular media. In the mid-1950s *Esquire* and *Life* magazines referred to working wives as a "menace" and to their employment as a "disease."[5] To these "experts" and social commentators, society would survive only if women kept their proper place. If they did not—well, awful things like juvenile delinquency would happen. A popular 1947 book by Ferdinand Lundberg and Marynia Farnham, *Modern Woman: The Lost Sex,* condemned feminism as "a deep illness," warned of the danger of masculinization that career women faced, and predicted "enormously dangerous consequences to the home [and] . . . children" caused by working wives and mothers.[6]

In spite of the tenacity with which many in society trumpeted what had become proper "traditional" spousal roles and in spite of their warnings of social anarchy if these roles changed, change did come. And with change came anxiety and confusion along with growth and liberation. By the early 1970s provocative titles began peppering the writings of social scientists: "The Future of Marriage"; "Does the Family Have a Future?"; "The Family Today: Is It an Endangered Species?"; and "The Family: Is It Obsolete?"[7] In the ensuing decades academics and journalists alike ritualistically began most articles on the family with a list of changes they saw occurring, changes that caused them to question the very survival of the institutions of marriage and family. One scholar asked, "Will marriage continue to exist in some form we can recognize?"[8] Another fretted, "Can the traditional nuclear family created by the legal act of marriage survive?"[9]

Several social scientists in the 1970s seemed already resigned to the impending demise of the family. The only question remaining was the timing of its inevitable end. "The family has endured from the Stone Age to the Space Age," wrote Edward Cornish in "The Future of the Family." "Today it faces greater challenges than ever before in history, and its continued existence can no longer be taken for granted."[10] Even more pessimistically, in 1971 Susan Keller wrote, "Hard as it may seem, perhaps some day we will cease to relate to families, just as we no longer relate ourselves to clans, and instead be bound up with some new, as yet unnamed principle of human association."[11]

Black families came in for an especially high dose of pessimism, beginning with the Moynihan Report in 1965, a controversial policy paper written for the Johnson administration that set the agenda for a debate about black families for decades.[12] In this policy paper sociologist Daniel Patrick Moynihan characterized black "lower-class" families as "highly unstable" and "matriarchal" and wondered about their imminent "breakdown."[13] Subsequent popular writings on black families generally failed to even make Moynihan's distinction between middle-class and "lower-class" families, expressing alarm over the state of *the* black family.

While black families have received an unusually high degree of negative press since the Moynihan Report, the earlier quotations reflect a more general angst during the past thirty years over the future of the American family. The American family system has certainly changed. But change and diversity are hardly new to families. Over the past 200 years American families have experienced two major transformations in the way members function and relate to each other and the larger society. The first shift occurred during the transition from a preindustrial to an industrial society in the first half of the nineteenth century; the second parallels the emergence of our postindustrial service economy in the twentieth century. In each transformation there have been wide variations across both class and race.[14] In the early nineteenth century it was white upper-middle-class families who led the way, introducing the cult of domesticity and ushering in what became known in the twentieth century as the "traditional" family. In the late nineteenth and early twentieth centuries it was black upper-middle-class wives who developed a new ideology of womanhood and in the process pioneered the model of the modern dual-career and dual-earner family. But it was not until the 1970s, following the social, cultural, and political upheavals of the 1960s and the emergence of the feminist movement, that white women abandoned the traditional family of the nineteenth century. In doing so they were not directly imitating black families. Rather, they were belatedly discovering what black women had already experienced, namely, that paid employment outside the home was the only path to equality both in and outside the home. The result has been a revolution that has completely transformed the American family.

DEFINING A FAMILY REVOLUTION

Pessimism about the future of the family during the 1970s was prompted primarily by the sharp rise in divorce rates. As demographers pored over tables of statistics in the late 1970s and early 1980s, they made a startling discovery. People were exiting marriages almost as rapidly as others were entering them. If the then-current divorce trends continued, the demographers predicted, half of all marriages contracted beginning in the late 1970s would eventually end in divorce, a far cry from 1940, when only one in four marriages ended that way.

The 1980s brought more change: a continued increase in single-parent families, delayed marriages, and a consequent growth in single households. By 1985 the median age at first marriage had risen to 25.5 years for men and 23.3 years for women, up from 23.2 years for men and 20.8 years for women in 1970.[15] With delayed marriage and divorce came an 80-percent growth in cohabitation, from 1,589,000 households in 1980 to 2,856,000 by 1990.[16] But in spite of the catchy sound bites such statistics make for the six o'clock news and popular talk shows, the late-twentieth-century family revolution lies not in the increase in single-parent families or even in the high divorce rate (which decreased to 40 percent in the 1990s). Nor is it to be found in the postponement of marriage or increasing cohabitation. While these are all important developments, by themselves they do not challenge or alter the basic functioning of the traditional family. Rather, the family revolution consists of a radical reshaping of the traditional two-parent nuclear family itself.

The philosopher Thomas Kuhn defined a scientific revolution as "noncumulative developmental episodes in which an older paradigm is replaced in whole or in part by an *incompatible* new one." [17] We might think of a paradigm as a design for living, a combination of values, attitudes, behaviors, and definitions of appropriate and expected behavior. In this case the paradigm that has been replaced includes the values, attitudes, and behaviors that defined spousal roles in the normative two-parent family from the mid-1850s to the 1950s. From this point of view, we can call the changes that have been occurring in the American family system a revolution. By 1996 only 21 percent of all families conformed to the traditional ideal of the nuclear family composed of a breadwinner father, an unemployed housewife, and children.[18]

Although there are wide variations among different classes and racial/ethnic groups, there is no doubt that spousal roles have been irreversibly transformed, so much so that the dual-worker family has now become the norm for families. In spite of newspaper headlines about the *new motherhood,* in spite of the stresses and strains accompanying this new model of the family, wives and mothers continue their movement into the labor force, with no signs of turning back. And they are making substantial contributions to their families' economies. In all classes and all racial/ethnic groups, dual-worker families now predominate.

ORIGINS OF THE TRADITIONAL FAMILY

To fully understand the extent of this revolution in family functioning, we must first explore the origins and development of the traditional family. Historians now agree that the traditional family as we came to know and practice it in the United States had its roots in English common law of the tenth or eleventh century, which at that time reflected Christian beliefs about marriage.[19] Christianity defined marriage as a monogamous holy union, a "sacrament." Those who chose to enter this union committed themselves to a lifetime together and to the procreation of children. Equally important and consequential, the spousal relationship was to be hierarchical. The husband was the legal head of the family; his wife and children his subordinates. This hierarchical relationship would one day be reflected in a bride's promise to "love, honor, and *obey*." Oblivious of this vow's origin in the English "common-law doctrine of coverture which established the legal fiction that a husband and wife took on a single legal identity upon marriage—the identity of the husband,"[20] brides eagerly gave up their own family names to assume those of their husbands and counted themselves lucky to become a new person, Mrs. John Smith or Mrs. Smith. Witnesses to the power of socialization, most wives and husbands took for granted the many legal ramifications of the subordinate status of wives, such as their inability to enter into independent contracts or to own and dispose of property.

This legal tradition also sanctioned a division of labor in the family based on gender. The husband was to be the family's provider, the wife its caretaker, the person responsible for the upkeep of the home, the nurturing of children, and the meeting of her husband's needs. In twentieth-century speech, this reality has been captured in catchy descriptions of the husband "ruling the roost" or "wearing the pants."

In practical terms, traditional family roles represented an unrealistic division of labor mandated more by theology and philosophy than by family needs. Prior to the nineteenth century, in the labor-intensive agricultural societies of preindustrial times when survival depended on the contributions of wives and children as well as husbands, only the nobility and the more successful merchants could adhere to this ideal of a strict division of labor. Most Europeans made their livelihood from small farms or crafts in urban centers. In these preindustrial economies, wives and children as well as husbands performed productive roles. Husbands were more likely to work in the field and at the various crafts, while wives wove material and made clothing for the family; produced candles, soap, linen, and other small items for the home; and cared for small children. The care of children, however, was not entirely a female role, since at an early age boys began working side by side with their fathers and girls with their mothers. Not infrequently, children left home to work as apprentices, domestics, or farm hands. The money earned was sent home as their contribution to the family economy. After describing the household economy of preindustrial Europe, three historians concluded, "In city and country, among propertied and propertyless, women of the popular classes had a vital economic role which gave them a recognized and powerful position within the household. . . . We *can* say . . . that women in these families were neither dependent nor powerless."[21]

Like their European counterparts, colonial families in Massachusetts, Pennsylvania, Maryland, and the other colonies were productive units. Recent historical research has uncovered evidence of a wide range of work performed by colonial women both inside and outside the home. The former included, as in Europe, the production of goods consumed by the family, but also much that was sold to others. Although historians argue about the extent of the sexual division of labor during colonial times and the typical work of males and females, there is no doubt that women engaged in a wide variety of activities outside the home.[22] They served as proprietors of taverns, innkeepers, teachers, tailors, and printers. Many of these women were widows with children and had no alternative means of support. But many male entrepreneurs found the assistance of their wives necessary for the success of the enterprise.

Underlying this discussion is the important fact that colonial families, like their European preindustrial counterparts, functioned as economic units in which all members had productive roles. Though the elements of the traditional family were clearly in place and sanctioned by law and religion during the seventeenth and eighteenth centuries, preindustrial economies limited their full adoption in all but a small circle of upper-class families.

INDUSTRIALIZATION SPAWNS DOMESTICITY AND THE GOOD PROVIDER ROLE

The catalyst for the expansion of the traditional family paradigm in the United States was the separation of the workplace from the home during the industrial revolution in the early nineteenth century. Although the majority of white males in 1800 were independent farmers or urban artisans, by the 1830s the first factories had begun to appear, and growing cities created a need for additional wage labor.[23] What was once a temporary position while a man waited for his chance to start a small family business or purchase land for tilling soon became the permanent condition of increasing numbers of American males. By 1870 the proportion of males working as wage laborers in the increasingly numerous factories and mines had risen to 61 percent, while that of the old middle class of independent farmers and artisans had declined from 80 to 33 percent.[24] The advent of large corporations created out of the first wave of mergers at the turn of the twentieth century increased the need for office managers and clerks, accountants and secretaries.[25] These and other salaried and independent professionals formed the core of a new urban middle class, who, like wage laborers, worked outside their homes.

It was the segregation of the work site from the home, historians now agree, that eventually led to an increasingly rigid separation of spousal roles. This process occurred rapidly after 1830 in the Northeast and Midwest, but with considerable variation between the middle and working classes. In the small middle class of this period, which foreshadowed the later emergence of the "new"[26] urban middle class of salaried workers in the late nineteenth century, the husband's ability to earn sufficient income to support his family's needs transformed him into what Jessie Bernard has called the "good provider."[27] Already by the 1840s and 1850s urban wives could now purchase in stores the yards of cloth that it once took hours to weave in the home. Soon other commodities such as soap, candles, and brooms could be found in urban stores, eliminating (for those who could afford it) the need for home production for personal use and for the rural cottage industry. The good provider became the husband who could earn enough income for his family to live in relative comfort, purchasing the goods they consumed. In the process the productive roles of wives and children disappeared. Middle-class homes became units of consumption rather than production. In such homes, the period of childhood grew longer and the wife's activities became increasingly confined to the nurturing of children, the care of the home, and the husband's needs. Women became housewives and full-time mothers. The collective economic unit and the shared productive roles of husbands, wives, and children were replaced by a rigid division of labor once found only in the upper class. The family pattern that was to become "traditional" in the twentieth century was born.

The Cult of Domesticity

On balance, these developments enhanced the position of men while diminishing that of women. In a world in which prestige and power were increasingly awarded to those who held occupations and earned income in the marketplace, middle-class wives found few avenues to either personal prestige or power. In the home the preindustrial shared economic partnership of spouses gave way to a distinction between paid and unpaid work. Housework became devalued because it was unpaid labor, and wives became dependent upon the earning power of their husbands. Even though women were accorded a lower status than men in preindustrial colonial societies, wives wielded a certain degree of power by virtue of their productive role in the family.[28] The relationship between spouses was one of mutual dependency borne out of their joint contribution to the family economic unit. Now the balance had decidedly tipped in favor of the husband, who became head not only legally but by virtue of his role as sole provider.

Such an unequal system required justification and persuasion if women were to acquiesce to it. This justification was found in a new ideology that began to appear in women's magazines, religious literature, and guidebooks to wifehood and motherhood between 1830 and 1860. "True Womanhood," these guidebooks emphasized, was to be found in the home, in the nurturing of children, and in the care of husbands. Marriage and motherhood were thus the proper—and even divinely ordained—roles of women. The women's magazines and religious sermons never tired of repeating this message with appropriate advice on the best ways to carry out these roles. Of motherhood, women read that "the best pleasures of a woman's life are to be found in the faithful discharge of her maternal duties."[29] On the faithful and selfless discharge of this duty depended the "future of civilization" itself.[30] It was even the source of power—at least vicarious power—through the later achievements of sons who became statesmen and business leaders.[31] Such an important role was, of course, a full-time job.

This emphasis on motherhood does not appear unusual today. Certainly it was taken for granted by women in the 1940s and 1950s. Historian Barbara Easton points out, however, that it would have sounded strange to their colonial ancestors of the seventeenth and eighteenth centuries. For them, motherhood was not the sole role of women, but rather blended with their many other roles in the interdependent households of the time: "In Puritan tracts on family life, men and women were as likely to be referred to as 'heads of the household' or 'parents,' as they were to be spoken of as 'husbands and wives' or 'mothers and fathers.' In these tracts there was little discussion of 'motherhood' or, for that matter 'fatherhood.'"[32] By the 1840s, however, motherhood was becoming for the middle-class white urban woman a full-time preoccupation with awesome implications for society. "Oh, mother," admonished one minister in 1850, "acquit thyself well in thy humble sphere, for thou mayest affect the world."[33]

Equally important to the women's magazine writers and ministers in the nineteenth century were a woman's responsibilities to her husband, who was portrayed as her undisputed superior, to whom she must be ever submissive and attentive. She was to support him in all he did and maintain his home as a haven to which he could retreat after the struggles of the day. As one minister urged, "How interesting and important are the duties devolved on females as WIVES . . . the counsellor and friend of the husband; who makes it her daily study to lighten his cares, to soothe his sorrows, and to augment his joys; who, like a guardian angel, watches over his interests, warns him against dangers, comforts him under trials; and by her pious, assiduous, and attractive deportment, constantly endeavors to render him more virtuous, more useful, more honourable, and more happy."[34]

The word that best captures the new roles of the nineteenth-century middle-class white woman is *domesticity*. To adequately discharge her sacred duties as wife and mother, she had to set aside all outside distractions and be willing to center all her energies on the home. In his treatise on *The Young Wife,* William Alcott wrote in 1837, "She cannot discharge the duties of a wife, much less those of a mother, unless she prefers home to all other places and is only led abroad from a sense of duty, and not from choice." [35] To prepare themselves for this role, girls were schooled in the decorative arts of needlework and floral arrangements, as well as the social graces appropriate for home entertainment. They were not to be too concerned about higher intellectual pursuits beyond the secondary level, however. That was an area reserved for their fathers, brothers, and future husbands.

Together with domesticity, the most important characteristic urged on those who would be true women was submissiveness. Young women were admonished in the most solemn tones at the beginning of their marriage, "Oh, young and lovely bride, watch well the first moments when your will conflicts with his to whom God and society have given the control. Reverence his *wishes* even when you do not his *opinions.*" [36] This theme of dependency and inferiority was ubiquitous in the literature of the 1830s and 1840s. "True feminine genius," wrote one author, "is ever timid, doubtful, and clingingly dependent; a perpetual childhood." [37] Another wrote, "A really sensible woman feels her dependence. She does what she can, but she is conscious of inferiority, and therefore grateful for support." [38] Today, when I read these quotes to my undergraduate students, there are snickers around the classroom. But in the nineteenth century, white middle-class women took this advice seriously.

It was not accidental that domesticity and dependency were being urged upon women in the early decades of the nineteenth century. The new responsibilities of motherhood as a full-time job and the care of the home as a haven for husbands developed to fill the void left by the loss of women's productive roles in the home, as well as a means of ensuring the dominance of men in an industrializing society. These new roles called for a different set of characteristics from those expected of preindustrial women. In place of the self-reliance, creativity, and resourcefulness required of women on small farms and urban households during colonial times, nineteenth-century urban women were urged to develop delicate graces and to cultivate the virtues of purity, piety, submissiveness, and domesticity. They were to shift from producing goods, which contributed to the survival of the entire family, to supporting the husband's productive role, upon which they were now completely dependent. By mid-nineteenth century, white women in the emerging urban middle-class were becoming consumers and household managers rather than valued producers. Although still a small percentage of the American population at the time, these families would influence family norms far beyond their numbers.[39]

As Barbara Easton points out, there was an alternative to domesticity: "As women's productive work was moved from the home to the factory, married women as well as single could have gone to work in the factories. Women could have gone to work in the towns as storekeepers, artisans, and professionals. Children could have been cared for in nurseries and kindergartens, by grandparents, or by their fathers."[40] Had wives been allowed to work outside the home, this rigid segregation of gender roles into domestic and productive spheres would not have developed and the traditional family would not have taken root in the middle and working classes.

EXCEPTIONS TO DOMESTICITY

In spite of its great influence, the ideology of domesticity was not a complete success. This was in part because its immediate target was the educated white middle class and in part because it did not fit the life experiences of working-class families. Additionally, a small number of white middle-class women active in the abolitionist movement also had feminist leanings. The reluctance of abolitionist groups generally to accept women in leadership roles, and in particular the refusal of the 1840 World Anti-Slavery Convention in London to seat women delegates led to the first attempt to organize a feminist movement.[41] Eight years later Elizabeth Cady Stanton organized the Seneca Falls Convention with the support of Lucretia Mott, who had been refused seating at the London Anti-Slavery Convention. Neither had experience in such an undertaking, and in the end the support of Frederick Douglass probably proved decisive in buoying Stanton's courage. The meeting was held in a Wesleyan chapel with many local farmers, women and men, attending. The proposal was broad, including a call for the franchise. Although this meeting is seen as the birth of the women's movement, it did not slow the tide of domesticity that swept up most white middle-class women and men in its path.

The women's magazines, religious literature, sermons, and books on womanhood and motherhood published between 1830 and 1860 were ubiquitous and drowned out the voices of feminists. Written for the white educated women of the middle class, who increasingly had time on their hands, they stridently promoted the cult of domesticity. Working-class women, especially immigrant and black working-class women, either lacked the literacy skills to read these treatises or were too engulfed by the struggle to make ends meet to find time for them. This does not mean that they were not influenced by this new ideology. They were, often through the working-class press. But, as historian Mary Ryan notes, they had "neither the pretense nor the possibility of conforming to the middle-class model of womanhood."[42]

For farm families, for the emerging native-born white working class, and especially for the immigrants who began arriving by the millions, family life continued the interdependence of the preindustrial era. A large proportion of the two and a half million immigrants who came from Ireland, Germany, and other parts of northwestern Europe between 1820 and 1860 settled on small farms. For them, the family's survival continued to depend upon the work of wives and children as well as husbands. As the pace of industrialization increased, however, more and more immigrants settled in cities. By the time the immigrant mix changed from northwestern Europeans to Italians, Jews, Poles, and others from southern and eastern Europe near the end of the century, the United States had become an industrialized nation. Most of these 22 million newcomers were unskilled workers who settled in the large industrial cities and mining towns of the northeast. The unskilled jobs at which most of these men toiled typically paid wages sufficient for the support of only one person.

When Henry Ford introduced his $5.00 a day wage in 1914 to reduce turnover, increase productivity, and avoid unionization, he did so under the guise of providing married men a "family wage," a wage that would eliminate the need for their wives' employment.[43] For those workers lucky enough to be employed in a Ford factory, this wage represented the culmination of the mostly unsuccessful struggle of working-class males throughout the nineteenth century to persuade employers to raise their wages to a level adequate for their families' support. Other Detroit auto workers at this time were not so fortunate, earning only the going wage of about $2.40 a day, a level that required additional income from family members to lift them out of poverty. Though workers continued to fight for a family wage, Martha May concludes, "Based on research to date in several fields, it seems clear that the [Ford Motor Company] family wage was an isolated, rather than a national, achievement for male workers."[44] In addition to low incomes, working-class males often experienced high unemployment rates. As a result, a large segment of working-class white families throughout the nineteenth and early twentieth centuries lived in poverty. The gap had to be filled through the combined efforts of other family members. One United States Senate study of workers in mining and manufacturing in 1913 found that only 38 percent of immigrant families were supported completely by husbands.[45]

Where suitable work for women was available, as in the textile mills of New England, working-class women often remained employed until marriage or the birth of their first child. Thereafter their employment was influenced by a variety of factors such as their husbands' occupation, the employment of teenage children, or their immigrant status.[46] Families headed by husbands who held unskilled jobs had a greater economic need, and these wives were more likely to be employed than those whose husbands were skilled craftsmen. But mothers with small children who needed to work could do so only if they could make suitable child care arrangements, typically care by a relative or an older child.

Nevertheless, even in the white working class, the cult of domesticity eventually took roots, as can be seen from a comparison of the employment patterns of native-born white working-class wives and immigrant wives in the late nineteenth and early twentieth centuries. Not yet fully aware of societal norms, wives in first-generation immigrant families were the most likely to be employed outside the home, but by the second generation, according to historian Tamara Hareven, "American values of domesticity had become dominant" and these wives also tended to remain home.[47] Americanization had a powerful influence on immigrants eager to be accepted in their adopted country. When these working-class wives remained home, however, other strategies were typically needed to supplement the husbands' income.

For these families, the preindustrial practice of truncated childhoods interrupted by work was the common practice. Young working-class girls and boys began toiling in their early teens or even sooner and contributed their meager earnings to the family pool.[48] Writing about working-class families in a small New Hampshire mill town in 1900, Hareven notes that employed children in their teens and early twenties who lived at home typically contributed "most, if not all, of their earnings to their families."[49] Reminiscing on his experience as an employed teenager, Thomas Bergeron commented, "He [Bergeron's father] always kept the $40 I gave him. He wouldn't give it to me. The old days it was that way. . . . Once in a while he'd give us a couple of dollars."[50] For these immigrant families (and for many native-born working-class families as well), educating their children beyond elementary school was a luxury they could ill afford. In 1890 fewer than one in ten were attending school.[51] Nationally in 1900, almost 20 percent of children aged 10 to 15 worked.[52] In some cities the figures were as high as 50 percent in some immigrant groups. Another survey of immigrant working girls in Pennsylvania in 1925 found an average of 2.4 workers per household.[53]

Taking in boarders became another working-class family strategy for supplementing the husband's income without wives leaving the home. In 1901 a Bureau of Labor Statistics study found that wives in nearly one-fourth of the urban families studied earned over one-third of the average annual family income by caring for boarders. In a study of working-class families in Pittsburgh in the late nineteenth century, historian S. J. Kleinberg paints a gloomy picture of these wives' life of drudgery. Cooking for boarders and the male members of the family often meant that "the millworker's wife rose at 5 or 6 A.M. to prepare breakfast. She continued cooking throughout the day, as men returned from the mills, children came home from school, and lunch buckets had to be prepared. Each man expected a hot dinner when he returned home."[54] Another study in 1907 found that half of all families in New York City took in one or more boarders.[55] Work at home, whether in the form of piecework or the care of boarders, was the typical compromise to maintaining a traditional family life among a large percentage of working-class white families at this time.

For most immigrant families, the overcrowded, unsanitary tenements in urban ghettoes were unlikely breeding grounds for the practice of the new domesticity. Mothers carrying buckets of water up three flights of stairs for cooking or waiting with children in line to use a communal bathtub had little time to devote to floral arrangements and needlepoint. Nor were long years of work in New England textile factories, endless hours bent over sewing machines in the garment district of New York City, or the ordeal of nineteenth- and early-twentieth-century domestic work a proper socialization for "true womanhood." Yet, by the late 1800s, domesticity had become part of the American ideology of family life rather than merely an ideology of the middle class. It was embraced by immigrants in the Americanization process as a goal to strive for, even while it was impossible to practice fully.

In time working-class immigrant husbands came to view the challenge to keep their wives at home as a test of their manhood and proof of their success as husbands. Young immigrant girls looked forward to the day when marriage would rescue them from the drudgery of low-paying factory or domestic work, and wives worked outside the home only as a last resort, returning to the home as soon as feasible. It was understood that widows, poor women, and black women (for reasons that will be discussed in chapter 3) were exempted from this ideal; but for middle-class and most working-class white women, work outside the home involved a loss of status and a sign of failure on the part of the male breadwinner.

Domesticity under Fire

In a sense, the traditional family has always walked a tightrope. Before the nineteenth century it was a way of life accessible only to the upper class. In the nineteenth and early twentieth centuries it could be comfortably lived only by the upper middle class, a small minority of all families. In the mid-nineteenth century the white middle class could hardly have comprised more than about 3 percent of the United States population. By 1910 only 24 percent of whites and 3 percent of blacks belonged to the middle class, and even fewer to the upper-middle class.[56] And though white working-class families accepted and practiced the cult of domestic-ity as often as possible, they did so by sacrificing the more adequate liv-ing standard they would have enjoyed had wives entered the labor force. It was a curious dilemma, a catch-22, that new immigrants and other white working-class families faced. To become true Americans meant adopting the ideal of the traditional family with rigidly differentiated spousal roles. At the same time, the low wages of working-class hus-bands made this a choice accompanied by a severe economic penalty—a lower living standard or outright poverty. It was a dilemma that was only partially alleviated by the compromise of sending children out into the workforce and taking in boarders.

At the turn of the twentieth century, therefore, the ideology of domes-ticity was still overwhelmingly effective. Although 75 percent of white families belonged to the working class or lived on a farm, only 3 percent of white married women worked outside the home in 1900. By the time society came to accept single women in the workplace in the 1920s, the percentage of employed white wives had risen to only 7 percent. In 1900, and for the next fifty years, a white family typically had to be in desperate straits for wives to brave the social stigma of working outside the home.[57]

Black wives, however, worked outside the home in large numbers at this time. Nationally, according to the United States Census, about 26 percent of black wives were employed outside the home in 1900.[58] But in some cities the proportion of employed black wives reached 65 per-cent.[59] Why black wives worked outside the home in such large num-bers in the early twentieth century while white wives of all classes over-whelmingly stayed home is one of the major questions addressed in this book. Although conventional wisdom suggests a straightforward eco-nomic motivation, I believe that the reason is far more complex. Spe-cifically, I contend, as I will detail in chapter 3, that just as a particular ideology of white womanhood influenced white wives' employment decisions, so too a particular ideology of black womanhood, developed within the black community, shaped black wives' orientation to paid work. In the course of their activities for racial uplift, as they spoke their minds and lived out their lives, black upper-middle-class wives developed and promulgated their own unique conception of true womanhood. It was a conception that united rather than separated the public and private spheres, a conception that championed a wider role for married women than domesticity. It argued for equality in marriage and valued employment as the key to achieving equality in marriage and society as well as to *fulfilling* lives for themselves. As we shall see, these upper-middle-class black wives embodied this ideal in dual-career marriages and urged their working-class sisters to follow their lead in accepting employment as a legitimate part of their roles as women. First, however, it is important to examine the development of black family life, especially in the postemancipation period, in both rural and urban areas.

2 Black Families: A Challenge to the Traditional Family Paradigm

Conservatives who opposed the employment of wives and mothers in the 1970s on the grounds that their employment outside the home would imperil traditional family relations were correct. They did not, however, notice that this "tradition" had been undermined long before the 1960s and 1970s. By exempting black wives from the cult of domesticity and the definition of "true womanhood," white society had made it easier for black families to depart from the nineteenth-century paradigm of the family and develop an alternative.

As they emerged from slavery, African Americans faced formidable obstacles in their attempts to preserve a two-parent family system they had developed and nurtured in spite of oppressive conditions. Freed from the constraints of the master-slave relationship, they looked forward to enacting their own strategy for survival and for the allocation of family roles. Because of the continued importance of cotton to the United States economy, however, the South and the North—through the Freedmen's Bureau—colluded to deny blacks property ownership and to define black wives as part of the agricultural labor force needed to rebuild the southern economy. Without land and faced with restrictive laws limiting their geographic mobility, most black families in the South had no choice initially but to submit to the peonage of the sharecropping system.

THE BLACK FAMILY IN SLAVERY

In *The Negro Family in the United States,* an otherwise solid work, E. Franklin Frazier argued that, deprived of their African culture, slaves had no choice but to develop a family system that was at best a weak and imperfect imitation of their masters'. With ultimate authority resting with slave masters, Frazier alleged, black males became mere shadowy figures. After the Civil War, in the absence of the authority and watchful eye of slave masters, even this "compromise" supposedly fell apart. In place of the stable two-parent family evident among whites, Frazier maintained, there arose a family system anchored in motherhood, a matriarchal system frequently including three generations of women.

But as historian Herbert Gutman has demonstrated, this image of the black family was constructed mainly out of conjecture and the flimsiest of "evidence"—"six pieces of historical evidence for the critical decades between 1870 and 1900: a letter from the Yankee schoolteacher Elizabeth Botume, an extract from A. T. Morgan's semifictional memoir *Yazoo* (1884), and two quotations each from Philip A. Bruce's *The Plantation Negro as Freedman* (1889) and J. Bradford Law's Department of Labor study, 'The Negroes of Cinclaire Central Factory and Calumet Plantation' (1902)."[1] Yet this image of a weak, female-headed black family structure dominated both social science and popular beliefs about black families well into the 1970s. In fact, this myth became the cornerstone of Daniel Patrick Moynihan's influential policy paper on the black family for the Johnson administration in 1965.[2]

Not until the publication of Herbert Gutman's groundbreaking study

in 1976, *The Black Family in Slavery and Freedom 1750–1925*, was this view
of the black family seriously challenged—indeed, fully discredited. Bas-
ing his study on the painstaking reconstruction and analysis of plantation records, Freedmen's Bureau records, and several United States
censuses, Gutman developed a picture of African American families during slavery and freedom quite at variance with the prevailing myth. He
demonstrated that, though severely constrained by an oppressive system
bent on extracting every ounce of labor from their weary bodies, slaves
nevertheless *acted* on their own behalf in the "spaces" allowed them.

The most important of these actions was the construction of a community that developed a culture of its own, a culture transmitted across
many generations of slaves throughout the South.[3] At the heart of this
community was a strong family and kinship system, marked by firm
bonds of intimacy, love, caring, and two-parent nuclear families. The role
of slaves in constructing their own family and kinship systems can be
seen in a variety of examples. For instance, slaves had a taboo against
first-cousin marriages, in contrast to this practice among the families of
white southern planters.[4] Also notable was slaves' practice of naming
children after their fathers or other relatives in the kin network, such as
uncles, aunts, and grandparents, indicating the existence of an enlarged
kin network. Naming sons after their fathers, Gutman points out, was a
practice "sufficiently powerful to affect behavior in the immediate post-
emancipation decades."[5]

Although their marriages were not legally recognized, slaves typically
considered them permanent unless terminated by death or the sale of
a spouse.[6] Many marriages endured with spouses belonging to different
masters and living on separate plantations in the same vicinity. When
separated by distances too great for visiting or by sale, spouses mourned
for each other and often communicated by letters dictated to others. The
pain accompanying separation is reflected in letters penned both before
and after the sale of a spouse. One husband living on a neighboring plantation who was being sold wrote to his wife:

> My Dear wife I take the pleasure of writing you these few [lines] with
> much regret to inform you that I am Sold to a man by the name of Peter-
> son atreader and Stays in new orleans. I am here yet But I expect to go

before long but when I get there I will write and let you know where I am. My dear I want to Send you Some things but I donot know who to Send them By but I will thry to get them to you and my children. Give my love to my father & mother and tell them good Bye for me. and if we Shall not meet in this world I hope to meet in heaven. My Dear wife for you and my Children my pen cannot Express the griffe I feel to be parted from you all I remain your truly husband until Death Abream Scriven.[7]

In one of the most touching exchanges between a husband and wife who had been separated by the sale of the wife and children before the Civil War, the husband, who had remarried, exchanged several letters with his former wife. In one letter, after expressing his grief over the sad turn of events, he added, "Send me some of the children's hair in a separate paper with their names on the paper."[8]

Gutman found ample evidence of long-lived slave marriages in the records of the Freedmen's Bureau. Among ex-slaves who registered marriages in North Carolina in 1866, for instance, 27 percent had been married from 10 to 19 years, 22 percent for more than 20 years, and 9 percent for over 30 years.[9] Records from other parts of the South revealed similarly enduring unions everywhere. Not only were slave marriages long-lasting, but fully three-fourths of slave families were headed by two parents.[10]

Contrary to the opinions of Frazier and other writers, slave husbands and fathers exercised authority within the slave community and family even though deprived of ultimate authority within the slave system. According to Gutman, the practice of naming sons for their fathers in itself "strongly disputes frequent assertions that assign a negligible role to slave fathers."[11] There is also evidence that black church rules required wives to take a submissive role.[12] The assertiveness of black males during the Civil War and their protective actions on behalf of their families also suggests that these men must have held an important place in their families during slavery.

Thousands of ex-slaves volunteered to fight in the Union Army, a fact that, in itself, demonstrates the assertiveness of male slaves. However, their temporary absence from their families coupled with their service in the cause of freedom often led to reprisals from slave owners against their families. Thousands of letters exchanged between ex-slave Union soldiers and their wives attest to their deep affection for each other and their grief at being separated. In less than a year, at least five thousand letters were written for illiterate black soldiers at Camp Nelson in Kentucky in 1864.[13]

Ex-slave wives with their children frequently visited their husbands in military camps, and thousands more fled plantations to join their husbands. Sometimes they were allowed to remain in camp, but frequently unsympathetic Union officers sent them away without shelter or adequate clothing. Ex-slave soldiers cared for their families as best they could under these circumstances. They frequently protested the mistreatment of their wives and children, and on one occasion threatened mutiny when a special order required that their wives leave the city of Natchez.[14] Regarding this incident, Gutman comments, "The ex-slave soldiers acted decisively. The first night after Kelly's edict was enforced, fifteen deserted their regiments. Three days later, other ex-slave soldiers, their exact number unknown, told their commanding officer that 'they could no longer endure the trial of seeing their wives and children driven into the streets, and if he would not at once interfere and protect them they should *positively* do it themselves.'"[15] A few days later the order was modified, and after some weeks several commanders were removed. These could not have been the actions of men unaccustomed to playing a major role in family affairs during slavery.

THE BLACK FAMILY IN JEOPARDY

Following the Civil War, black families in the South were placed in greater jeopardy than at any time in their existence in the United States. Many ex-slave soldiers, upon returning to get their wives and children, were physically abused, shot at, and run off by planters irate at the loss of their cheap labor supply. When some wives attempted to leave plantations to join their husbands, their ex-masters refused to allow them to take their children under threat of "jail or death."[16]

A further threat to black families was the sexual exploitation of black women. "Military occupation and emancipation," Gutman explains, "unsettled the exploitative sexual ties that had bound unknown numbers of slave women to owners and other whites."[17] Both during and immediately after the war, black women continued to be sexually abused by whites. The summer of 1865 was particularly bad for black women, prompting a black Mobile correspondent for the New Orleans *Tribune* to plead with federal authorities for the protection of black women, warning, "We have sworn before God to protect inviolate our wives and daughters."[18] Black women frequently complained on their own behalf to the Freedmen's Bureau about continued sexual exploitation by white men. So serious was the problem that black delegates to the Mississippi and Arkansas Constitutional Conventions urged passage of stringent laws against concubinage. Not surprisingly, their efforts were unsuccessful.[19]

Forced indenture of children proved to be yet another attempt by white planters to limit the freedom and integrity of ex-slave families and retain a supply of cheap labor. Before the Civil War, many states had "apprenticeship laws" that gave local judges the power to forcibly remove children of free blacks from their homes, under the guise that a child could be better cared for by a white person. Immediately upon emancipation, whites all over the South invoked such laws to obtain free labor, even if it was only from children. Safeguards such as parental consent were generally ignored, so that thousands of families found their children forcibly removed from their homes and bound over to whites in a state of virtual slavery. The numerous complaints of parents generally went unheeded, and the practice continued until the Supreme Court struck it down in 1867.[20]

The Strength of Ex-Slave Families

In spite of these considerable obstacles, ex-slaves managed to preserve the strong family system they had created during slavery. As historian Jacqueline Jones states, "Though the black family suffered a series of disruptions provoked by Confederates and Yankees alike, it emerged as a strong and vital institution once the conflict had ended."[21] At no time did ex-slaves falter in their commitment to the two-parent family. All over the South, thousands of couples came forward to legalize their marriages by registering them with the Freedmen's Bureau during and immediately following the close of the Civil War. In so doing, ex-slaves demonstrated their commitment to their current spouses as well as to the institution of marriage. Where the payment of a fee was required, they often presented as payment some commodity such as "six eggs" or a "quart of strawberries."[22] The eagerness with which they came forward to register their marriages in the spring of 1866 led one judge in Greensboro, North Carolina, to remark, "Let the marriage bonds be dissolved throughout the State of New York to-day, and it may be doubted if as large a proportion of her intelligent white citizens would choose again their old partners."[23] About a year earlier a Union Army officer in Mississippi had noted that ex-slaves had "an almost universal anxiety . . . to abide by first connections. Many, both men and women with whom I am acquainted, whose wives or husbands the rebels have driven off, firmly refuse to form new connections, and declare their purpose to keep faith to absent ones."[24]

African Americans continued to register new marriages in the decades following emancipation, demonstrating the effectiveness of traditions passed down over the generations. Even in states such as North Carolina, which permitted common-law marriages, Gutman emphasizes, ex-slaves placed "a high value on legal marriage, at least as high as their urban and rural white neighbors," registering new marriages "in exact proportion to their number in the population."[25]

Evidence from many sources confirms the continuation of the two-parent family among blacks in the decades following emancipation and well into the twentieth century. Gutman, who studied nearly nineteen thousand black households in the North and the South covering the period 1855 to 1880, found that from 70 to 90 percent of black families were headed by two parents.[26] In the South those families included primarily adult blacks who had been born during slavery, a fact that provides strong support for the idea that the two-parent black family system developed during slavery. Researching the same period, Jones found that in 1870 "80 percent of black households in the Cotton Belt included a male head and his wife (a proportion identical to that in the neighboring white population)."[27] Finally, the federal census reveals that this pattern continued among black families in the Cotton Belt of the South to the end of the nineteenth century. Fully 86.4 percent of black families in 1880 and 82.5 percent in 1900 remained dual-parent families.[28]

That the predominance of two-parent black families was not confined to areas of heavy black concentration—such as the South's Cotton Belt— is confirmed by statistics covering the same period for Buffalo, Boston, cities in the Ohio Valley, and Philadelphia. In Buffalo and in seven cities of the Ohio Valley (Steubenville, Wheeling, Marietta, Portsmouth, Pittsburgh, Cincinnati, and Louisville) studied by Paul Lammermeier, the majority of African American households and families were headed by a husband and wife during the 1870s and 1880s.[29] The range of dual-headed families was from 71.5 percent in Cincinnati in 1870 to 85.5 percent in Buffalo in 1875 and in Pittsburgh in 1880.

Similarly high percentages of dual-headed black families were found in Philadelphia for the years 1850 and 1880.[30] This analysis of family structure in Philadelphia is particularly valuable for its comparisons of black families with three groups of whites: Irish immigrants, German immigrants, and native-born whites. The researchers found that although the largest percentage of female-headed families were found among blacks (25.3% in 1880), female headship varied widely among whites, with native-born whites (13.6%) and Irish (12.7%) having the next highest incidence of female-headed families and Germans the lowest (8.3%). These racial differences declined significantly when the economic conditions of blacks and whites were taken into consideration. That is, the poorer the families, the higher the percentage of female heads. Thus, the greater poverty of blacks accounted for some of the difference between blacks and whites. Another contributing factor was the higher male mortality rate among blacks than whites.[31]

For the early twentieth century, historian Kenneth Kusmer's careful analysis of the 1930 census reveals mixed patterns.[32] In some cases the percentage of female-headed families was actually lower among blacks. Thus, women headed 15.4 percent of black and 16.2 percent of native-born white families of foreign or mixed parentage in Buffalo. In Cincinnati, foreign-born whites and blacks had about the same percentage of female-headed families—18.4 and 18.9 percent, respectively. In Cleveland, the percentages were 14.7 percent for native-born whites, 11.7 percent among foreign-born whites, and 17.2 percent among blacks. The highest percentage of black female-headed families (33.7) was found in urban areas of Georgia, while the highest percentage of white female-headed families (23.3) occurred in Cincinnati.

From his investigation of black family structure Gutman concluded, "The typical Afro-American household changed its shape in the half century between 1880 and 1930. But at all times—and in all settings—the typical black household (always a lower-class household) had in it two parents and was not 'unorganized and disorganized.'"[33] Gutman based his conclusion on an analysis of the complete censuses of black populations in a variety of localities in South Carolina, Mississippi, Alabama, and Virginia, as well as Buffalo and New York City in the North.[34]

THE BRIEF RISE AND RAPID FALL OF BLACK DOMESTICITY: WORK AND FAMILY IN THE POST-EMANCIPATION PERIOD

In attempting to redefine their family roles after emancipation, former slaves encountered especially difficult obstacles when their own wishes clashed with the economic interests of southern planters and northern reconstructionists. This was the case when they attempted to redefine their own work roles. During slavery, both males and females had been defined primarily as laborers, of value to masters in proportion to their economic productivity. The roles of husband, wife, father, and mother were secondary. Although slaves, as Gutman has demonstrated, developed a strong two-parent family system, they nevertheless lacked ultimate control over their time and the roles they adopted. In the minds of ex-slaves, therefore, emancipation offered an opportunity to assume control over their own destiny: freedom of movement, freedom to live their lives as they desired, and freedom to determine their own familial roles. This redefinition led large numbers of black wives and mothers to refuse to work in the fields throughout the South, much to the chagrin of southern planters and northern reconstructionists alike.

Southern planters saw this action as an attack on their cheap labor supply. All across the South, planters complained about the refusal of black wives to work. "The women," one lamented, "say that they never mean to do any more outdoor work, that white men support their wives, and they mean that their husbands shall support them."[35] This was not a decision made by wives alone. Planters frequently acknowledged the role of husbands in keeping their wives at home. One Boston cotton broker noted that "planters hiring twenty hands, have to support on an average twenty-five to thirty negro women and children *in idleness,* as the freedmen will not permit their wives and children to work in the fields."[36] Northern reconstructionists were equally dismayed at freedmen's attempts to redefine black women's roles. Rather than embarking on a program of land redistribution to former slave families (the promised forty acres and a mule), they introduced an experiment in "free" black labor to rebuild the South that envisioned the employment of women as well as men.

In reality, this system of contract labor was hardly free, since it deprived African Americans of the right to negotiate for higher wages or go on strike. Typically, contracts contained very restrictive provisions. Workers were confined to the plantation, needed permission to go into town or to visit relatives, had to retire at a certain hour at night, and were bound by contract to work for a year at a time.[37] The reluctance of ex-slaves to return to the plantation fields was overcome by a variety of devices and pressures from both the Freedmen's Bureau and southern legislatures. The Freedmen's Bureau employed both persuasion and pressure. Typical of the first strategy was exhortation by the bureau office in South Carolina: "Freedmen, let not a day pass ere you find some work for your hands to do, and do it with all your might. Plough and plant dig and hoe, cut and gather in the harvest. Let it be seen that where in slavery there was raised a blade of corn or a pound of cotton, in freedom there will be two."[38]

Through a strange twist, "freedom" had taken on a new meaning, quite divergent from that assumed by ex-slaves. Where persuasion failed, punitive vagrancy laws were enacted by southern legislatures with at least the tacit support of the Freedmen's Bureau. These statutes both restricted the movement of freedmen and hindered their efforts to buy or rent land.[39] Nor had blacks entirely escaped the harsh physical punishments of slavery. Black women who remained home often found themselves coerced by hired "riders," who went from cabin to cabin in an attempt to force wives into the fields. And Freedmen's Bureau agents often looked the other way when planters administered physical punishment to workers.

By tying the economic recovery of the South to a system not of land redistribution but of forced contract wage labor utilizing both husbands and wives, the Freedmen's Bureau made it difficult for ex-slaves to redefine their own family roles. Like southern planters, the Freedmen's Bureau was concerned that the wives' preference to remain at home caring for their households and children would "subvert the free labor experiment." Both planters and reconstructionists therefore condemned such domesticity and fostered a view of all black women, including wives and mothers, as laborers. At a time when an ideology of domesticity was being actively promoted for white middle-class women, black women were being defined as part of the agricultural labor force, exempt from the ideals of full-time domesticity and true womanhood. Even northern teachers who came to the South to minister to blacks held the belief that "hard manual labor would refresh the souls of individual black women and men even as it restored the postwar southern economy."[40]

Thus, both planters and reconstructionists spoke in disparaging terms of black women who chose to stay out of the fields. They were criticized for being "out of the field doing nothing," ridiculed for "playing the lady," and considered "idle" and "lazy." Planters complained about the "evil of female loaferism" and worried about the loss of as much as one-third of their labor force. "You will never see three million bales of cotton raised in the South again unless the labor system is improved," complained one Georgia planter.[41] *Improved*, of course, meant returning black wives and children to the fields.

Reconstruction has often been portrayed as a radical northern effort in black empowerment that failed only because of southern intransigence. In reality, the North never fully committed itself to protecting the interests of freed blacks or to providing them with the means of self-sufficiency—land. The much-vaunted forty acres and a mule was never a serious commitment. Even the limited effort to redistribute confiscated Confederate land to freed blacks by Otis Howard, commissioner of the Freedmen's Bureau, was quickly rescinded by order of President Andrew Johnson.[42] Equally unsuccessful was the effort of a group of sixty wealthy blacks in New Orleans early in 1865 to secure land for ex-slaves by leasing abandoned plantations and renting them to freed black families. The experiment came to an abrupt end when the Freedmen's Bureau returned the plantations to their former owners.[43]

The goal of Reconstruction quietly became the rebuilding of the southern economy rather than the creation of independent and self-sufficient freedmen. As sociologist Stephen Steinberg points out, the invention of spinning machinery, the power loom, and finally the cotton gin by Eli Whitney in 1793 raised cotton to the status of the major United States export in the nineteenth century. By 1860 cotton constituted 60 percent of all exports.[44] Cotton was king because it had become the major catalyst for the industrialization of both the United States and England. The growth of the textile industry in the British Isles and the New England states depended on a steady supply of cotton from the South. Economic development in the United States had become linked to the southern cotton economy. In the end, the economic interests of the North won out over the legitimate claims of blacks, and Reconstruction turned to restoring the southern economy and the flow of cotton to foreign markets and northern mills rather than to promoting the independence of blacks.

Under these economic conditions, attempts by black families to conform to the cult of domesticity were short-lived. Jacqueline Jones notes that "the failure of the federal government to institute a comprehensive land confiscation and redistribution program, combined with southern whites' systematic refusal to sell property or extend credit to the former slaves,"[45] doomed their efforts to redefine family roles and conform to the new norms of domesticity. In an agricultural economy, and at a time when land ownership was an important means of achieving self-sufficiency and autonomy, the majority of black families found themselves blocked at every turn. The only feasible option for most freedmen was wage labor on their former plantations.

By 1870, the economic structure of the "New South" had settled into an uneasy compromise. Sharecropping had become the dominant mode of production, defining the relationship between blacks and whites, and black families had become the principal labor force of this system. It was a compromise, historians agree, that met only the minimum desires of planters for a reliable and cheap labor force and of black families for independence in decisions affecting family work roles and geographic mobility. Though the terms of this contractual arrangement varied, a fifty-fifty pattern eventually prevailed, whereby families received small parcels of land to cultivate, along with rations and supplies, in exchange for half the crop. In practice the sharecropping system was as exploitative as contract labor. Sharecroppers were routinely cheated of their meager wages, paid in kind, and forced to buy provisions from the plantation store at inflated prices that frequently left families penniless or in debt at the end of the year.

African American families nevertheless attempted to set their own priorities within the constraints of this system. Although they had not become independent landowners, the sharecropping system at least enabled them to function as family units and exercise a minimum degree of control over the labor of individual members. Wives were assigned primary responsibility for domestic duties, while care of the fields and contact with whites became the major roles of husbands. As acknowledged heads of their families, Jones notes, fathers "had the last word in deciding which children went to the fields, when, and for how long."[46]

In practice, however, black families—91 percent of whom lived in rural areas—resembled preindustrial family units more than the newly emerged white middle-class urban family characterized by rigidly defined breadwinner/homemaker roles. Like preindustrial families, black families functioned as economic units in which the needs of the family typically took precedence over individual desires. Wives, though primarily responsible for home and children, often shifted their efforts between home, field, or other cash-producing activities as family needs dictated, causing overseers to complain about their late arrival to and early departure from the field.

Though it was not uncommon for plantations to rely on the paid labor of women and children, in this period it was chiefly black families—the backbone of the South's plantation economy—upon whom this burden fell. By designing a system that kept blacks poor, planters maintained a cheap, dependent labor pool. Their very poverty made it necessary for wives and children to work to a far greater degree than their white counterparts, who more frequently owned land. Thus in 1870, when over 40 percent of black married women reported jobs to census takers, most as field laborers, 98.4 percent of rural white wives reported that they were "keeping house."[47] Additionally, 24.3 percent of rural black families, compared with only 13.8 percent of white rural families, had at least one child under sixteen who worked outside the home.[48]

BLACK WORKING-CLASS FAMILIES
AND THE CULT OF DOMESTICITY

To escape the virtual peonage to which they were subjected in the rural South, many African American families migrated to the cities. The numbers making this move were not great at first, but blacks had increased to 30 percent of the South's urban population by 1890.[49] Many more left the South altogether. In 1879 some sixty thousand blacks left for Texas, Arkansas, Oklahoma, Nebraska, and Kansas.[50] Perhaps the best documented group are those who journeyed to Kansas, a move referred to by contemporaries as the Great Exodus.[51] From eyewitness accounts and interviews with migrants, these blacks clearly were escaping oppression. They recounted stories of poverty, lynching, rape, and fear of death. For one migrant who left with his wife and two children, it was the fact that he "was never able to buy anything to eat" because he "didn't have any money."[52] Another lamented, "We lived and breathed along. Could barely live and that was all."[53] But more than poverty and the absence of political rights, it was, in the words of Tandy, a black man collecting affidavits from migrants, "the terrors of Mississippi and Louisiana" that drove these blacks to migrate.[54] "I think I am too good a man to stay down there and be killed," one male migrant from Mississippi complained, "and don't intend to do it. Couldn't carry me back South unless they would chain and carry me back."[55]

A deteriorating agricultural economy added to the misery of black families in the late nineteenth and early twentieth centuries, and millions more left the South for the industrial cities of the Midwest and Northeast.[56] A contemporary verse gave voice to the frustrations of southern blacks:

> Boll-weevil in de cotton
> Cut worm in de cotton,
> Debil in de white man,
> Wah's goin' on.[57]

By chance, this exodus peaked just when the labor demand in the North was increasing due to a cut in European immigration during the First World War. In the cities blacks encountered greater diversity and even some increase in educational opportunities for their children. Yet, in both the South and the North, urban black working-class families, like their white counterparts, typically found that a husband's income was inadequate to meet a family's needs. Faced with this situation, however, black and white families pursued different strategies for survival.

The major difference in black and white families' strategies revolved around the cult of domesticity. As we saw in chapter 1, white working-class families, both native-born and immigrant, developed family work strategies that would enable them to *conform* to the cult of domesticity. They were more likely to send children out to work than wives or mothers, and often added income from boarders. Such was the influence of the cult of domesticity on white immigrant families, according to historian Tamara Hareven, that even in Manchester, New Hampshire—a city where jobs for women in textile factories were plentiful—"only almost one-quarter of all wives were employed" in 1900, a proportion that was nevertheless more than four times that for the United States as a whole.[58] Among wives whose husbands were present the employment rate was only 12.6 percent.[59] The low employment rate of white working-class wives did not result from the success of their husbands, as we saw in chapter 1, since at the turn of the century most working-class males—white or black—did not earn sufficient income to support a family.

In the late nineteenth and early twentieth centuries black males often experienced even worse employment conditions than white immigrant males. The firm foothold in the skilled trades that black males had gained during slavery gradually eroded in the decades following emancipation.[60] At the close of the Civil War, although not evenly distributed across all crafts, five out of every six artisans in the South were black.[61] Through a variety of ruses, including barring blacks from unions, denying them work, and enforcing discriminatory licensing statutes, black artisans had been reduced to 5 percent of the southern, urban artisan class by 1900.[62] In the few cities where they were able to maintain a foothold, it was often by accepting lower wages for the same work. Black carpenters, for instance, were paid $1.82 to $2.50 per day, while white carpenters received $2.07 to $4.00 per day.[63] Throughout the South in the late nineteenth century the experience of black males was the same. Discrimination confined them to unskilled labor and locked them out of factory work in the emerging cotton mills. In some southern cities black males suffered high rates of unemployment.[64]

In the industrial cities of the North—Chicago, Philadelphia, Cleveland, New York, Detroit, and Pittsburgh—black males found work but were usually restricted to unskilled labor, the lowest position in the class structure. In Detroit, the great post–Civil War labor demand generated by the automobile and other manufacturing industries was filled almost entirely by white immigrants. In 1910 only twenty-five black males could be found among the ten thousand operatives and laborers in Detroit's automobile factories.[65] When the influx of immigrants was stemmed during the First World War, employers sent recruiters South to fill their labor needs, but often employed these black recruits only in the most unskilled industrial jobs.

The experience of black males in Detroit was repeated in other industrial cities throughout the North, where they were either shut out of the growing number of industrial jobs or employed only in the most unskilled and dangerous work in steel mills, slaughterhouses, meat-packing plants, and other factories. According to historian Herbert Gutman, 86 percent of black males in the Tenderloin and San Juan Hill districts of Manhattan in 1905 were employed as laborers or service workers.[66] Attempts to increase their numbers in the skilled trades were effectively thwarted by discriminatory unions.[67] Prior to the First World War, black males even found themselves edged out of competition by immigrants for choice nonindustrial jobs where they had once held a firm footing—jobs such as barbers, apartment house doormen, elevator operators, and waiters and cooks in expensive hotels.[68]

A Comparison of Black and White Family Strategies

Faced with the need to supplement the husband's income, black working-class families, like comparable white families, employed a variety of strategies. Since the cult of domesticity was not intended to include black women, however, black families were able to create their own survival strategies free of this constraint. Most often, black urban working-class families chose to have wives employed and to send their children to school, such was the emphasis placed on education. Like immigrant families, black families also took in boarders, especially in the North.[69]

In the urban South black women had to content themselves with whatever work was available. Typically this meant employment as domestics and laundresses, low-status work that whites—even immigrant whites—shunned at all costs. By 1900, 90 percent of domestic servants in southern cities were black,[70] as were the majority of laundresses. Domestic work was especially disagreeable, involving a constant struggle between servants attempting to maintain some self-esteem and control over their work and white mistresses bent on extracting as much labor as possible.

Additionally, black wives who worked as domestics found their own roles as wives and mothers undermined while they tended the kitchens and children of white families, often laboring from five or six in the morning to eight at night. When they returned home at the end of this long day, there was often little time left for their own children. Child care during the day was an especially big problem, as their employers frowned on the presence of children at work. Neighbors, relatives, or older siblings had to be relied upon for child care, or the children were left alone to fend for themselves.[71]

As in the South, the family strategy of black working-class families in the North led wives into the labor force far more frequently than native-white or immigrant working-class wives. In 1911, for instance, 54 percent of black wives in Philadelphia were employed, compared with 8 percent of Italian and 28 percent of Irish wives. In New York City during the same year 51 percent of black wives were employed, compared with 30 percent of German and 5 percent of Irish wives.[72] These black wives who worked in northern cities found their opportunities almost as limited as in the South. During the first decades of the twentieth century, a period when immigrant women were abandoning domestic work for factories and native-born white women were moving into clerical and sales work, the majority of black women could find work only as domestics and washer-women. After the First World War, over one-half of domestics in Phila-delphia and more than one-fifth in New York and Chicago were black women.[73]

The few who found work in factories (5.5 percent in 1930 compared with 27.1 percent of immigrant and 19 percent of native-born white women) were confined to the most menial tasks, such as sweeping fac-tory floors, scrubbing equipment, and disposing of refuse.[74] So distaste-ful was domestic work, however, that black women chose these jobs whenever possible. Their attitude was typified by the statement of a black woman working in a Chicago box factory in 1920: "I'll never work in nobody's kitchen but my own any more. No indeed! That's the one thing that makes me stick to this job."[75] In spite of their educational par-ity with the daughters of immigrant and native-born white working-class families, the daughters of black migrants were generally excluded from clerical and sales employment in all but the small black enterprises of the growing northern ghettoes.[76]

Domesticity versus Work

The high rate of employment of black working-class wives compared with their white counterparts did not necessarily indicate a preference for employment among these black women at that time. Given the type of work available to black women in the North and South, they had little

incentive to seek employment, and whenever possible they chose to remain at home, caring for their families. They achieved this as often as
possible by choosing to do laundry in their own homes rather than domestic work in the homes of middle-class whites.[77] Though it involved
grueling, heavy work—boiling, scrubbing, rinsing, starching, and ironing in the hot climate of the South—laundry work at least allowed them
some control over their time and gave mothers the opportunity to remain
at home, where they could care for their children while earning a few
dollars.

In the North this work was complicated by the absence of yards and
front porches for washing and drying clothes and by the small size of urban apartments. Invariably, laundry work made the already difficult task
of keeping order in cramped quarters even more burdensome. In those
households with boarders, black wives found it even more difficult to
balance the demands of boarders, the care of home and children, and
sometimes even laundry work. Yet social workers of the period commented on the efforts of black wives and mothers to create a pleasant,
homelike atmosphere under difficult circumstances. "Even the very poor-
est Negro homes," wrote social worker Helen Tucker of the Pittsburgh
black community, "are usually clean inside and out and have a home-like
air—[there is] always some attempt at ornamentation, oftenest expressed
by a fancy lamp. . . ."[78] In her book on blacks in New York City, *Half a
Man,* Mary Ovington described how black wives "adorned walls with
colorful cards and photographs and found places for knickknacks and
other 'pretty things.'"[79]

Another indication that black working-class wives did not prefer work
at this time is the correlation of their employment rates to their husbands'
employment. Historian Jacqueline Jones notes that black wives' employment varied with the local work opportunities of their husbands. Their
employment rates were especially high in cities like New York (46 percent in 1920), where little else than low-paying service jobs was available
to black males. In cities such as Pittsburgh and Detroit, where higher-
paying industrial jobs could be found, only 25.5 percent of black married
women worked.[80] Unlike white working-class wives, however, these
black working-class wives were motivated to remain at home in this pe-

riod less to conform to the cult of domesticity than to escape oppressive and demeaning work and to be able to care properly for their children.

In the late nineteenth and early twentieth centuries blacks and whites lived in different societal and community environments. While white immigrants often lived in ethnic communities, their work took them into the larger white society. There they encountered the norms of the larger American society as they rubbed shoulders with native-born white workers, sent their children to public schools, often themselves attended Americanization classes, and read the working-class newspapers. These publications reflected for them the values of white middle-class society and paralleled the advice on true womanhood white upper-middle-class wives had received decades earlier. In Pittsburgh, a city dominated by the manufacturing of iron, steel, and glass, *The People's Monthly* praised the life of the workingman's wife as "eminently a home life."[81] Reminiscent of upper-middle-class writers who praised upper-middle-class mothers as the keepers of civilization, the *National Labor Tribune* enthused that the faithful fulfillment of the working-class wife's domestic role would reverberate beyond the confines of her home, resulting in "less crime and vice, less ruined characters and stained consciences, less misery and wretchedness, more Godliness, more happiness."[82]

A wife was also urged to be subordinate to her husband, to be a "meet helper." The *Commoner and Glass Worker* went so far as to carry a column in the late 1880s entitled "The Working Man's Wife," in which wives received regular advice on the more efficient organization of their domestic chores.[83] One column admonished, "a bit of necessary wearing apparel for the homemaker is a bridle for the tongue."[84] According to historian S. J. Kleinberg, "The popular press advised working-class women to finish all the chores before the husband arrived home from his hard day's work in the mill, mine, glass house or railroad yard."[85] Such advice was meted out to wives who typically rose about 5:00 or 6:00 A.M. and did not retire until about 9:00 P.M.[86] That these wives absorbed this information and so patterned their lives is evidenced by their diffidence when writing letters to the newspapers, often prefacing their remarks with such expressions as "I am but a woman, but . . .".[87]

The selling of the Americanization process became especially intense during this period as native-born whites watched with apprehension the arrival of millions of immigrants with different linguistic, religious, and cultural backgrounds. For their part, these immigrants from southern and eastern Europe, escaping poverty and political persecution, were eager to become part of their new country. Adopting the new norms governing family life and spousal roles was seen as part of the process of becoming true Americans.

Working-class blacks lived in different environments from whites. The most immediate was the black community itself, a community that had emerged from slavery less than a half century earlier. It was a community beset and sometimes physically assaulted by a hostile white society. And while blacks aspired to full participation in the larger American society, that possibility was clearly more remote for them than for white immigrants. In the South they were locked in the vise of Jim Crow. In the North they experienced more freedom but were nonetheless often denied access to the educational establishment and other institutions of society. Again and again they experienced the disappointment of being passed over by white employers for newly arrived immigrants. When employed in the same factories as immigrants, black males and females were invariably assigned the least skilled jobs. The upward mobility of black families was thus stymied at its very source—the opportunity for husbands and wives to gain good and secure employment and thus sponsor their sons' and daughters' movement up the occupational ladder. Instead, they were forced to stand by helplessly as their sons and daughters remained shut out of the growing number of skilled and clerical jobs becoming available at that time. Though American society was often hostile to white immigrants, those immigrants could at least glimpse a better future in the education of their sons and daughters and the work available in a burgeoning industrial economy.

Unlike white immigrants, whom native-born whites attempted to incorporate into the larger society through the Americanization process, blacks were actively excluded. They had no hope that their families would be included under the same norms that governed the roles of white husbands and wives. Indeed, white society, in both the North and the South, by denying black males the same access to jobs as white males, pursued policies that resulted in a large supply of female domestic workers. And as immigrant women moved to factory employment, northern white middle-class families frequently turned to black females from the South for cheap domestic labor.[88]

By the beginning of the twentieth century (the period of massive white immigration from southeastern Europe), the employment of black working-class wives had become acceptable, though not necessarily desirable. Again, given the type of low-status and disagreeable jobs available to working-class black women, employment could not have been an attractive prospect during this period. At the same time, it is impossible to fully explain differences in the employment rates of black and white immigrant working-class wives in terms of economic need alone. Historian Elizabeth Pleck has pointed out that during this period, among working-class urban families at the same level of economic need and under similar demographic conditions, black wives worked in much higher proportions than white immigrant wives, a point to which I will return in chapter 4.[89]

Many factors influenced the acceptability of wives' employment among black families at this time. As we have seen, the cult of domesticity was not applied to black wives, and they were forced to participate in fieldwork as sharecroppers during the postemancipation period. Like preindustrial white farm families and white settlers in the West, sharecroppers depended on the effort of all family members for economic survival. And like white farm families everywhere, the fieldwork of black sharecropper wives was ancillary to that of their husbands as well as seasonal. But they did divide their time as needed between household duties and fieldwork. In her study of black women in the postbellum South, Jones describes a normal planting season scene: ". . . a typical division of labor included a father who 'ran furrows' using a plow drawn by a mule or oxen, a small child who followed him dropping seeds or 'potato slips' on the ground, and 'at each step the mother covering them with a cumbersome hoe or setting out the plants by piercing holes in the ground with a sharp stick, inserting the roots, and packing the earth with deft movements of the hand.'"[90] Harvest time, which "lasted from August to December" with two to four cotton pickings a year, again required the efforts of all family members.[91] Jones summarizes the responsibilities of black sharecropper wives during this period:

> As productive members of the household economy, black women helped to fulfill the economic as well as the emotional needs of their families. . . . These needs changed over the life course of individual families and clans. So too did the demands upon women fluctuate in the cabin and out in the cotton field, from season to season and from year to year. Thus the responsibilities of wives and mothers reflected considerations related to their families' immediate daily welfare, the fortunes of their kinfolk, and the staple-crop planting and harvesting cycle. Within this constantly shifting matrix of obligations, black women performed housekeeping and child care tasks, earned modest sums of cash, and worked in the fields.[92]

When blacks migrated to the cities, they simply transferred their recent experience as sharecroppers to the urban setting. There, black husbands often expected their wives to seek employment, at least temporarily, to contribute to the family economy. As already noted, blacks saw education as the only opportunity for their sons and daughters to escape their own fate, so they were more likely than white immigrants to send their children to school rather than out into the work force.[93] Finally, since black families were excluded from the cult of domesticity, black working-class husbands—unlike white working-class husbands—did not lose status within the black community when their wives worked.

The survival strategies of black working-class families were not without ambivalence. They do suggest that black working-class wives' employment decisions—unlike those of white wives—were less a response to the cult of domesticity than part of a strategy to meet family needs within a hostile white society. Still, freed from the constraints of the cult of domesticity, African Americans could view the employment of wives as acceptable, though not necessarily desirable, and could mix employment with domestic work as family need dictated. Given the limited options open to working-class families for supplementing the low incomes of male heads, the employment of wives seemed the most appropriate. There is no reason to believe that white working-class families would not have made the same choice had it not been for the cult of domesticity. The income received from boarders, according to Hareven, did not equal the wages a wife could earn. In her study of white immigrants in Manchester, New Hampshire, Hareven found it required the wages of three or more teenage children to equal those of one adult woman.[94]

It remained for upper-middle-class black wives to elevate the *acceptable* to the *desirable* in the early decades of the twentieth century. Married to professional males, even though these men often earned less than comparable white males, they could have lived reasonably comfortable lives, well above the living standard of black working-class families. They could have, therefore, chosen conformity to the cult of domesticity. Instead, they chose employment and viewed it as a desirable addition to their domestic roles. Admittedly, these women, unlike their working-class sisters, were college educated and could pursue intrinsically satisfying professional careers. But their contribution lies in developing a competing ideology to the cult of domesticity.

3 Black Women and a New Definition of Womanhood

A popular novel of 1852 chirped that the white heroine, Eoline, "with her fair hair, and celestial blue eyes bending over the harp . . . really seemed 'little lower than the angels,' and an aureola of purity and piety appeared to beam around her brow."[1] By contrast, in another popular antebellum novel, *Maum Guinea and Her Plantation Children* (1861), black women are excluded from the category of true womanhood without debate: "The idea of modesty and virtue in a Louisiana colored-girl might well be ridiculed; as a general thing, she has neither."[2] Decades later, in 1902, a commentator for the popular magazine *The Independent* noted, "I sometimes hear of a virtuous Negro woman, but the idea is absolutely inconceivable to me. . . . I cannot imagine such a creature as a virtuous Negro woman."[3] Another writer, reflecting early-twentieth-century white male stereotypes of black and white women, remarked that, like white women,

56

"Black women had the brains of a child, [and] the passions of a woman" but, unlike white women, were "steeped in centuries of ignorance and savagery, and wrapped about with immoral vices."[4]

Faced with the prevailing views of white society that placed them outside the boundaries of true womanhood, black women had no choice but to defend their virtue. Middle-class black women led this defense, communicating their response in words and in the actions of their daily lives. In doing so they went well beyond defending their own virtue to espouse a broader conception of womanhood that anticipated modern views by more than half a century. Their vision of womanhood combined the public and the private spheres and eventually took for granted a role for women as paid workers outside the home. More than merely an abstract vision, it was a philosophy of womanhood embodied in the lives of countless middle-class black women in both the late nineteenth and the early twentieth centuries.

VIRTUE DEFENDED

Although black women were seen as devoid of all four of the cardinal virtues of true womanhood—piety, purity, submissiveness, and domesticity—white attention centered on purity. As Hazel Carby suggests, this stemmed in part from the role assigned to black women in the plantation economy. She argues that "two very different but interdependent codes of sexuality operated in the antebellum South, producing opposite definitions of motherhood and womanhood for white and black women which coalesce in the figures of the slave and the mistress."[5] In this scheme, white mistresses gave birth to heirs, slave women to property. A slave woman who attempted to preserve her virtue or sexual autonomy was a threat to the plantation economy. In the words of Harriet Jacobs's slave narrative, *Incidents in the Life of a Slave Girl* (1861), it was "deemed a crime in her [the slave woman] to wish to be virtuous."[6]

Linda Brent, the pseudonym Jacobs used to portray her own life, was an ex-slave struggling to survive economically and protect herself and her daughter from sexual exploitation. In telling her story, she recounts the

difficulty all black women faced in practicing the virtues of true womanhood. The contrasting contexts of black and white women's lives called
for different, even opposite, responses. While submissiveness and passiv-
ity brought protection to the white mistress, these characteristics merely
exposed black women to sexual and economic exploitation. Black women,
therefore, had to develop strength rather than glory in fragility, and had
to be active and assertive rather than passive and submissive.

Though "conventional principles of morality were rendered impossible by the conditions of the slave," as Jacobs argued,[7] Linda Brent embodied the virtues required by black women to survive with dignity in
a hostile environment. It was a world in which "Freedom replaced and
transcended purity."[8] In the conventional sentimental novels of the period, white heroines who lost their purity chose death or went mad. Black
women saw death as an alternative to slavery. "As I passed the wreck of
the old meeting house," Linda Brent mused, "where, before Nat Turner's
time, the slaves had been allowed to meet for worship, I seemed to hear
my father's voice come from it, bidding me not to tarry till I reached
freedom or the grave."[9] Painfully aware of her inability to meet the standards of conventional white womanhood ("I do not sit with my children in a home of my own. I still long for a hearthstone of my own, however humble."[10]), Linda Brent nevertheless represented a fundamental
challenge to this ideology and the beginnings of an alternative, broader
definition of womanhood, one that incorporated resourcefulness and
independence.

Three decades later, in the 1890s, black women found reasons to defend their moral integrity with new urgency against attacks from all
sides. Views such as those in *The Independent* noted earlier were given
respectability by a report of the Slater Fund, a foundation that supported
welfare projects for blacks in this period. The foundation asserted without argument, "The negro women of the South are subject to temptations . . . which come to them from the days of their race enslavement. . . .
To meet such temptations the negro woman can only offer the resistance
of a low moral standard, an inheritance from the system of slavery, made
still lower from a lifelong residence in a one-room cabin."[11]

At the 1893 World Columbian Exposition in Chicago, where black women were effectively barred from the exhibits on the achievements of American women, the few black women allowed to address a women's convention there felt compelled to publicly challenge these views. One speaker, Fannie Barrier Williams, shocked her audience by her forthrightness. "I regret the necessity of speaking of the moral question of our women," but "the morality of our home life has been commented on so disparagingly and meanly that we are placed in the unfortunate position of being defenders of our name." [12] She went on to emphasize that black women continued to be the victims of sexual harassment by white men and chided her white female audience for failing to protect their black sisters. In the same vein, black activist and educator Anna Julia Cooper told the audience that it was not a question of "temptations" as much as it was "the painful, patient, and silent toil of mothers to gain title to the bodies of their daughters." [13] Williams was later to write on the same theme. "It is a significant and shameful fact that I am constantly in receipt of letters from the still unprotected women in the South, begging me to find employment for their daughters . . . to save them from going into the homes of the South as servants as there is nothing to save them from dishonor and degradation." [14] Another black male writer was moved to reveal in *The Independent:* "I know of more than one colored woman who was openly importuned by White women to become the mistress of their husbands, on the ground that they, the white wives, were afraid that, if their husbands did not associate with colored women they would certainly do so with outside white women. . . . And the white wives, for reasons which ought to be perfectly obvious, preferred to have all their husbands do wrong with colored women in order to keep their husbands *straight!*" [15] The attacks on black women's virtue came to a head with a letter written by James Jacks, president of the Missouri Press Association, in which he alleged, "The Negroes in this country were wholly devoid of morality, the women were prostitutes and all were natural thieves and liars." [16] These remarks, coming from such a prominent individual, drew an immediate reaction from black women throughout the country. The most visible was Josephine St. Pierre Ruffin's invitation to black club women to a national convention in Boston in 1895; one hundred women from ten states came to Boston in response. In a memorable address to

representatives of some twenty clubs, Ruffin directly attacked the scur-
rilous accusations:

> Now for the sake of the thousands of self-sacrificing young women
> teaching and preaching in lonely southern backwoods, for the noble
> army of mothers who gave birth to these girls, mothers whose intelli-
> gence is only limited by their opportunity to get at books, for the cul-
> tured women who have carried off the honors at school here and often
> abroad, for the sake of our own dignity, the dignity of our race and the
> future good name of our children, it is "meet, right and our bounden
> duty" to stand forth and declare ourselves and our principles, to teach
> an ignorant and suspicious world that our aims and interests are iden-
> tical with those of all good, aspiring women. Too long have we been
> silent under unjust and unholy charges. . . . It is to break this silence,
> not by noisy protestations of what we are not, but by a dignified show-
> ing of what we are and hope to become, that we are impelled to take
> this step, to make of this gathering an object lesson to the world.[17]

At the end of three days of meetings, the National Federation of Afro-
American Women was founded, uniting thirty-six black women's clubs
in twelve states.[18] The following year, the National Federation merged
with the National League of Colored Women to form the National Association of Colored Women (NACW).

RACIAL UPLIFT: IN DEFENSE
OF THE BLACK COMMUNITY

While the catalyst for these national organizations was in part the felt
need of black women to defend themselves against moral attacks by
whites, they soon went beyond this narrow goal. Twenty years after its
founding, the NACW had grown to fifty thousand members in twenty-
eight federations and more than one thousand clubs.[19] The founding
of these organizations represented a steady movement by middle-class
black women to assume more active roles in the community. Historian
Deborah Gray White argues that black club women "insisted that only
black women could save the black race," a position that inspired them to
pursue an almost feverish pace of activities.[20]

These clubs, however, were not the first attempts by black women to participate actively in their communities. Since the late 1700s black women had been active in mutual-aid societies in the North, and in the 1830s northern black women organized anti-slavery societies. In 1880 Mary Ann Shadd Cary and six other women founded the Colored Women's Progressive Franchise Association in Washington, D.C. Among its stated goals were equal rights for women, including the vote, and the even broader feminist objective of taking "an aggressive stand against the assumption that men only begin and conduct industrial and other things."[21] Giving expression to this goal were a growing number of black women professionals, including the first female physicians to practice in the South.[22] By the turn of the twentieth century, the National Business League, founded by Booker T. Washington, could report that there were "160 Black female physicians, seven dentists, ten lawyers, 164 ministers, assorted journalists, writers, artists, 1,185 musicians and teachers of music, and 13,525 school instructors."[23]

Black women's activism was spurred by the urgency of the struggle for equality, which had led to a greater acceptance of black female involvement in the abolitionist movement. At a time when patriarchal notions of women's domestic role dominated, historian Paula Giddings asserts, "There is no question that there was greater acceptance among Black men of women in activist roles than there was in the broader society."[24] This is not to say that all black men accepted women as equals or the activist roles that many were taking. But when faced with resistance, black women often *demanded* acceptance of their involvement. In 1849, for example, at a black convention in Ohio, "Black women, led by Jane P. Merritt, threatened to boycott the meetings if they were not given a more substantial voice in the proceedings."[25]

In the postbellum period black women continued their struggle for an equal voice in activities for racial uplift in both secular and religious organizations. Historian Evelyn Brooks Higginbotham has offered a detailed account of the successful struggle of black women in the Baptist Church during the late nineteenth century to win acceptance of independent organizations led by themselves.[26] These women's organizations then played a significant role not only in missionary activities, but also in general racial uplift activities in both rural and urban areas.[27]

Expanding Roles

By the turn of the twentieth century, the increasing oppression of the black community led black women to expand their activities even more and to engage in a variety of community self-help and social service programs. At the 1899 Hampton Negro Conference, Lucy C. Laney, an educator and feminist, suggested that educated black women had special roles to play on behalf of racial uplift. They should be active in teaching, setting up church activities, giving advice through public speeches, and providing assistance in developing better hygiene habits.[28]

The black women's club movement, spurred by Ida B. Wells's antilynching campaign and by attacks on black women's virtue,[29] soon embraced a wide variety of community service projects. One of the most active and influential groups was the Tuskegee Woman's Club, founded in 1895 by Margaret M. Washington, wife of Booker T. Washington. Initiated as an exclusive club for the self-improvement of women faculty and faculty wives, it soon branched out to involve members in community services. One project was opening a school for children on the nearby Russel Plantation. For twelve years, club members spent every weekend promoting a variety of activities for all residents of the plantation.[30] Within the city of Tuskegee itself, club members' projects included starting a public library and reading room, developing a program of home visits, and setting up a "lab for the instruction of housekeeping tips, activities for girls and boys, the *Tuskegee Messenger*, and especially a Town Night School. The Town Night School provided an education to many who would otherwise not have been able to attend school."[31]

In Hampton, Virginia, black women initiated several black women's and girls' clubs to promote personal development. In 1912 several of these women wrote a guide, "Community Clubs for Women and Girls," that federal extension agents eventually adopted in their promotion of women's and girls' clubs. Lizzie A. Jenkins, the assistant district agent of the Federal Extension Service, summarized her activities for 1915.

"During this year I have traveled 12,259 miles by rail, 1,200 miles by team [horse drawn carriages], visited 200 homes, 50 clubs, talked with 1,000 club members, 20 superintendents, visited 145 schools, spoken at 50 other meetings with an estimated attendance of 15,339, wrote 814 letters, sent 159 circular letters and assisted with 23 county exhibits, as well as assisting with the exhibits at the Farmers' Conference."[32]

While Jenkins, as an administrator of the Federal Extension program, may have been unusually active, black club women all over the country were engaged in similar community self-help activities. In Baltimore, women's clubs were especially active on behalf of poor children, eventually purchasing a 10.5 acre farm outside the city in 1905 as a retreat for them.[33] In Atlanta, Georgia, the Neighborhood Union, founded by Lugenia Hope (wife of Atlanta University president John Hope) in 1907, was especially instrumental in improving the health conditions of black residents. In cooperation with the Atlanta Anti-Tuberculosis Association, in which she held a full-time position, Lugenia Hope organized a major cleanup of black neighborhoods in 1921 under the rubric of "Negro National Health Week."[34] The Neighborhood Union not only succeeded in securing the passage of several local ordinances to promote the health of black residents, but also opened the only health facility for black residents in Atlanta.

BLACK WOMEN AND THE SUFFRAGE MOVEMENT

In their struggle for their own rights, black women moved into the political fray and eagerly joined the movement for passage of a constitutional amendment giving women the right to vote. Unlike white women suffragists, who focused exclusively on the benefits of the vote for their sex, black women saw the franchise as a means of improving the condition of the black community generally. For them, race and gender issues were inseparable. As historian Rosalyn Terborg-Penn emphasizes, black feminists believed that by "increasing the black electorate" they "would not only uplift the women of the race, but help the children and the men as well."[35]

Prominent black women leaders as well as national and regional organizations threw their support behind the suffrage movement. At least twenty black suffrage organizations were founded, and black women participated in rallies and demonstrations and gave public speeches.[36] Ironically, they often found themselves battling white women suffragists as well as men. Southern white women opposed including black women under a federal suffrage as a matter of principle. Northern white women suffragists, eager to retain the support of southern white women, leaned toward accepting a wording of the amendment that would have allowed the southern states to determine their own position on giving black women the vote, a move that would have certainly led to their exclusion.[37]

After the Nineteenth Amendment was ratified in 1920 in its original form, black women braved formidable obstacles in registering to vote. All across the South white registrars used "subterfuge and trickery" to hinder them from registering, including a "grandmother clause" in North Carolina, literacy tests in Virginia, and a $300 poll tax in Columbia, South Carolina. In Columbia, black women "waited up to twelve hours to register" while white women were registered first.[38] In their struggle to register, black women appealed to the NAACP, signed affidavits against registrars who disqualified them, and finally asked for assistance from national white women suffrage leaders. They were especially disappointed in this last attempt. After fighting side by side with white women suffragists for passage of the Nineteenth Amendment, they were rebuffed by the National Woman's Party leadership with the argument that theirs was a race rather than a women's rights issue.[39] Thus, white women continued to separate issues of race and sex that black women saw as inseparable.

CHALLENGING THE PRIMACY OF DOMESTICITY

A conflicting conception of the relationship between gender and race issues was not the only major difference in the approaches of black and white women to their roles in the family and society. For most white women, their domestic roles as wives and mothers remained primary. In the late nineteenth century, as they began increasingly to argue for acceptance of their involvement on behalf of child-labor reform and growing urban problems, white women often defended these activities as extensions of their housekeeping role. Historian Barbara Harris comments, "The [white women] pioneers in women's education, who probably did more than anyone else in this period to effect change in the female sphere, advocated education for women and their entrance into the teaching profession on the basis of the values proclaimed by the cult of true womanhood. In a similar way, females defended their careers as authors and their involvement in charitable, religious, temperance, and moral reform societies."[40] Paula Giddings notes that in this way white women were able "to become more active outside the home while still preserving the probity of 'true womanhood.'"[41] From the birth of white feminism at the Seneca Falls Convention in 1848, white feminists had a difficult time advancing their goals. Their numbers were few and their members often divided over the propriety of challenging the cult of domesticity. Harris notes, "The advocates of woman's rights remained a small minority of American women, which is one reason for their limited success."[42] Historian Estelle Freedman suggests, "Most [white] feminists did not adopt the radical demands for equal status with men that originated at the Seneca Falls Convention of 1848."[43] Rather than a period of direct challenge of male supremacy or the cult of domesticity, she argues, the late nineteenth century was a period of institution building among women. This was the period of the women's club movement. Initially devoted primarily to culture and self-improvement, many of these clubs became active in urban reform and such issues as moral purity, temperance, and education.[44]

Not until the suffrage movement of the late nineteenth century were white feminists able to develop a unified movement. But with the merging in 1890 of the radical National Women Suffrage Association led by Elizabeth Cady Stanton and Susan B. Anthony with the American Women Suffrage Association led by Lucy Stone, the new National American Women Suffrage Association focused on the single issue of suffrage at the expense of the broader agenda promoted earlier by Stanton and Anthony. Its success in winning the franchise also spelled the end of this phase of the feminist movement. Broader issues of equality would not take shape again until the 1960s.

In the late nineteenth century the cult of domesticity remained primary even for white women graduates of progressive women's colleges such as Vassar, Smith, and Wellesley. For them, no less than for those with only a high-school education, "A Woman's Kingdom" was "a well-ordered home."[45] In a student essay, one Vassar student answered her rhetorical question, "Has the educated woman a duty towards the kitchen?" by emphasizing that the kitchen was "exactly where the college woman belonged" for "the orderly, disciplined, independent graduate is the woman best prepared to manage the home, in which lies the salvation of the world."[46] This essay reflects the dilemma faced by these young white women graduates. They found little support in white society to combine marriage and career. In *Beyond Her Sphere* historian Barbara Harris comments, "To a degree that is hard for us to appreciate, a [white] woman had to make a choice: she either married and had children, or she remained single and had a career. . . . Yet, after their exhilarating years at college, many women were far too committed to the pursuit of knowledge or the practical application of their education to retreat willingly to the narrow confines of Victorian domesticity. And so, in surprising numbers, they chose the other alternative and rejected marriage."[47] Historian Carl Degler estimates that in 1900 25 percent of white women college graduates and 50 percent of those receiving Ph.D.s remained single. Graduates of elite women's colleges in the East were even less likely to marry: 45 and 57 percent, respectively, of Bryn Mawr and Wellesley graduates between 1889 and 1909. While the increasing numbers of white women receiving college degrees did contribute to the ranks of activists, this did not result in a frontal attack on the cult of domesticity. In fact, a number of prominent feminists such as Angelina Grimké and Antoinette Brown Blackwell "disappeared from the ranks of feminist leaders after their marriages," and Alice Freeman Palmer, the president of Wellesley College, resigned after her marriage in 1887 to Herbert Palmer, a philosophy professor at Harvard.[48] Society sanctioned only three courses for the middle-class white woman in the Progressive period: "marriage, charity work or teaching."[49] Marriage and motherhood stood as the highest calling. If there were no economic need for them to work, single women were encouraged to do volunteer charity work. For those who needed an independent income, teaching was the only acceptable occupation.

Historian John Rousmaniere suggests that the white college-educated women involved in the early settlement house movement saw themselves as fulfilling the "service norm" so prominent among middle-class women of the day. At the same time, he argues, it was their sense of uniqueness as college-educated women and their felt isolation upon returning home that led them to this form of service. The settlement houses, located as they were in white immigrant, working-class slums, catered to these women's sense of noblesse oblige; they derived a sense of accomplishment from providing an example of genteel middle-class virtues to the poor. Yet the settlement houses also played into a sense of adventure, leading one resident to write, "We feel that we know life for the first time."[50] For all their felt uniqueness, however, with some notable exceptions these women's lives usually offered no fundamental challenge to the basic assumptions of true womanhood. Residency in settlement houses was for the most part of short duration, and most volunteers eventually embraced their true roles of wife and mother without significant outside involvement. The exceptions were women like Jane Addams, Florence Kelley, Julia Lathrop, and Grace Abbott, who became major figures in the public sphere. Although their lives disputed the doctrine of white women's confinement to the private sphere, the challenge was limited in that most of them did not themselves combine the two spheres of marriage and a public life. Although Florence Kelley was a divorced mother, she nevertheless upheld "the American tradition that men support their families, the wives throughout life," and bemoaned the "retrograde movement" against man as the breadwinner.[51]

Most college-educated black middle-class women also felt a unique sense of mission. They accepted Lucy Laney's 1899 challenge to lift up their race and saw themselves walking in the footsteps of black women activists and feminists of previous generations. But their efforts were not simply "charity work"; their focus was on "racial uplift" on behalf of themselves as well as of the economically less fortunate members of their race.[52] The black women's club movement, in contrast to the white women's, tended to concern themselves from the beginning with the "social and legal problems that confronted both black women and men."[53] While there was certainly some elitism in the NACW's motto, "Lifting as We Climb," these activists were always conscious that they shared a common experience of exploitation and discrimination with the masses and could not completely retreat to the safe haven of their middle-class homes.[54] On the way to meetings they shared the black experience of riding in segregated cars or of being ejected if they tried to do otherwise, as Ida B. Wells did in 1884.[55] Unlike white women for whom, as black feminist Frances Ellen Watkins Harper had emphasized in 1869, "the priorities in the struggle for human rights were sex, not race,"[56] black women could not separate these twin sources of their oppression. They understood that, together with their working-class sisters, they were assumed by whites to have "low animalistic urges." Their exclusion from the category of true womanhood was no less complete than for their less educated black sisters.

It is not surprising, therefore, that the most independent and radical of black female activists led the way in challenging the icons of true womanhood, including on occasion motherhood and marriage. Not only did they chafe under their exclusion from true womanhood, they viewed its tenets as strictures to their efforts on behalf of racial uplift and their own freedom and integrity as women. In 1894 *The Woman's Era* (a black women's magazine) set forth the heretical opinion that "not all women are intended for mothers. Some of us have not the temperament for family life. . . . Clubs will make women think seriously of their future lives, and not make girls think their only alternative is to marry."[57] Anna Julia Cooper, one of the most dynamic women of the period, who had been married and widowed, added that a woman was not "compelled to look to sexual love as the one sensation capable of giving tone and relish, movement and vim to the life she leads. Her horizon is extended."[58] Elsewhere Cooper advised black women that if they married they should seek egalitarian relationships. "The question is not now with the woman 'How shall I so cramp, stunt, and simplify and nullify myself as to make me eligible to the honor of being swallowed up into some little man?' but the problem . . . rests with the man as to how he can so develop . . . to reach the ideal of a generation of women who demand the noblest, grandest and best achievements of which he is capable."[59]

And yet black activists were far more likely to combine marriage and activism than white activists. Although a number of prominent white feminists like Elizabeth Cady Stanton and Lucy Stone were married, as Barbara Harris notes, white middle-class women in the late nineteenth and early twentieth centuries tended to see marriage and career as alternatives. Historian Linda Gordon found this to be the case in her study of sixty-nine black and seventy-six white activists in national welfare reform between 1890 and 1945. Only 34 percent of the white activists had ever been married, compared to 85 percent of the black activists. Most of these women (83 percent of blacks and 86 percent of whites) were college educated.[60] She also found that "The white women [reformers], with few exceptions, tended to view married women's economic dependence on men as desirable, and their employment as a misfortune. . . ."[61] On the other hand, although there were exceptions, Gordon writes, ". . . most black women activists projected a favorable view of working women and women's professional aspirations."[62] Nor could it be claimed that these black activists worked out of necessity, since the majority were married to prominent men "who could support them."[63]

Witness Ida B. Wells-Barnett (married to the publisher of Chicago's leading black newspaper) in 1896, her six-month-old son in tow, stumping from city to city making political speeches on behalf of the Illinois Women's State Central Committee. And Mary Church Terrell dismissing the opinion of those who suggested that studying higher mathematics would make her unappealing as a marriage partner with a curt, "I'd take a chance and run the risk."[64] She did eventually marry and raised a daughter and an adopted child. Her husband, Robert Terrell, a Harvard graduate, was a school principal, a lawyer, and eventually a municipal court judge in Washington, D.C. A biographer later wrote of Mary Terrell's life, "But absorbing as motherhood was, it never became a full-time occupation."[65] While this could also be said of Stanton, perhaps what most distinguished black from white feminists and activists was the larger number of the former who unequivocally challenged domesticity and the greater receptivity they found for their views in the black community. As a result, while the cult of domesticity remained dominant in the white community at the turn of the twentieth century, it did not hold sway within the black community.

Rejection of the Public/Private Dichotomy

Black women of the nineteenth and early twentieth centuries saw their efforts on behalf of the black community as necessary for their own survival, rather than as noblesse oblige. "Self preservation," wrote Mary Church Terrell in 1902, "demands that [black women] go among the lowly, illiterate and even the vicious, to whom they are bound by ties of race and sex . . . to reclaim them."[66] These women rejected the confinement to the private sphere mandated by the cult of domesticity. They felt women could enter the public sphere without detriment to the home. As historian Elsa Barkley Brown has emphasized, black women believed that "Only a strong and unified community made up of both women and men could wield the power necessary to allow black people to shape their own lives. Therefore, only when women were able to exercise their full strength would the community be at its full strength. . . ."[67]

In her study of black communities in Illinois during the late Victorian era (1880–1910), historian Shirley Carlson contrasts the black and white communities' expectations of the "ideal woman" at that time:

> The black community's appreciation for and development of the feminine intellect contrasted sharply with the views of the larger society. In the latter, intelligence was regarded as a masculine quality that would "defeminize" women. The ideal white woman, being married, confined herself almost exclusively to the private domain of the household. She was demure, perhaps even self-effacing. She often deferred to her husband's presumably superior judgment, rather than formulating her own views and vocally expressing them, as black women often did. A woman in the larger society might skillfully manipulate her husband for her own purposes, but she was not supposed to confront or challenge him directly. Black women were often direct, and frequently won community approval for this quality, especially when such a characteristic was directed toward achieving racial uplift. Further, even after her mar-

riage, a black woman might remain in the public domain, possibly in paid employment. The ideal black woman's domain, then, was both the private and public spheres. She was wife and mother, but she could also assume other roles such as schoolteacher, social activist, or business-woman, among others. And she was intelligent.[68]

In their struggle for an expansion of roles beyond the domestic sphere, black women sometimes had to contend with opposition from within the black community, especially from men, as well as with the larger society's definition of women's proper role. When Ida Wells-Barnett was elected financial secretary of the Afro-American Council, the *Colored American* newspaper suggested that a man should hold the position. While recognizing that "She is a woman of unusual mental powers," the newspaper argued that "the proprieties would have been observed by giving her an assignment more in keeping with the popular idea of women's work and which would not interfere so disastrously with her domestic duties."[69]

Feminist Maggie Lena Walker, the first woman in the nation (and the first African American, male or female) to establish and head a bank and founder of the Richmond Council of Colored Women in Virginia, also met with male opposition in her efforts for racial uplift and expanded women's roles. She too opposed these limitations to the domestic sphere, contending, "Men should not be so pessimistic and down on women's clubs. They don't seek to destroy the home or disgrace the race."[70] The Woman's Union, a Richmond female insurance company founded in 1898, took as its motto, "The Hand That Rocks the Cradle Rules the World." As Brown has clarified, however, "unlike nineteenth-century white women's rendering of that expression to signify the limitation of woman's influence to that which she had by virtue of rearing her sons, the idea as these women conceived it transcended the separation of private and public spheres and spoke to the idea that women, while not abandoning their roles as wives and mothers, could also move into economic and political activities in ways that would support rather than conflict with family and community."[71]

Although many black males, like most white males, opposed the expansion of black women's roles, many other black males supported women's activism and even criticized their brethren for their opposition. Echoing Maggie Walker's sentiments, T. Thomas Fortune wrote, "The race could not succeed nor build strong citizens, until we have a race of women competent to do more than hear a brood of negative men."[72] Support for women's suffrage was especially strong among black males. Few agreed with Representative Clark, a white congressman from Florida, who said in 1915, "I do not wish to say the day will come when the women of my race in my state shall trail skirts in the muck and mire of partisan politics. I prefer to look to the American woman as she always has been, occupying her proud state as queen of the American home, instead of regarding her as a ward politician in the cities."[73] Black men saw women's suffrage as advancing the political empowerment of the race. For black women, suffrage promised to be a potent weapon in their fight for their rights, for education and jobs.[74]

A Threefold Commitment

An expanded role for black women did not end at the ballot box or in activities promoting racial uplift. Black middle-class women demanded a place for themselves in the paid labor force. Theirs was a threefold commitment to family, career, and social movements. According to historian Rosalyn Terborg-Penn, "most black feminists and leaders had been wives and mothers who worked yet found time not only to struggle for the good of their sex, but for their race." Such a threefold commitment "was not common among white women."[75]

In her study of eighty African American women throughout the country who worked in "the feminized professions" (such as teaching) between the 1880s and the 1950s, historian Stephanie Shaw comments on the way they were socialized to lives dedicated to home, work, and community. When these women were children, she indicates, "the model of womanhood held before [them] was one of achievement in *both* public and private spheres. Parents cast domesticity as a complement rather than a contradiction to success in public arenas."[76] Later, in her discussion of one woman whose husband opposed her desire to work outside the home, Shaw observes, "It seems, then, that Henry Riddick subscribed to an old tradition (which was becoming less and less influential in general, and which *had never been a real tradition among most black families*) wherein the wife of a 'good' husband did not need to work for pay."[77]

An analysis of the lives of 108 of the first generation of black clubwomen bears this out. "The career-oriented clubwomen," comments Paula Giddings, "seemed to have no ambivalence concerning their right to work, whether necessity dictated it or not."[78] According to Giddings, three-quarters of these 108 early clubwomen were married, and almost three-quarters worked outside the home, while one-quarter had children.

A number of these clubwomen and other black women activists not only had careers but also spoke forcefully about the importance of work, demonstrating surprisingly progressive attitudes with a very modern ring. "The old doctrine that a man marries a woman to support her," quipped Walker, "is pretty nearly thread-bare to-day."[79] "Every dollar a woman makes," she declared in a 1912 speech to the Federation of Colored Women's Clubs, "some man gets the direct benefit of same. Every woman was by Divine Providence created for some man; not for some man to marry, take home and support, but for the purpose of using her powers, ability, health and strength, to forward the financial . . . success of the partnership into which she may go, if she will. . . ."[80] Being married with three sons and an adopted daughter did not in any way dampen her commitment to gender equality and an expanded role for wives.

Such views were not new. In a pamphlet entitled *The Awakening of the Afro-American Woman,* written in 1897 to celebrate the earlier founding of the National Association of Colored Women, Victoria Earle Matthews referred to black women as "co-breadwinners in their families."[81] Almost twenty years earlier, in 1878, feminist writer and activist Frances Ellen Harper sounded a similar theme of equality when she insisted, "The women as a class are quite equal to the men in energy and executive ability." She went on to recount instances of black women managing small and large farms in the postbellum period.[82]

It is clear that in the process of racial uplift work, black middle-class women also included membership in the labor force as part of their identity. They were well ahead of their time in realizing that their membership in the paid labor force was critical to achieving true equality with men. For this reason, the National Association of Wage Earners insisted that all black women should be able to support themselves.[83] Sadie T. M. Alexander, the first black woman to practice law in Pennsylvania, was quite explicit in drawing the connection between work and equality. In 1930 she noted that some nonprofessional women were quick to leave the labor force as soon as they could afford to. Instead, she insisted, these women needed to remain continually attached to the labor force in order to realize long-term gains. Since a rapidly industrializing world rated housework as "valueless consumption," she reasoned, women had to "place themselves again among the producers of the world" and to do work "that resulted in the production of goods that have a price value." Far from being harmful to the home, she maintained, "The satisfaction which comes to the woman in realizing that she is a producer makes for peace and happiness, the chief requisites in any home." Countering the argument that children would be damaged if their mothers worked outside the home, she contended, "The derogatory effects of the mother being out of the home are overbalanced by the increased family income, which makes possible the securing of at least the necessities of life, and perhaps a few luxuries."[84]

Although they may have been more articulate than most, Sadie Alexander, Anna Julia Cooper, Ida Wells-Barnett, and Maggie Lena Walker were not atypical of black women. Other middle-class black women and legions of less educated black women embodied these principles of black womanhood in their daily lives. They resisted the prevailing cult of domesticity in the larger society and on occasion even stood up to both family and community opposition. In the process they helped define a new, more expanded view of womanhood and offered their own living examples of this new womanhood. Yet, as Stephanie Shaw documents, their commitment to both the public and the private spheres sometimes entailed considerable stress and disappointment. As a result, some of these women were forced to give up, or at least temporarily suspend, their careers, while others enjoyed the tacit or active support of husbands who were willing to increase their share of domestic work "as the women relinquished it."[85] In the end, Shaw comments, "each woman had to devise a strategy that would allow her to fulfill personal, family, and community roles within her particular situation."[86]

Like Mary Church Terrell, a number of women began their fight for careers when still very young and continued this battle throughout their lives. Braving the opposition of family and friends, Terrell dared to earn an A.B. degree in mathematics from Oberlin, even though "It was held by most people that women were unfitted to do their work in the home if they studied Latin, Greek and higher mathematics." Upon graduation, she defied her father's furious objection to her employment and took a teaching job at Wilberforce College. For her act of rebellion she was "disinherited" by her irate father, who "refused to write to me for a year." [87] But Terrell enjoyed the full support of her husband, Robert.

In 1963 in *The Feminine Mystique*, Betty Friedan wrote, "I never knew a woman, when I was growing up, who used her mind, played her own part in the world, and also loved, and had children." [88] Her experience, however, was only of white middle-class women. In fact, many black middle-class women did fit this description, and Friedan's lack of acquaintance with these women attests to the deep chasm that has historically separated the worlds of black and white women. As W. E. B. Du Bois commented as early as 1924, "Negro women more than the women of any other group in America are the protagonists in the fight for an economically independent womanhood in modern countries.... The matter of economic independence is, of course, the central fact in the struggle of women for equality." [89]

DEFINING BLACK WOMANHOOD

In the late 1930s when Mary McLeod Bethune, the acknowledged leader of black women at the time and an adviser to President Franklin Roosevelt on matters affecting the black community, referred to herself as the representative of "Negro womanhood" and asserted that black women had "room in their lives to be wives and mothers as well as to have careers," she was not announcing a new idea.[90] As Terborg-Penn emphasizes:

> ... most black feminists and leaders had been wives and mothers who worked yet found time not only to struggle for the good of their sex, but for their race. Until the 1970s, however, this threefold commitment—

to family and to career and to one or more social movements—was not common among white women. The key to the uniqueness among black feminists of this period appears to be their link with the past. The generation of the woman suffrage era had learned from their late nineteenth-century foremothers in the black women's club movement, just as the generation of the post World War I era had learned and accepted the experiences of the preceding generation. Theirs was a sense of continuity, a sense of group consciousness that transcended class.[91]

This "sense of continuity" with past generations of black women was clearly articulated in 1917 by Mary Talbert, president of the NACW. Launching an NACW campaign to save the home of the late Frederick Douglass, she said, "We realize today is the psychological moment for us women to show our true worth and prove that Negro women of today measure up to those sainted women of our race, who passed through the fire of slavery and its galling remembrances."[92] Talbert certainly lived up to her words, going on to direct the NAACP's antilynching campaign and becoming the first woman to receive the NAACP's Spingarn Medal for her achievements.

What then is the expanded definition of true womanhood found in these black middle-class women's words and embodied in their lives? First, they tended to define womanhood in an inclusive rather than exclusive sense. Within white society, true womanhood was defined so narrowly that it excluded all but a small minority of white upper- and upper-middle-class women with husbands who were able to support them economically. Immigrant women and poor women—of any color —did not fit this definition. Nor did black women as a whole, regardless of class, because they were all seen as lacking an essential characteristic of true womanhood—virtue. For black women, however, true womanhood transcended class and race boundaries. Anna Julia Cooper called for "reverence for woman as woman regardless of rank, wealth, or culture."[93] Unlike white women, black women refused to isolate gender issues from other forms of oppression such as race and nationality, including the struggles of colonized nations of Africa and other parts of the world. Women's issues, they suggested, were tied to issues of oppression, whatever form that oppression might assume.

As discussed above, black women organized to defend their virtue against the vicious attacks of white society. They pointed out—Fannie Barrier Williams and Ida B. Wells-Barnett forcefully among them—that the real culprits were white males who continued to harass and prey upon them with the tacit support of white women. At times they also chastised black males for failing to protect them. Black women obviously saw themselves as virtuous, both individually and as a group. Yet, apart from defending themselves against these attacks, black women did not dwell upon virtue in defining womanhood. Theirs was not the sexless purity forced on white women by white males who placed their women on pedestals while seeking out black women for their pleasure. Nor did they feel it necessary to equate womanhood with the absence of a natural sex drive. As historian Barbara Berg has noted, "The cult of purity denied that [white] women had natural sex drives."[94] The most widely quoted book on sexuality in mid-nineteenth century, by Dr. William Acton, accepted the prevailing belief that "the best [white] mothers, wives and managers of households know little or nothing of sexual indulgence. Love of home, children and domestic duties are the only passions they feel."[95] The approach of elite black women predated by several generations the demand of white women in the 1970s to be viewed as total human beings with healthy sexuality.

The traditional white ideology of true womanhood separated the active world of men from the passive world of women. As we have seen, women's activities were confined to the home, where their greatest achievement was maintaining their own virtue and decorum and rearing future generations of male leaders. Although elite black women did not reject their domestic roles as such, many expanded permissible public activities beyond charity work to encompass employment and participation in social progress. They founded such organizations as the Atlanta Congress of Colored Women, which historian Erlene Stetson claims was the first grassroots women's movement organized "for social and political good."[96]

The tendency of black women to define womanhood inclusively and to see their roles extending beyond the boundaries of the home led them naturally to include other characteristics in their vision. One of these was intellectual equality . While the "true" woman was portrayed as submissive ("conscious of inferiority, and therefore grateful for support"),[97] according to literary scholar Hazel Carby, black women such as Anna Julia Cooper argued for a "partnership with husbands on a plane of intellectual equality."[98] Such equality could not exist without the pursuit of education, particularly higher education, and participation in the labor force. Cooper, like many other black women, saw men's opposition to higher education for women as an attempt to make them conform to a narrow view of women as "sexual objects for exchange in the marriage market."[99] Education for women at all levels became a preoccupation for many black feminists and activists. Not a few—like Anna Cooper, Mary L. Europe, and Estelle Pinckney Webster—devoted their entire lives to promoting it, especially among young girls. Womanhood, as conceived by black women, was compatible with—indeed, required—intellectual equality. In this they were supported by the black community. While expansion of educational opportunities for women was a preoccupation of white feminists in the nineteenth century, as I noted above, a college education tended to create a dilemma in the lives of white women who found little community support for combining marriage and career. In contrast, as Shirley Carlson emphasizes, "The black community did not regard intelligence and femininity as conflicting values, as the larger society did. That society often expressed the fear that intelligent women would develop masculine characteristics—a thickening waist, a diminution of breasts and hips, and finally, even the growth of facial hair. Blacks seemed to have had no such trepidations, or at least they were willing to have their women take these risks."[100]

In addition to women's right to an education, Cooper, Walker, Alexander, Terrell, the leaders of the National Association of Wage Earners, and countless other black feminists and activists insisted on their right to work outside the home. They dared to continue very active lives after marriage. Middle-class black women's insistence on the right to pursue careers paralleled their view that a true woman could move in both the private and the public spheres and that marriage did not require submissiveness or subordination. In fact, as Shirley Carlson has observed in her study of black women in Illinois in the late Victorian period, many activist black women "continued to be identified by their maiden names—usually as their middle names or as part of their hyphenated surnames—indicating that their own identities were not subsumed in their husbands.'"[101]

While the views of black women on womanhood were all unusual for their time, their insistence on the right of all women—including wives and mothers—to work outside the home was the most revolutionary. In their view the need for paid work was not merely a response to economic circumstances, but the fulfillment of women's right to self-actualization. Middle-class black women like Ida B. Wells-Barnett, Margaret Washington, and Mary Church Terrell, married to men who were well able to support them, continued to pursue careers throughout their lives, and some did so even as they reared children. These women were far ahead of their time, foreshadowing societal changes that would not occur within the white community for several generations.

WORK AND THE FAMILY

Black women's position on their role as co-breadwinners was not reached without ambivalence and debate, however. As I pointed out in chapter 2, after emancipation some black women took the cult of domesticity as their model and refused to work in the fields, declaring that their husbands should support them just as white husbands supported their wives. Yet the conventional orthodoxy of true womanhood never took a firm hold within the black community. During this same period some women, as Frances Ellen Harper remarked, did "double duty," a "man's share in the field and a woman's part at home,"[102] and still others could be found managing sizable plantations. In the ensuing decades, rather than debate women's proper role, black people's energies turned toward the struggle to expand occupational opportunities for both sexes and to address the needs of the black community. Instead of viewing women as frail, ethereal creatures, the black community developed what educator Jeanne Noble has called a "social system" that "rewarded the enterprising, clever, ambitious woman."[103] This community support was often expressed in newspaper articles encouraging African American women to pursue higher education and praising outstanding women for their intelligence. In 1900 the Chicago *Broad Ax* commented on the graduation of Minnie Kelly: "Among the graduates of the Art Institute of Chicago at Fullerton Memorial recently was Miss Minnie C. Kelly. Miss Kelly is a native of Padukah, Kentucky and a graduate of Tuskegee Institute. Before taking up her studies in Chicago, Miss Kelly lived in St. Louis." [104] On the graduation of Miss M. A. Taylor from the University of Chicago in 1910, the publisher and editor of the *Defender,* Robert Abbott, wrote, "There is nothing so encouraging to the loyal members of the race when at spring time we watch with pride the goodly number of college men and women who stretch forth their hands for the conventional sheepskin." [105] Not only single women, but also married women, according to Carlson, were praised for their intellectual achievements. "Mrs. George E. Taylor of Oakloosa, Iowa," according to the July 7, 1900, *Broad Ax* "accompanied her husband to the Kansas City Convention. . . . Mrs. Taylor is well educated and being handsome she possesses all the qualifications which go to make up a *true woman.*" [106] Carlson points out that "admonitions to well-educated single women sometimes suggested that they select a mate who could appreciate their career aspirations." [107]

Rather than accepting white society's views of paid work outside the home as deviant, therefore, black women fashioned a competing ideology of womanhood—one that supported the needs of an oppressed black community and their own desire for gender equality. Middle-class black women, especially, often supported by the black community, developed a consciousness of themselves as persons who were competent and capable of being influential. They believed in higher education as a means of sharpening their talents, and in a sexist world that looked on men as superior, they dared to see themselves as equals both in and out of marriage.

This new ideology of womanhood came to have a profound impact on the conception of black families and gender roles. Black women's insistence on their role as co-breadwinners clearly foreshadows today's dual-career and dual-worker families. Since our conception of the family is inseparably tied to our views of women's and men's roles, the broader definition of womanhood advocated by black women was also an argument against the traditional family. The cult of domesticity was anchored in a patriarchal notion of women as subordinate to men in both the family and the larger society. The broader definition of womanhood championed by black middle-class women struck a blow for an expansion of women's rights in society and a more egalitarian position in the home, making for a far more progressive system among blacks at this time than among whites.

4 The New Family Paradigm Takes Root and Spreads

The emergence of dual-worker and dual-career black couples in the late nineteenth and early twentieth centuries struck at the heart of the traditional family. The very existence and growing acceptance of these couples within the black community challenged white society's most cherished beliefs about the family: its hierarchical nature and asymmetrical roles. Whereas champions of the traditional family defended the primacy of the husband and the subordination of the wife as the ideal arrangement, black dual-career and dual-worker families offered living examples of more egalitarian arrangements. Within these new families, hierarchy was yielding to greater flexibility, particularly in sharing the breadwinner role. A new family paradigm had emerged in direct opposition to the traditional one.

Although in the early twentieth century few whites were prepared to accept this new paradigm, as I have shown in chapter 3 it was well on its way to becoming the norm among middle-class black families and within the larger black community. The first generation of black club women—women born between 1860 and 1885—embraced this model of marriage and family life, and many became its propagandists. In this chapter, using twentieth-century census data, I will trace the spread of this paradigm as it was increasingly embraced by black and eventually by white families. More specifically, in light of my argument that black middle-class women fashioned and promoted a new feminist ideology that championed egalitarianism within the family and a broader, more active role for themselves in society, I will explore the extent to which support for this argument can be found in statistics on the employment of black and white wives in different classes over the past half-century. In particular, I will test the extent to which we can attribute the participation of wives in the labor force to ideology as opposed to economic need or other factors.

IDEOLOGY VERSUS ECONOMIC NEED IN WIVES' EMPLOYMENT

In the nineteenth and early twentieth centuries, as the American working class took shape in the cauldron of the industrial revolution, Karl Marx's prediction of an exploited proletariat materialized. Expanding United States industries developed an insatiable hunger for low-skilled and unskilled workers, who were rewarded with long hours and low pay. Without legal labor unions to fight effectively for higher wages and more humane working conditions, the typical United States factory worker had difficulty earning enough to support his family. With the average wage of male unskilled workers—the majority of all workers—sufficient only to support a single individual, prospects for a comfortable life were remote within the working class, whether native-born white, immigrant, or black.[1] Although the work day was gradually shortened from the ten or twelve hours common in the nineteenth and early twentieth centuries, the mechanization of United States industry typified by the Ford Motor

Company's assembly lines reduced skill requirements to a minimum and rendered most production workers interchangeable and powerless to improve their lot. Only in the small emerging middle class, where males earned many times the income of blue-collar workers, did husbands earn enough to support a family in comfort. In 1890 even clerical employees earned almost double the wages of blue-collar workers.[2]

Given these conditions, working-class wives—whether native-born white, immigrant, or black—had a powerful incentive to enter the paid labor force. Yet when faced with the same objective conditions, white immigrant and native-born wives invariably were employed far less frequently than black wives. In her comparison of black and Italian families in southern and northern cities during 1896 and 1911, historian Elizabeth Pleck found significantly lower employment rates among working-class Italian wives, even though their husbands often earned less and had higher unemployment rates than black husbands. With apparent surprise, she notes:

> . . . even with husbands earning identical incomes, a black wife was more likely to work than an Italian wife. Among the poorest families in 1896, those with husbands earning less than $200 a year, almost all black wives in Atlanta, Nashville, or Cambridge were working, whereas the same desperation sent only a fifth of Italian wives in Chicago to work. *At all income levels . . . black wives were far more likely to work than Italian wives.*[3]

Pleck further observes that "when her husband became unemployed, a black wife was more likely to work than an Italian wife" and that "even with young children at home, black mothers more often took paid jobs than Italian mothers."[4] Low levels of employment were likewise found among the wives of Polish, German, Irish, and Russian Jewish immigrants. In no case did immigrant wives work at the same rate as black wives. Pleck found that though both black and Italian wives responded similarly to the same economic conditions—amount of wealth, husband's income and unemployment, presence of small children, and wages—Italian wives with identical family circumstances were far less likely to work than black wives. That is, both Italian and black wives were more likely to work when their husbands were unemployed or women's wages high. Both were also deterred from working when husbands' incomes were high or small children were present. Nevertheless, faced with the same incentives or deterrents, black wives were more likely to work than Italian or other immigrant wives.

After considering the various factors known to influence wives' employment rates, Pleck concludes that "no single economic or demographic condition accounts for the higher rate of wage earning among black than Italian wives." Pleck also considers the argument that black wives were more likely to work because of the shorter duration of black women's marriages as a result of death, desertion, or separation. After reviewing relevant data on black families in Boston, she concludes, "Boston black wives whose husbands had left them by 1900 were no more likely to have been employed in 1880 than black wives in stable marriages lasting the two decades. . . . In sum, a [black] wife's wage earning bore little connection to her husband's subsequent absence."[5] Nor does it appear that black and immigrant wives' employment differences can be explained simply by differences in cultural attitudes toward women's employment. In Italy at the time, Pleck observes, "Peasant wives . . . were expected to contribute to the family by field work as well as their performance of traditional female tasks;" and in America young single Italian women were often employed until marriage. Indeed, Pleck observes that "Italian wives were no more confined to the home than other immigrant wives."[6] At the same time she recognizes the resistance of both black wives and their husbands to wives' working in the fields after emancipation. Pleck's data for the late nineteenth and early twentieth centuries offer evidence that the widely held belief that black wives were more likely to work than white wives simply because of economic need is at best an oversimplification of far more complex motivation.

How then can the discrepancy in the employment rates of black and Italian immigrant wives be explained? Since wives in other immigrant groups also showed a similar avoidance of outside work, it seems plausible that immigrant wives, being white themselves, identified more strongly than blacks with the domestic ideology of the white middle class. As I noted in chapter 2, like the middle-class press, immigrant working-class newspapers urged their readers to observe the cult of domesticity. In 1900 the *National Labor Tribune* in Pittsburgh cautioned its readers that when women tended to their domestic duties there resulted "more of all that tends to make life worth living."[7] That these women read these admonitions is evidenced by their many letters to these newspapers. Similarly, historian Tamara Hareven found evidence of the penetration of the cult of domesticity in the lives of working-class families in Manchester, New Hampshire, in the same period. She observes, "By the second generation, American values of domesticity had become dominant over the desire for maximum employment of the family."[8] These studies attest to the eagerness of immigrants to be accepted as full-fledged white Americans, an eagerness that led to the adoption of a domestic pattern ill-suited to their economic situation.

Faced with the dilemma of their economic need and adherence to the new domestic norms, immigrant families had to make compromises. As discussed in chapter 1, most frequently this took the form of sending their children into the workforce or taking in boarders. For instance, altł. ugh only 8 percent of German wives in Chicago worked outside the home in 1911, 44 percent had working children, and 11 percent took in boarders. Similarly, though only 16 percent of Italian wives in Boston worked during that year, 25 percent of Italian families had children at work, and 39 percent had boarders.[9] The need for additional income, as Hareven found, often conflicted with a child's desire for an education. One young immigrant girl offered subtle resistance, but in the end was forced to take employment in a local mill:

> At first, I didn't want to go to work. I was only sixteen when my mother sent me down to the mill. I wanted to continue with high school, but she wouldn't send me. She'd say, "You don't need an education to get married and wash diapers." I thought if I didn't find a job, maybe she'd let me go back to school. So in the morning, I'd leave and walk uptown the minute the stores were open. I'd go from one store to another just looking. Then at noontime, I'd come home. I did that for three or four days. My mother asked, "Did you find a job?" and I said I hadn't. . . . When my sister Flora came home for dinner, my mother said, "Why don't you take her with you?" Flora brought me to the employment office, and they sent me to the rayon plant.[10]

Black families, on the other hand, not being part of the white community, did not experience the same pressures to keep wives and mothers out of the workforce. The cult of domesticity did not apply to them. While preferring to remain at home with their children, black working-class wives who went out of the home to work were not as likely to threaten their husbands' manhood or violate black community norms of their proper role. Bowing to the harsh reality of urban life north and south, black husbands often encouraged their wives to work. This is evident in letters from potential black migrants to the black newspaper, the *Chicago Defender,* inquiring about work in that city. Letters written by husbands to the paper, historian Jacqueline Jones observes, described their wives as "very industrious," "a very good cook . . . [with] lots of references," or "a good launders." Although husbands complained about the forced employment of their wives in the fields, their letters, according to Jones, indicated "that most men expected their wives to continue to contribute to the family income, at least temporarily, in their new northern home." [11] It was left to black middle-class wives to transform what had become acceptable, though not desirable, among black working-class wives to the level of desirable.

IDEOLOGY AND WIVES' EMPLOYMENT RATES, 1940 TO 1994

United States census employment statistics reveal just how powerful a force the ideology of domesticity remained in the lives of white wives as late as 1940 (figure 3).[12] In that year, nationally, only one in ten white wives dared to risk the social disapproval of friends and neighbors by entering the labor force. Black wives, on the other hand, were more than twice as likely to be at work outside the home. Over the next fifty-four years, however, white wives abandoned the domestic sphere for work outside the home at the average rate of approximately nine percentage points per decade. By 1990 over half of all white wives had jobs and were thus no longer living in traditional families. This gradual movement away from the traditional to the modern family paradigm was paced by black wives who, throughout most of this period, remained roughly ten years ahead of whites in their employment rates. Not until the 1980s were there signs of convergence in the proportions of black and white

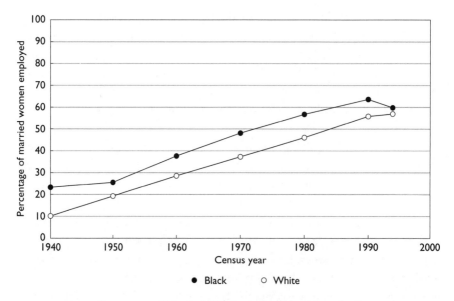

FIGURE 3.   Percentage of Married Women in the Labor Force, by Race, 1940–1994

NOTE: Unless otherwise indicated, all graphs are based on the author's analysis.

wives employed, primarily due to an acceleration of the pace at which white middle-class wives entered the labor force and, to some extent, from a slight decline in the rate of increase in the participation of middle-class black wives.

Class and Domesticity

The trend away from domesticity toward the modern paradigm of the family occurred among all classes, but it was among middle-class families that the new paradigm was most readily adopted.[13] Throughout the period studied, among both black and white families, middle-class wives were far more likely to have left the home for the labor force than those in the working class—a fact that flies in the face of a simple "need hypothesis" of wives' employment (see appendix figures B1 and B2). In 1940 the employment rates of middle-class wives compared with those of working-class wives were 10 percent higher among black wives and 8 percent higher among white wives. This gap continued to widen steadily in the ensuing decades. Thus we have the anomaly that wives in families with the least economic need—middle-class families—were the most likely to work outside the home. How can this be explained?

The neoclassical economic model sees the participation of wives in the labor force as a tradeoff between the value placed on "nonmarket time" (time spent on housework and child care) and the value placed on "market time" (time spent employed outside the home).[14] The value of nonmarket time is itself affected by a variety of factors, especially the availability of nonmarket income—usually that of husbands. Although this model has a certain logical appeal, it is difficult to test, and—even more problematic—it fails to account for differences in the labor force participation of black and white wives faced with the same constraints. Economists Francine Blau and Marianne Ferber acknowledge this when they admit, "The reasons for the higher participation rate of black married women are not fully understood. . . ."[15] As I intend to show, only blacks' and whites' different ideologies concerning women's roles and the family can explain these observed racial differences in employment. In turn, class differences in the labor force participation of wives relate to variations in the strength of these ideologies among different classes.

THE POWER OF IDEOLOGY

In the previous chapter I argued that black middle-class women developed a competing ideology of feminism that championed both egalitarianism in the family and an expanded role for women in society. Central to this enlarged role was employment outside the home and the pursuit of a career. These women peppered their speeches and essays with such terms as "co-breadwinners," "equality" with men, "ability," and a "threefold commitment" to family, career, and social movements. They embodied their convictions in active careers while married and raising children. Women like Philadelphia lawyer and assistant city solicitor Sadie T. M. Alexander chided some of her working-class sisters for their lack of attachment to the labor force, arguing that since housework was little valued, women had to "place themselves again among the producers of the world" and engage in work "that resulted in the production of goods that have a price value."[16] White feminists like Charlotte Perkins Gilman and Elizabeth Cady Stanton also urged that married women had a right to pursue careers. Both were exceptional women who played major roles in advancing women's causes. Stanton was a leader in the suffrage movement and Gilman a writer and lecturer whose 1898 book, *Women and Economics,* was very influential in promoting ideas of equality.[17] Yet neither they nor other white feminists of the late nineteenth and early twentieth centuries were able to mount an effective attack on the cult of domesticity or to have the same impact on white society that black women had on black society. This was in part because relatively few white activists opposed domesticity, as was discussed in the previous chapter, in part because of differences among white feminists over the goals of the feminist movement, and in part because of the strength of white society's resistance to feminism and the issue of equality. As a result, the cult of domesticity maintained its grip on white women's lives until the 1960s.

In contrast, the pioneering black women of the late nineteenth and early twentieth centuries were followed by a host of others who typified this new ideology of womanhood. They married, bore children, pursued careers, and wielded influence within the black community far beyond their numbers. By 1940 almost four out of ten black middle-class wives fit this model, compared with fewer than two in ten whites (see figure 4). It would require another twenty years before white middle-class wives would embrace this new model of womanhood to the same extent. In fact, throughout the next fifty-four years, black middle-class wives' rate of employment stayed about two decades ahead of their white counterparts'. In 1960 almost 60 percent of black middle-class families had adopted the modern paradigm, compared with about 38 percent of white middle-class families. By 1994 only about 14 percent of two-parent black middle-class families fit the traditional model, while about 24 percent of white middle-class families still did.

The pioneers of the new family paradigm were *upper*-middle-class black professional women. It was they who had the education and experience to accomplish this. They not only had careers, but assertively defended the legitimacy of their lives. By 1940 some 40 percent of these women were pursuing careers while raising families, and many were liv-

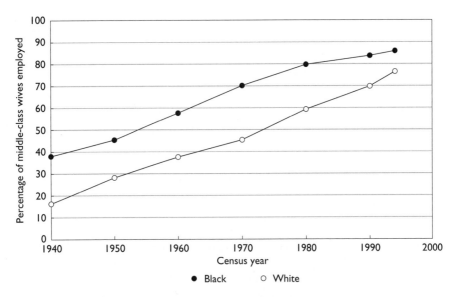

FIGURE 4. Percentage of Middle-Class Wives in the Labor Force, by Race, 1940–1994

ing the threefold commitment of the early club women to family, career, and social movement (see appendix figure B3). Indeed, women like Mary Church Terrell were still very much in the forefront of this movement at the time.[18] As a group, upper-middle-class black wives in 1940 were a full thirty years ahead of white upper-middle-class wives in their adoption of the new family paradigm. As will be discussed below, only in the 1970s and 1980s did signs of a narrowing of this gap appear, prompted by the feminist movement and a severe economic downturn.

The slow pace with which upper-middle-class white women abandoned the traditional paradigm can be seen from a comparison of the employment rates of upper- and lower-middle-class wives. Upper-middle-class wives, married to husbands in professional and managerial positions, had little need to work compared with wives in the lower middle class—those whose husbands performed sales or clerical work. Yet careful analysis of census data from 1940 to 1994 shows clearly that upper-middle-class black wives were far more likely to work outside the home than those in the lower middle class (figure 5). This remained

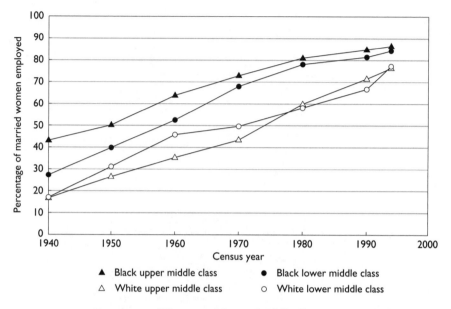

FIGURE 5.   Percentage of Upper- and Lower-Middle-Class Wives in the Labor
Force, by Race, 1940–1994

true even after the 1964 Civil Rights Act outlawing discrimination in employment made clerical work in white establishments available to black
women.

There was an opposite trend among whites. Although in 1940 white
wives in both upper- and lower-middle-class families held equally to
their traditional roles (figure 5), over the next thirty years it was lower-
middle-class white wives who were more likely to move out of the home
into the workforce. This was true during the war years, when married
women were encouraged to leave home to meet the nation's labor needs,
and continued during the prosperous postwar decades of the 1950s and
1960s, when they were encouraged to return to their homes and real income rose significantly for workers of all classes. Thus, during the period
of greatest prosperity—the 1950s and 1960s—upper-middle-class black
wives were the most likely to work outside the home, while upper-
middle-class white wives were the least likely to work outside the home.
Not until the late 1970s did the pattern reverse and the proportion of white

upper-middle-class wives working outside the home exceed that of white lower-middle-class wives. As will be seen below, however, it was only those upper-middle-class white wives without children whose labor force participation rates exceeded that of lower-middle-class wives in 1980 (see appendix figures B3 and B4).

Why did these upper-middle-class wives who had little need to leave the home for the world of work behave in opposite ways? Or, in terms of the family paradigms, why were upper-middle-class white wives so reluctant to abandon the traditional paradigm? The answer lies largely in the opposite ideological stances of black and white women. Upper-middle-class whites developed the ideology of domesticity, an ideology gradually adopted by white families of other classes. Black upper-middle-class wives, on the other hand, rejected domesticity and produced their own competing ideology—an ideology that encouraged combining work outside the home with marriage and family. Although some white feminists in the late nineteenth and early twentieth centuries called for change, their voices were easily drowned out by adherents of domesticity.

The 1950s and the Recommitment to Domesticity

During the prosperous postwar decade of the 1950s, there was a resurgence of interest in the traditional family, expressed in an ideology that Betty Friedan has called the "feminine mystique." It was a decade when women married at a younger age, bore their first child earlier, and had more children than in the 1940s. As we saw in chapter 1, prominent magazines like *Life* and *Esquire* had harsh words for married women who were tempted to stray from their domestic role. Television sitcoms entertained Americans nightly with amusing domestic scenes, and advertisers sold everything from kitchen stoves to automobiles with images of the domestic wife and mother. Of their constant barrage Friedan comments, "Their unremitting harangue is hard to escape in this day of mass communications; they have seared the feminine mystique deep into every woman's mind, and into the minds of her husband, her children, her neighbors. . . . They have made it part of the fabric of her everyday life, taunting her because she is not a better housewife, does not love her family enough, is growing old." [19]

Advertisers blared:

Can a woman ever feel right cooking on a dirty range? Until today, no range could ever be kept really clean. Now new RCA Whirlpool ranges have oven doors that lift off, broiler drawers that can be cleaned at the sink, drip pans that slide out easily. . . . The first range that any woman can keep completely clean easily . . . and make everything cooked taste better.[20]

With clothes, ads provided ready-made identities to housewives:

Who is she? She gets as excited as her six-year old about the opening of school. She reckons her days in trains met, lunches packed, fingers bandaged, and 1,001 details. She could be you, needing a special kind of clothes for your busy, rewarding life.[21]

While hardly any woman could be entirely immune to these constant blandishments, the white upper-middle-class mother apparently was most susceptible. Only 27 percent had taken jobs by 1960, compared to 35 percent of lower-middle-class white mothers and 64 percent of upper-middle-class black mothers (appendix figure B3). Nevertheless, the 1950s proved to be the "last stand" of the cult of domesticity. Women who had heard the message of Rosie the Riveter beckoning them into defense plants during the war years and felt themselves enlarged and empowered by the success of building ships could not easily erase these images from their minds. Had other challenges to the status quo not followed this experience, however, the feminine mystique still might have triumphed. But there ensued the Civil Rights Movement in which many young white middle-class women participated, followed by the founding of the National Organization for Women (NOW) in 1963 and the feminist movement. These movements were joined by the youth movement, Vietnam protests, and the years of cultural upheaval that followed. In such a cauldron of change domesticity was seriously challenged, if not mortally wounded. It did not die easily, however.

The Importance of Husbands' Attitudes

In addition to the ideology of wives, their husbands' attitudes toward their employment have been an important factor in the process of family change. I have already noted historian Jacqueline Jones's finding that, among black families migrating north, most husbands expected their wives to work, at least temporarily. Even in the nineteenth century, black middle-class women who wished to work outside the home often found support from sympathetic husbands. In a study of the employment of black and white wives in the mid-1970s, Margaret Platt Jendrek and I found that black husbands were generally more supportive of their wives' employment than white husbands.[22] Black middle-class husbands were far more likely than white middle-class husbands to either express a preference for their wives' employment or remain neutral— 68 percent and 55 percent, respectively. Even black working-class husbands were more likely than white middle-class husbands to express a preference for their wives' working. White working-class husbands proved to be the most traditional, with almost two-thirds (61 percent) opposing their wives' employment. In other words, a husband's attitude toward his wife's employment varied by both his race and class position.

The reactions of wives to their husbands' wishes also differed by race and class. White middle-class wives' actions were far more likely to correspond to their husbands' wishes than black middle-class wives' actions were. When middle-class husbands expressed a preference for their wives' remaining at home, 89 percent of white wives did so, but among the black husbands with this preference, only 56 percent of their wives remained at home. Most white middle-class wives (70 percent) likewise tended to stay out of the labor force if their husbands were neutral about their working. In contrast, the majority of black middle-class wives whose husbands were neutral (74 percent) chose employment. Although not as pronounced, the same racial difference in their reactions to their husbands' attitudes appears among black and white working-class wives. Thus, a decade after the social and cultural revolutions of the mid-1960s and well into the era of the feminist movement, Jendrek and I found that white wives were far less likely than black wives to gain spousal support for their employment aspirations.

These findings shed further light on differences in the employment rates of middle- and working-class wives. Among both blacks and whites, middle-class wives have encountered less resistance from their husbands to their aspirations for expanded roles than have working-class wives.

Family change has therefore occurred more rapidly within the middle class. And it has occurred earliest and most fully within the black middle class, where wives found the greatest support for their adoption of the new family paradigm.

A crucial test of the modern family paradigm constructed by black women is how motherhood affects their employment. In the traditional view of the family, women's proper role is in the home, caring for both the husband and the children. These twin roles, it was often argued, are divinely ordained and offer a woman's supreme fulfillment. The very future of civilization, nineteenth-century white women were reminded, depended on their faithful discharge of maternal responsibilities.

Though white society gradually softened its attitude toward the employment of single women, it did not compromise over the norms governing motherhood in the nineteenth and early twentieth centuries. The prevailing opinion was that if single women worked, they had to be protected from conditions that might endanger their future motherhood. The result, historian Alice Kessler-Harris explains, was "protective legislation" passed by state governments barring women from certain occupations such as night work and jobs that required lifting heavy loads that were thought to be injurious to their health and thus a threat to their future role as mothers.[23] By 1915 single middle-class white women were grudgingly accepted as part of the labor force—provided they restricted their employment to "appropriate" occupations, such as teaching and office work, and provided they were willing to leave the labor force upon marriage so as to properly discharge their ultimate duties of wife and mother.

In the face of a serious labor shortage during the Second World War, the norm was relaxed a bit, and married women were encouraged to enter the labor force to replace their husbands, fathers, and brothers in arms. Rosie the Riveter became a symbol of those women who responded. But work in defense factories or offices was not viewed as an expansion of women's roles. Theirs was a noble, patriotic "sacrifice." Even in this time of grave need, however, it was a sacrifice from which mothers were often barred. The last bastion of the woman's traditional role, therefore, was motherhood.

Black middle-class women in the late nineteenth and early twentieth centuries did not see an expanded work role as incompatible with motherhood. Many of these women, like Maggie Lena Walker, explicitly rejected the notion that outside work was detrimental to their role as wives and mothers. Others, like Susan Smith McKinney Steward, a physician, demonstrated this belief by a life combining medicine and marriage. Of her life, the author of a black women's club publication wrote, "She had fairly outdone her white sisters in proving that a married woman can successfully follow more than one profession without neglecting her family."[24] That such women were often conscious of their progressive stance is evident from Steward's comments on the marriageability of black women physicians. "Fortunate are the men who marry these women from an economic standpoint at least. They are blessed in a threefold measure, in that they take unto themselves a wife, a trained nurse, and a doctor." But she cautioned that these women should take care to avoid becoming "unevenly yoked" because "such a companion [would] prove to be a millstone hanged around her neck." Indeed, these women typically married men who were equally successful.[25] As noted in the previous chapter, college educated white women, especially those with postgraduate degrees, often remained single, due to more limited support in the white community for combining marriage and career than in the black community. For example, Howard University medical school maintained a gender-blind admissions policy supported by the school's medical alumni association that decried discrimination against women "as being unmanly and unworthy of the [medical] profession," and announced, "we accord to all persons the same rights and immunities that we demand for ourselves."[26] Few medical schools were so progressive at the time. And their policy of teaching both men and women in the same classes was in part responsible for the refusal of the Association of American Medical Colleges to seat their delegation at its annual convention in 1877.

If the views of black and white middle-class wives on womanhood and family were as different as they appear, we should find black mothers far more likely to work outside the home than white mothers. As Elizabeth Pleck's research has demonstrated, this was certainly true in the late nineteenth and early twentieth centuries.[27] Did the pattern that Pleck observed continue later in the twentieth century? Further, was this the case among middle-class black and white wives who had no real economic need to work outside the home? To what extent have these opposing views been espoused and followed by black and white women over the past fifty-some years? If black and white women did indeed subscribe to opposing beliefs about their roles and the family, we should find that even when children were present black women—especially middle-class black women—would be more likely than white women to enter the labor force.

Working Mothers with Children, 1940 to 1994

If we look at the work patterns of married women in their peak childbearing years, ages twenty-five to forty-four, we find that among both blacks and whites, women with children have been less likely to work than those without children. This might at first suggest that the different ideologies held by black and white women have had no effect on the employment of mothers, but this is not the case. The employment gap between those with and without children has been significantly wider among whites than blacks. Although both black and white mothers were less likely to work outside the home than married women without children, the presence of children has been a weaker deterrent to employment for black than white mothers. Analysis of the employment rates of all black and white mothers between the ages of twenty-five and forty-four demonstrates that the patterns in 1896 and 1911 that Pleck observed have continued throughout the twentieth century. Indeed, among all mothers combined—regardless of class—the employment rates of black mothers remained about ten years ahead of white mothers throughout this period, including the 1960s and 1970s, when the domestic ideology came under especially sharp attack from white feminists. These patterns continue to hold true when the middle and working classes are considered separately. In both classes a higher percentage of black than white mothers worked outside the home. This in itself is strong evidence that the competing ideologies of black and white women had consequences on the way they lived and on family life in general.

Still, this is not the entire story. I have argued repeatedly that the competing ideologies of womanhood had their greatest impact among women in the class where the ideologies originated—the middle class, and especially the upper middle class. Because of their higher education, upper-middle-class women were more likely to come into contact with literature promoting these ideologies and to be involved in promoting these views themselves. At the same time, they were likely to be married to men whose incomes made it unnecessary for them to work outside the home. If these women entered the labor force, then, it was from choice rather than necessity. Data from the 1940 census support this view. With 34 percent of their members at work outside the home in 1940, middle-class black mothers were the most likely among all mothers to have rejected the ideology of women's traditional homemaker role. It would be almost thirty years before an equivalent percentage of white middle-class mothers would enter the labor force (see appendix figure B5). The employment gap was even greater among upper-middle-class wives: 40 percent of black upper-middle-class wives with children were at work in 1940, compared with only 10 percent of white upper-middle-class wives. In subsequent decades, white middle-class mothers left the home for the marketplace at a faster rate than those in the working class but nevertheless remained two to three decades behind black middle-class mothers in their rejection of domesticity. By 1990, when 73 percent of white middle-class mothers had entered the workforce (a level reached by black middle-class mothers around 1970), it was clear that white as well as black women had decisively rejected the traditional family paradigm. Especially in the middle class, a traditional family was now almost an anachronism.

The above comparisons include wives with children of all ages. The effect of the competing ideologies of black and white womanhood can be tested even more stringently by comparing the employment rates of wives with children of different ages. The expected pattern would find wives without children the most likely to be employed, those with preschool-aged children the least likely to work outside the home, and those with children in school falling somewhere in between. This pattern is clearly evident among white middle-class wives (figure 6). (Those with children under age six include all mothers with a preschool child, whether or not an older child is also present.) Relatively few white wives (19 percent) with preschool-aged children were at work in 1960 (the first year for which such data are available). Those with preschool-aged children were about one and a half times less likely to be in the labor force than mothers with school-aged children, and more than two and a half times less likely to be employed than those wives without children. The mid-twentieth century version of the ideology of domesticity, belief in what psychologist Susan Basow calls the myth that only mothers can properly care for small children, seems clearly evident among white middle-class wives in 1960 as well as in 1970.[28] Thereafter it weakens noticeably to the point that almost 70 percent of white middle-class mothers with preschool children are in the workforce by 1994.

In sharp contrast to the pattern found among white middle-class mothers, half of black middle-class mothers of preschool-aged children were already in the labor force in 1960 (figure 7). These mothers were only about a third less likely to be employed than those with school-aged children and about half as likely to be employed as those wives without children at home. The relatively small differences in the employment rates of the three categories of wives—those without children, those with school-aged children, and those with preschool children—suggest how complete the acceptance of the modern family paradigm of the family was becoming among blacks by 1960.

The effects of the competing ideologies seem even more striking in comparisons of the employment rates of black and white middle-class wives with preschool and school-aged children. In 1960 black middle-class wives with preschool children had higher employment rates than white wives with either preschool or school-aged children. The employment rate of black wives with school-aged children was as high as that of white middle-class wives without children. These differences in the employment rates of black and white mothers persisted into the 1990s. Not only did black and white middle-class wives hold opposing role ideolo-

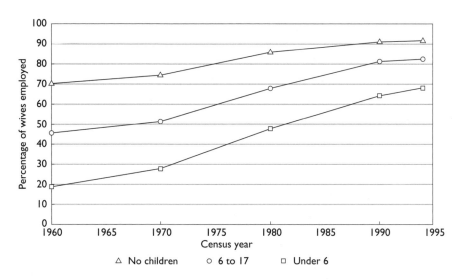

FIGURE 6. Percentage of White Middle-Class Wives Employed, Aged 25 to 44, by Age of Children, 1960–1994

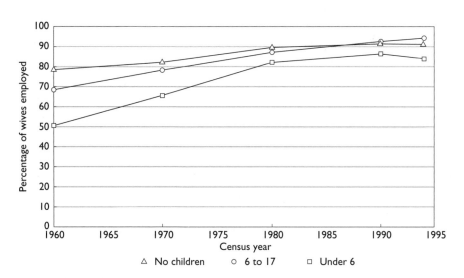

FIGURE 7. Percentage of Black Middle-Class Wives Employed, Aged 25 to 44, by Age of Children, 1960–1994

gies; these ideologies appear to have resulted in very different behaviors and to have profoundly affected the functioning of their families. White wives with children, especially small children, tended to accept mothering and homemaking as their sole roles until at least 1970, while black wives for over three decades have combined these roles with work outside the home, much as the first generation of club women did in the late nineteenth and early twentieth centuries. Not until the 1970s did white mothers with preschool-aged children begin entering the labor force in large numbers. For these mothers, the proportion employed rose from 19 percent in 1960 to 48 percent in 1980. As will become increasingly clear, the 1970s marked the turning point for white wives, who more and more abandoned the traditional family.

Comparing the Employment of Upper- and Lower-Middle-Class Wives and Mothers

The work decisions of upper-middle-class wives are, I believe, powerful indicators of the force of competing domestic ideologies. Because these women are married to men who earn the highest incomes of all workers—professional men and men in management—they have no real economic need to work. Their decision to work can therefore be viewed as flowing more directly from their beliefs about their proper roles than the work decisions of women in other classes, who are likely to be influenced also by economic need. This is true even when upper-middle-class wives are compared with wives in the lower middle class. Although more economically secure than working-class wives, lower-middle-class wives still do not have the security of upper-middle-class wives. Their husbands' positions in sales, clerical, and other administrative and professional support areas command neither the high salaries of professionals and managers nor the same job security or mobility opportunities. Consequently, lower-middle-class wives may feel some pressure to work.

If, then, economic need is the primary motivator for the entrance of wives into the labor force, we should expect to find a higher proportion of lower-than-upper-middle-class wives at work outside the home. That is precisely what occurred among whites, at least until recently. As we saw in figure 5, from 1940 to almost 1980 lower-middle-class white wives entered the labor force faster than upper-middle-class white wives. Thereafter, upper-middle-class white wives joined the workforce at a slightly higher rate. Yet these statistics include wives of all ages, both with and without children. The picture changes when we compare the employment patterns of only wives who are in their primary childbearing years, ages twenty-five to forty-four (see appendix figures B3 and B4). Among white women, we find that after 1970 upper-middle-class wives *without* children became more likely to abandon domesticity than lower-middle-class wives, but this was not true of upper-middle-class white wives *with* children until almost 1990. All in all, among whites, upper-middle-class wives have shown a stronger tendency to conform to the traditional family than wives in the lower middle class.[29]

Just the opposite was true among blacks. Whether we look at all upper- and lower-middle-class black wives (see figure 5) or just those aged twenty-five to forty-four with and without children (see appendix figures B3 and B4), we discover that throughout this period upper-middle-class black wives were more likely to combine marriage and motherhood with employment than those in the lower middle class. Unlike whites, black wives with the least economic need to be employed have been the most likely to enter the workforce. These opposite employment behaviors of black and white wives can be explained only by the competing ideologies of womanhood and the family that they espoused. Adhering to the cult of domesticity, white middle-class wives defined their role in life as caretakers of the home and children, and most remained at home until about 1970. In contrast, having long espoused an enlarged role for women, black middle-class wives acted on the belief that a woman should develop herself as a total person even if she has children. It was around the issue of combining motherhood and employment that the ideologies most clearly diverged by the mid-twentieth century, and it is in this area that the behaviors of upper-middle-class black and white women have been so different, even opposite. By 1970, among upper-middle-class wives age twenty-five to forty-four with children, over 70 percent of the black women chose to combine work and motherhood, while an almost equal percentage of their white counterparts continued to obey the cult of domesticity and stayed out of the labor force.

The 1970s and Beyond: The Demise of the Traditional Family

It took the upheavals of the 1960s—and the feminist movement of the late 1960s and 1970s in particular—to persuade white middle-class women to finally abandon domesticity in favor of the "new womanhood" and the new family paradigm. If white middle-class mothers had been the group most deterred from working outside the home by tradition, then we should expect that the assault on domesticity in the 1970s would have its greatest impact on them. This indeed was the case. Between 1940 and 1970 they entered the labor force at a rate of about 10 percent per decade. But their participation rate suddenly jumped by 20 percent in the 1970s and by another 14 percent in the 1980s (see appendix figure B5).

As we have already seen above, white middle-class wives both with and without children left the home for the marketplace in large numbers, but those with children—including preschool-aged children—made the biggest gains of all (see figure 6). By 1980 almost half of these white middle-class mothers with children under age six were at work outside the home, the majority of them (60.7 percent) full time. It is also true that during the 1970s and 1980s even middle-class families found their high living standards assailed by a declining economy—a fact that certainly motivated many wives to enter the labor force. Still, in no other class did wives with children forsake the haven of domesticity for the workplace to the same degree. White middle-class mothers' dramatic shift away from domesticity in the 1970s and 1980s seems motivated in large part by their belated acceptance of the new ideologies of womanhood and the family now being loudly championed by white feminists.

EXPLAINING THE EMPLOYMENT OF
BLACK AND WHITE WIVES: IDEOLOGY
VERSUS OTHER INFLUENCES

Can we so easily dismiss other influences on a wife's decision to work? To what extent have black and white wives also been swayed by considerations such as their husbands' income or their own marketable skills and education? And what about the availability and cost of child care?

Researchers have found that all of these factors affect a wife's employment decision to some extent. How much, then, has a wife's decision to enter the labor force been motivated by her ideology and how much by other factors? Which has been the most important? Has some factor other than ideology, such as her education or the level of her husband's income, been the principal motivator behind a wife's employment decisions?

We must untangle the effects of these various influences and estimate their relative importance. The neoclassical model used by economists sees the problem as one of a wife's maximizing her utility or satisfaction. In the vocabulary of economists, *utility* or *satisfaction* refers to the package of commodities or goods and services that she can consume because of her choice between remaining at home ("nonmarket time") and employment ("market time"), or some combination of the two.[30] In making her decision a wife will be influenced by the value of her nonmarket time or time at home, which in turn is influenced by her tastes and preferences and the demands placed on her time at home by children, housework, meals, and so forth. According to this model, the availability of "nonmarket income," particularly the amount of income earned by her husband, is also crucially important in her choice between homemaking (nonmarket time) or employment (market time). The higher her husband's income (nonmarket income) the less likely she is to choose employment (market time). On the other hand, her choice of market time is seen as primarily influenced by the value of her market time as measured by the wage rate she can expect. The higher the wage she can earn, the more likely she is to devote at least part of her time to the market.

This all seems very logical and may well explain some women's choices, as well as some of the differences in women's choices across classes (other factors held constant). For instance, women with more education can earn higher incomes, and education is highly correlated with class. This relationship may partially explain the higher employment rate of middle- than working-class wives. The neoclassical model, however, does not consider the husband's taste, as manifested in his support or opposition to his wife's employment. Beyond this, the neoclassical model has at least three major flaws. First, it assumes that women prefer or place a higher value on nonmarket time and therefore need a special incentive to choose market time (employment) over remaining at home, an incentive such as insufficient nonmarket (husbands's) income. Second, a woman's taste or preference never explicitly enters into the model as a measured factor, and therefore its effect is never directly calculated. Third, as I noted above, the neoclassical model cannot explain why black women with the same constraints (children, husband's income) and incentives (available wage rate) as white women tend to work at higher rates. Pleck's 1978 study observed this late-nineteenth- and early-twentieth-century enigma, and it has puzzled economists ever since.[31]

I argue that the assumption of a wife's preference for remaining at home (nonmarket time) historically has not held for a large percentage of middle-class black women. Rather, the preference of middle-class black women has long been to combine market time (employment) with nonmarket time. An accurate understanding of the observed difference in the employment decisions of black and white wives therefore requires that their preferences be somehow explicitly incorporated into the model. I contend that an effective measure of a wife's preference is her ideology of womanhood and that her ideology may well have greater impact on her decision than other factors such as nonmarket income. As an indicator of a wife's preference or ideology, I will use her *employment decision in the presence of children.* The ultimate expression of the ideology of domesticity and true womanhood, as we have seen, was a woman's duty to motherhood and home.

The model of married women's labor force participation that I propose can be tested using a multivariate statistical technique (logistic regression) that simultaneously measures the effects of several factors on a wife's employment decision. This technique is a version of multiple regression designed for problems that involve a dichotomous dependent variable. In this case we are interested in explaining a woman's decision to enter the labor force or remain at home. This approach is useful here for two reasons. First, by concurrently measuring the effects of several factors on a wife's work decision (her children, her education, and her husband's income), we are more closely modeling real-life decision making, where an individual weighs several factors at once. Second, the technique makes it possible to isolate the influence of each individual factor represented in the equation and measure its unique contribution, net of the other factors. When a married woman wrestles with the decision to work outside the home or remain at home, she presumably considers her own beliefs about her roles as woman, wife, and mother; her husband's income (need); her own skills and education (marketability); her husband's attitude; and the availability and cost of child care. Since census data do not include measures of a husband's attitude toward his wife's employment or available child care, these two factors will be omitted. However, the impact of her husband's income, her own education, her class position, and the presence of children will be included. Given that my main concern has been to determine the extent to which competing ideologies motivate black and white women considering employment, the problem is to separate the effect of children from the three other factors. Using logistic regression, we can control for the effects of these other factors and observe the additional outcome related to the presence or absence of children. With this method, we can be confident that the observed effects of children are not confused with outcomes due to a woman's educational level, her husband's income, or her class position.

Figure 8 presents the results of this analysis, showing the effects of the presence of children on the odds of employment among black and white middle-class wives, over and above the effects of these women's own education and their husbands' income (see also table C1 in appendix C). The percentages shown are all negative, indicating that both black and white middle-class wives with children are less likely to work than those without children. The actual percentages tell us how much less likely. For instance, in 1960 black middle-class wives with children were 66 percent less likely to work than black middle-class wives without children; white middle-class wives with children were 80 percent less likely to work than white middle-class wives without children.

This finding is not surprising given our earlier observations of the gap between the employment rates of wives with and without children, and it certainly corresponds to our everyday experience. Every mother has at some time or other struggled, often painfully, with this decision, regardless of her education, her husband's income, or her class position. In the present multivariate analysis, however, we are trying to determine whether this employment gap could be due to other factors besides children. Our findings clearly show that, even after taking into account the effects of a wife's education and her husband's income, the influence of

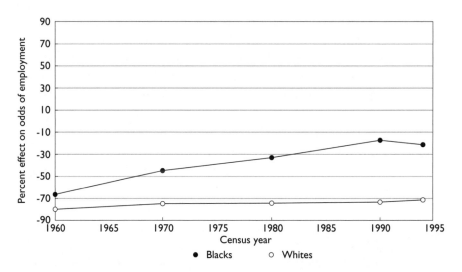

FIGURE 8.   The Effect of Children on the Odds of Employment of Middle-Class Wives, Aged 25 to 44, by Race

children on her work decision remains very strong. It is also clear that the presence of children is far more likely to deter white wives than black wives from leaving home for the work world.

After 1960, the deterrent effect of children on a black middle-class wife's employment declines rapidly to only 17 percent in 1990, indicating that by 1990 a black middle-class wife with children was only 17 percent less likely to work than one without children. Among white middle-class wives, the negative effect of children on employment also declines, but not as sharply. A white middle-class wife with children was still 73 percent less likely to work than her counterpart without children in 1990. Does this mean that most middle-class white mothers were remaining true to the maternal role assigned to them by the traditional family paradigm even in the 1990s? Not really. The increased employment of white middle-class mothers, aged twenty-five to forty-four, from under 30 percent in 1960 to about 75 percent in 1994 tells us differently.

Figure 8 actually reflects two trends: the increasing tendency over time among all wives to reject the traditional paradigm, and the impact of children on this trend. The logistic regression represented in the figure measures the impact of children on the overall trend toward wives' in-

creasing employment by comparing the chance of employment of mothers to nonmothers. As we have seen, by 1990 differences in the employment rates of black middle-class mothers and nonmothers had almost
disappeared (figure 7), while a declining but substantial gap remained
in the employment rates of white middle-class mothers and nonmothers (figure 6). If we think of the effect of children, especially small children, on a wife's employment as the litmus test of the traditional paradigm, the tendencies observed in figure 8 support the contention that
black women—regardless of maternal status—rejected domesticity earlier and more completely than white women. Since the majority of black
middle-class wives without children (78.3 percent)—as well as those
with school-aged children (68.3 percent)—were already working in 1960,
most of the room for change was among those with preschool-aged children (50.6 percent). These mothers of small children moved rapidly into
the labor force over the next 30 years at a rate that almost converged with
nonmothers in the 1980s.

Among white middle-class wives *without children* 70 percent were
at work outside the home in 1960—a percentage only marginally higher
than black middle-class wives *with* school-aged children (68 percent) (figure 7). Less than half of white wives with school-aged children worked,
and only one in five mothers of small children was employed. With the
majority of white middle-class wives with children and almost a third
without children still living in traditional families in 1960, there was
ample room for *both* nonmothers and mothers to reject the traditional
paradigm. They did so over the next thirty years at about the same rate,
producing only a small change in their relative odds of employment. So,
even though 68 percent of white middle-class mothers with small children were working by 1994, they nevertheless remained far less likely to
work than those without children (71 percent less likely).

The Employment of Mothers with Preschool
vs. Mothers with School-aged Children

In the above analysis I compared the odds of employment of nonmothers
versus mothers with children of any age under 18 years. An even more
stringent test of the effects of the two ideologies would be to compare the

employment odds of wives with preschool-aged children with the employment odds of wives without children. If the cult of domesticity is still operative, it likely has taken its last stand on the issue of the employment of mothers of small children. Jan Jarboe Russell, who coined the term "Mommy Wars," recounts an incident in a supermarket checkout counter. Dressed in her office attire of suit and pumps she was rewarded for her casual question to another women in line, "What do you do?" with a curt "I stay home with my children, which is what you should do," and a head of lettuce hurled at her.[32]

If black middle-class wives indeed rejected the ideology of domesticity earlier and more completely than white middle-class wives, we should expect that the presence of preschool children would be a greater deterrent to the employment of white than black wives. To test this possibility I calculated the odds of employment separately for middle-class mothers of preschool and school-aged children compared with the odds of employment of nonmothers, controlling for the effects of a mother's education and her husband's income (see appendix figure B6 and table C2).

In 1960 the chance of a white middle-class wife with a preschool-aged child being employed was 90 percent less than the chance of a white middle-class wife with no children at home. As expected, the differential was far less for a black middle-class wife with a preschooler, who was only 76 percent less likely to be in the workforce than a black wife without children. So, well before the feminist revolution of the mid-1960s to 1970s, there was a considerable gap between blacks and whites in the abandonment of the traditional family by those wives to whom the cult of domesticity most applied.

This is all the more striking since it comes at the end of the 1950s, a period during which American society rededicated itself to the traditional family and was entertained nightly by such televised icons as *Ozzie and Harriet, Father Knows Best,* and *Leave It to Beaver.* As we saw in chapter 1, wives during the 1950s were subjected to a great deal of propaganda urging them to adhere strictly to their domestic role. Small wonder, then, that in 1960 most white middle-class wives with preschool children remained at home. (Nor is it surprising that even white middle-class wives with school-aged children were still almost 60 percent less likely to be employed than those without children.) What is remarkable, however, is that in 1960 close to 51 percent of black middle-class wives with preschoolers were in the workforce (compared with only 19 percent of their white counterparts). Clearly, within that group of middle-class wives to whom the domestic ideology most applied, black and white mothers made different choices.

The 1960s brought little change in the lives of white middle-class mothers of small children. Their employment rate rose only slightly (from 19 to 27.6 percent), and they remained 86 percent less likely to be employed than their counterparts without children in 1970. During the 1970s, when the feminist movement rose to its height, both white wives without children and those with preschoolers entered the workforce in larger numbers and at about the same rate. As a result, the difference between the chance that a white middle-class wife with a small child would be employed and the chance that a wife without children would be employed remained almost the same as a decade earlier. By 1990 white middle-class mothers with preschool children were still 83 percent less likely to have joined the workforce than those without children. White middle-class wives with school-aged children, however, did show a slight increase in relative employment, so that by 1990 they were only 52 percent less likely to be employed than those without children.

After 1960 not only did black middle-class wives with preschool-aged children enter the workforce at a much faster rate than their white counterparts, but they did so more rapidly than black middle-class wives without children. By 1990 a black middle-class wife with a preschooler was only 42 percent less likely to be employed than one without children. If we take the employment of middle-class wives with preschool-aged children as the litmus test of the strength of the cult of domesticity, then clearly black mothers abandoned this ideology sooner and more completely than white wives. Or, to put it slightly differently, we might say that because of their different ideology of womanhood, black wives possessed a greater preference for employment than white wives with similar nonmarket (husband's) income, educational levels, and motherhood status. For black wives, employment seems to have been desirable regardless of these other factors.

5 Dual-Career Couples: Prototypes of the Modern Family

The most striking contrast between the traditional and the modern family is the employment of wives. The modern family, unlike the traditional family, has two earners, with wives, whether middle or working class, sharing the breadwinner role. Even though such families began appearing among African Americans at the end of the nineteenth century, only in the late 1960s did social scientists take an interest in this new family form. Not surprisingly, middle-class dual-career families grabbed the spotlight. The employment of working-class wives was easy to excuse on the grounds of economic need. But when white middle-class wives entered the workforce in substantial numbers, social scientists took note. Attention turned from acceptance of wives' employment in the working class out of need, to enthusiasm over the liberation of middle-class white wives. With the help that comes from 20–20 hindsight this is not surprising. In light of the social and cultural upheavals of the 1960s, including the emerging feminist movement, social scientists were prepared for a fresh perspective on the family.

In the first book on middle-class dual-income families, entitled simply *Dual-Career Families,* British anthropologists Rhona and Robert Rapoport gushed over what they perceived as a radical new family form. These families were different from the traditional family, they argued, because "both heads of household pursue careers and at the same time maintain a family life together."[1] It was not that employed wives were a rarity at the time. As we saw in the previous chapter, about a third of all white and almost half of all black wives were in the labor force by 1970. Indeed, among the upper middle class, about 43.4 percent of white and 72.8 percent of black wives were employed in 1970. What excited the Rapoports was the promise, or at least the possibility, these families offered of a total shift from the hierarchically structured traditional family to one characterized by egalitarian relationships.

While any employment of married women outside the home was at the time, in effect, a radical shift from traditional family norms, did these families in fact function in an egalitarian fashion? In this chapter I will explore the spread and functioning of the modern family. How, for example, have husbands and wives adapted to wives' expanded roles? What difficulties have wives encountered, and how have they dealt with these obstacles? What impact has this had on the marital relationship itself, especially the balance of power? Finally, what differences, if any, have emerged in dual-income families by race and class?

DUAL CAREERS: THE NEW MATH OF THE MODERN FAMILY

I have been arguing that black middle-class women pioneered the family revolution by developing a new ideology of womanhood and family roles. Only this new ideology, I believe, fully explains the differences in their employment history and that of white middle-class wives. Inherent in my argument is the conclusion that the mechanism for family change has been the employment of wives. While the cult of domesticity kept white wives out of the labor force, the ideology of a three-fold commitment to work, family, and community prompted black wives to take jobs outside the home—as a right rather than as a need. If ideology was the underlying force driving family change, the actual employment of wives was the catalyst for that change.

When a wife enters the labor force, she sets off a chain reaction that affects not only her own roles but those of her husband. By giving her access to new economic and psychological resources, employment changes the balance of power in her marriage. In the traditional family the gender division of labor placed most resources in the husband's hands, leaving the wife relatively powerless, particularly when she had to care for small children. An employed wife, by contrast, is engaged in activities that society rewards with income and status. Work outside the home gives her new experiences, and her accomplishments become new sources of self-esteem. Employed women express this in different ways. One woman interviewed by sociologist Arlie Hochschild spoke enthusiastically of her career at Fortune 500 Amerco, contrasting it with homemaking and appearing a bit apologetic. "I'm very good at what I do, and people at work appreciate that. I don't get the same feelings of accomplishment at home. I wish I did. I envy women who do. They have the harder job, but I find home boring. I don't have anything to do but wait until Hannah wakes up."[2] Some husbands recognize the benefit to their marriage that results from their wife's employment. "She has a sense of a full partnership and she should. . . . I think the partnership would be less equal if she didn't work, because she would sense herself as being far less equal if she were not working and having that self-esteem."[3]

The Rapoports referred to the dual-career couples in their study as "pioneers" and as "ordinary people who [had] created something extraordinary," not so much because they were employed but because their occupations required a great deal of personal commitment and time.[4] Because careers—in contrast to jobs—are highly structured, with an individual progressing through a series of developmental stages or promotions, years away from work for child rearing can seriously impede a woman's career mobility. The very nature of careers, therefore, pressures women to remain continuously employed, with only a brief interruption for childbearing. In the corporate world, sociologist Rosanna Hertz has suggested, careers are organized around a "male career model" that assumes a married male rather than either a female careerist or a dual-career couple.[5] This model makes no allowance for family obligations, parental responsibilities, or a life outside the corporate organization, so career women may be especially penalized for withdrawing temporarily to bear and rear children.

Although Hertz focused on dual-career families in the corporate world, it can be argued that all professional and managerial careers are structured around a male model, creating pressures for female careerists to follow a continuous pattern of employment. Certainly, this generates stress for employed wives and especially for mothers, yet it also produces pressure for changing husbands' roles toward truly egalitarian marriages. One husband in Amerco who had summoned the courage to ask his boss for paternity leave began promoting the idea among coworkers. "I was talking to a guy on the company softball team I play on. His wife is expecting, and the guy was saying, 'Oh, I could never ask for paternity leave. My boss wouldn't let me.' I said, 'How do you know? Did you ask him?' 'No, no, but he just wouldn't let me.' So I told him, 'Asking is the hardest part. *Ask* him!'"[6]

A thirty-eight-year-old engineer with Polaroid in a Boston suburb decided to put his family first. "I used to think I'd put up with endless hours forever. I once saw myself as a manager. Now I manage my family. I took a half-day last week. [To attend to family matters.] It's viewed more positively here, and believe me, I've seen it viewed more negatively elsewhere. It's not that I've dropped my career. I'm doing well here and the fringe benefits are great, but family is first."[7]

Because a wife's career employment generates this pressure for change, dual-career families might be considered prototypes of the modern family, families in which the breadwinning and homemaking functions are shared equally rather than segregated by gender. Admittedly, truly egalitarian marriages have proved to be an elusive goal, the Holy Grail of the modern family. Yet, it is this notion of dual-career couples as the "seedbed" of the modern egalitarian family that prompted Hertz to refer to them as "more equal than others."[8]

Indeed, whether a wife works at a career or a job, her very involvement in the labor force makes it difficult or even impossible for her to continue her traditional role of housewife in the same fashion. Her employment therefore creates pressure for her husband to expand his own activities into homemaking, edging little by little toward egalitarianism.

Sociologist Lillian Rubin often discovered a clear understanding of equity among the working-class wives she interviewed for her book, *Families on the Fault Line,* even though these wives could not always achieve this goal. "Sure, he helps me out," one woman said resentfully. "He'll give the kids a bath or help with the dishes. But only when I ask him. He doesn't have to *ask* me to go to work every day, does he? Why should I have to ask him?"[9] Rubin found that some husbands admitted the equity of their own role extension, even though reluctantly. "I don't know, as long as she's got a job, too, I guess it's right that I should help out in the house," remarked one twenty-eight-year-old white warehouse worker. "But that doesn't mean I've got to like it."[10]

The Growth of Black and White Dual-Career Families

The Rapoports and other analysts of dual-career families in the early 1970s all expressed a sense of newness and discovery. All, likewise, focused on small samples of white upper-middle-class couples: the Rapoports studied eighteen British couples in depth; Cynthia Epstein examined the lives of twelve lawyer couples, all partners in New York City practices.[11] Margaret Poloma and Neal Garland investigated the career orientations of fifty-three women in dual-career marriages; and Rebecca and Jeff Bryson and Mark and Barbara Licht looked at one hundred couples in which both spouses were psychologists. After a brief hiatus, other studies followed in the late 1970s, many by practitioners in the counseling field who saw a need to respond to the unique problems experienced by such couples.[12] None of these studies included African Americans, giving the impression that dual-career couples had emerged only among whites.

In fact, dual-career couples were not new among either whites or blacks in 1970. If we define dual-career couples as upper-middle-class couples with both spouses employed in professional or managerial occupations, then 14 percent of black and 5 percent of white upper-middle-class couples were already in that category in 1940. Interestingly, the proportion (14 percent) of black dual-career couples in 1940 was not matched by whites until three decades later, in the early 1970s, when the first articles on dual-career couples began appearing. By that time more than a fifth of upper-middle-class black families were headed by dual-career couples. This was to be expected, given the employment patterns discussed in the previous chapter and the different ideologies of black and white wives. During the 1970s, however, prompted in part by the feminist movement, upper-middle-class white wives entered the labor force in such large numbers that by 1980 the percentage of white dual-career couples (24.6) was slightly higher than that of black (23.4). The gap widened in the 1980s as college-educated white wives continued to move away from the traditional family. By 1990 almost a third of upper-middle-class white and over a fifth of upper-middle-class black families were dual-career.[13]

These percentages may seem small, but that belies their significance. Upper-middle-class families include three categories: (1) dual-career couples, (2) couples in which one spouse is a professional or manager while the other has a lower-middle-class (clerical or sales) or blue-collar job, and (3) couples with only a male breadwinner, who is a professional or manager.[14] Since 1940 both dual-career and dual-worker families have increased among whites and blacks, but more rapidly among blacks (see figures 9 and 10). Correspondingly, upper-middle-class families with a sole male breadwinner have decreased, again more rapidly among blacks than whites.

In 1940, among upper-middle-class black families, 14.2 percent were dual-career, 33.3 percent dual-worker, and 52.6 percent headed by a male breadwinner. In contrast, among upper-middle-class white families, just 4.8 percent were dual-career, 12.7 percent dual-worker, and 82.5 percent headed by a male breadwinner. By 1990 dual-career and dual-worker families predominated among both blacks and whites, leaving only about 10.9 percent of black and 22.5 percent of white upper-middle-class families still following the traditional pattern. With the continuation of these dual-income families' growth in the 1990s, the transformation of family roles is nearly complete.

Although a larger percentage of these new families has been dual-worker families than dual-career families, dual-career families have captured the spotlight because they have had the least necessity for wives

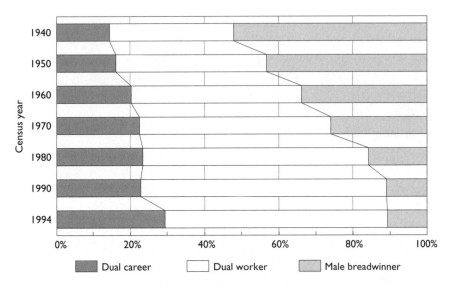

FIGURE 9. Distribution of Black Upper-Middle-Class Families, with Wives Aged 25 to 44, by Husbands' and Wives' Employment

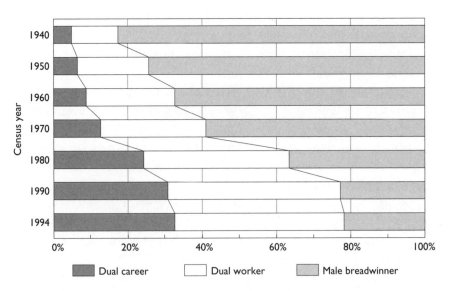

FIGURE 10. Distribution of White Upper-Middle-Class Families, with Wives Aged 25 to 44, by Husbands' and Wives' Employment

to be employed. In most cases husbands earn sufficient income to support their families in considerable comfort, so the wives can truly choose whether to remain at home or enter the workforce. These are the families that I see as prototypes of the modern family. The families represented in figures 9 and 10 include only those with wives who are twenty-five to forty-four years old. These are wives in their prime childbearing years who either have children or plan to have them. While childless professional couples are certainly counted in the dual-career category, researchers have tended to focus on couples with children. The extra workload, time constraints, and day care problems generated by the presence of children especially complicate these couples' lives. Professional wives under age twenty-five are less likely to have commenced childbearing, while those over age forty-four are likely to be parenting children in their late high school or early college years, when juggling child care arrangements is no longer an issue. Except for white wives in 1960, roughly 80 percent or more of both black and white wives had children in the home throughout this period; close to 40 percent had at least one child under six years old.[15]

As noted earlier, while dual-career families may be viewed as prototypes of the modern family, they are only a small fraction of the broader category of dual-worker families, families in which both spouses are employed outside the home, whether at a career or a job. Like upper-middle-class families, both black and white lower-middle-class and working-class families steadily abandoned the traditional pattern and moved into the ranks of dual-worker families after 1940 (see appendix figures B7 and B8). By 1990 almost 80 percent of black and 70 percent of white lower-middle-class families shared the breadwinner role. Within the working class, in about 60 percent of both black and white two-parent families, both spouses were employed. Again, we see that working-class families retained the most commitment to the traditional paradigm of the family.

THE SLOW LIBERATION OF WHITE WIVES

Earlier I suggested that the employment of wives has been the catalyst for family change. If this is so, what shifts have occurred inside the marital relationship as wives increasingly share the breadwinner role? Has the balance of power altered in significant ways? Feminists like Simone de Beauvoir and Betty Friedan have argued that women will never be truly equal to men until they attain equality in the family. Some feminists have even gone so far as to speak of women's "enslavement" in the family. In a less extreme but telling passage, Beauvoir wrote, "Many young households give the impression of being on the basis of perfect equality. But as long as the man retains economic responsibility for the couple, this is only an illusion." [16]

Today, the employment of wives appears to hold the key to ending the illusion. If the breadwinner role has given the husband power and control in the traditional family, then by sharing this role the wife breaks his stranglehold on control and authority. Pinpointing the traditional husband's power, Beauvoir observed, "It is he who decides where they will live, according to the demands of his work; she follows him from city to country or vice versa to distinct possessions, to foreign countries; their standard of living is set according to his income; the daily, weekly, annual rhythms are set by his occupations; associations and friendships most often depend upon his profession." [17]

Admittedly, Beauvoir was writing about the traditional upper-middle-class family in France, a small fraction of all families when she wrote in the late 1940s. Male control, however, has not been confined to upper-middle-class husbands with high-paying, prestigious occupations. Working-class wives have also been powerless. Commenting on white working-class families in Pittsburgh in the late nineteenth century, S. J. Kleinberg notes that the "industrial world penetrated the household and structured women's tasks around men's employment." Theirs were "unequal worlds where wages were the measure of the man but the women could only wait for their husbands to bring home the money that they then managed." [18] Middle class or working class, the traditional family placed women in a state of dependency.

What happens to the balance of power when wives go to work? Do they gain more influence? Do they become equal partners with their husbands? Or is marital equality a pipe dream, beyond the grasp of even the contemporary dual-earner couple?

Going against the Grain

White wives who entered the labor force in the 1960s and early 1970s were still going against the grain. They may not have been pioneers exactly, but the white community and white families still offered little support for employed wives, especially those with children. This was true even in dual-career marriages—with professional women married to professional men. These women's lack of support and the resulting strain affected their lives in a variety of ways. Many who worked before marriage and in the early years of their marriage "chose" to return to the conventional role of housewife when children arrived.[19] Employment until the birth of children was society's earliest concession to married women's aspirations. While not completely denying them the right to employment, it relegated this activity to the periphery of their real life's work: being wives and mothers. It was a kind of a "conventional" pattern, a "new traditionalism," that gave a slight nod to a woman's aspirations, then nipped them in the bud.

Some middle-class wives, however, refused to abandon their careers forever and returned to work after the birth of a child. During this period, reentry into the labor force was most frequently timed to coincide with the enrollment of the youngest child in school. It was this new compromise, the compromise of "interrupted careers," that the Rapoports suggested was gaining broad societal approval in the early 1970s. In 1970, 34.6 percent of middle-class white wives with school-aged children were employed full time, compared to 63.5 percent of those with no children at home and only 17.3 percent of those with preschool children. While ensuring that a woman fulfilled society's expectations of her mothering role when her children were small, this compromise enabled her to utilize her talents to some degree.[20] It was, however, a compromise with considerable personal cost. Depending on the number of children borne, such wives might be out of the labor force from five to fifteen years—a rather long interruption for any worker, but especially for those attempting to build careers. Relatively few white wives in the 1960s or early 1970s had the courage and support to defy gender norms altogether and remain continuously employed with only a brief maternity leave.

The Rapoports estimated that in their British study only 5 percent of the women with small children worked continuously in the late 1960s.[21] Lacking representative samples and in-depth studies of work careers, it is difficult to determine the percentage of American wives pursuing continuous careers at that time. As a rough estimate, we can use the percentage of wives with preschool-aged children who were employed full time. We do not know how long these women were out of the labor force for childbirth, but we do know that at the time of the census they were employed full time while caring for one or more preschoolers. It would appear, therefore, that the interruption of their employment was minimal. At least, these were women who did not wait until their children entered school to return to work.

Strikingly, in 1960 and 1970 only 10.4 and 17.2 percent, respectively, of white middle-class wives pursued continuous employment. Their proportion grew moderately during the 1970s to 22.4 percent in 1980, then—reflecting in part the rapid economic changes of the 1980s—nearly doubled, to 43.1 percent, by 1990. Comparing the proportions of full-time upper- and lower-middle-class wives with small children shows a pattern we have already observed (figure 5): a higher percentage of lower-middle-class than upper-middle-class wives were continuously employed until the mid- to late 1980s.

Generally, compared with middle-class wives, a smaller percentage of working-class wives had continuous employment. Sociologist Myra Marx Ferree has argued persuasively that the lives of women in these two classes are so different that the dual-career model is entirely inappropriate for working-class women.[22] Unlike middle-class women, working-class women cannot pursue careers because they lack the educational criteria for professional employment. Their jobs tend to be intrinsically less rewarding than those held by middle-class, especially upper-middle-class, women. This may be why working-class wives tend to value their roles both as housewives and workers, deriving unique benefits from each. Even more important, working-class families often do not have the income to afford the type of child care that would free the wife to pursue a continuous work career when their children are small.

In her study of working-class families, *Families on the Fault Line*, sociologist Lillian Rubin found that working-class spouses often resorted to shift work to enable wives to hold full-time jobs and yet provide continuous supervision of their children. This was true for about 20 percent of the families interviewed. "Now between the two of us working," one thirty-year-old black postal clerk complained, "we don't make enough money to pay for child care and have anything left over, so this [shift work] is the only way we can manage."[23] At the same time Rubin found that working-class husbands and wives—especially husbands—were more likely than their middle-class counterparts to subscribe to the traditional model of the family and to view a wife's employment as a temporary expedient until the husband found a job or gained a higher income. A twenty-nine-year-old white drill press operator fumed, "I know my wife works all day, just like I do, but it's not the same. She doesn't *have* to do it. I mean, she *has* to because we need the money, but it's different. It's not really her job to have to be working; it's mine. Know what I mean? I'm not saying it right; I mean, it's the man who's supposed to support his family, so I've got to be responsible for that, not her. And that makes one damn big difference."[24]

The fact that working-class males are less and less able to increase their earning power keeps their wives working. Economist Frank Levy points out in *Dollars and Dreams* that from about 1973 "inflation-adjusted wages have stagnated and, in many cases declined."[25] The problem has been especially severe for blue-collar workers who compete for jobs with other workers in the global economy.[26] The family's inability to afford reliable child care, especially for preschoolers, leads to more interrupted work careers for these wives than for those in the middle class, who are often able to purchase the services of au pairs or nannies. Thus even during the difficult economy of the 1980s, not even 25 percent of white working-class wives pursued continuous employment, compared with 42 percent of middle-class wives. For dual-career couples, even a daytime sitter can bring peace of mind when a family can afford the cost, as one woman in a dual-career marriage explained. "The ideal is to have someone in your home—the ideal for the person working, because then you work harder. You are not worried about what is going on at home. People are not calling you to tell you about your kids, which happens frequently at daycare. You don't have to run and pick them up if they are throwing up, or whatever. All that kind of stuff relieves you to do a good job, and that is what I think you pay for."[27] Inhouse sitters facilitate varying working hours, as one husband noted with satisfaction. "For example, she can be relied on to stay late when sometimes, unexpectedly, my wife or I don't get home till eight-thirty or nine o'clock. She stays till one of us gets there."[28]

Looking at wives' "attachment" to the labor force, we can see the Rapoports' three patterns—conventional, interrupted, and continuous—as outlining a progressive movement away from the norms of the traditional family. This movement is far from complete. Only with societal support for continuous careers will married women gain the same opportunity as married men for personal career development and, with it, the possibility of egalitarian marriages. While continuous careers for men are taken for granted and facilitated by the traditional assignment of housework and child care to wives, women usually do not have the help of a "wife" at home and frequently receive no structural support from the workplace for their parenting role. Thus dual-career marriages, in the words of one writer, suggest a "paradox of marriage as the union of two husbands and no wife."[29] To be successful, women must accommodate the demanding and greedy male career model of the workplace while finding scant relief from their traditional mothering and homemaking obligations. All of the early studies of dual-career couples found that wives continued to have primary responsibility for the home.

Domesticity's Lingering Hold

In her study of lawyers in the early 1970s, Epstein found that the wives not only maintained primary responsibility for the home and child care but also played a secondary role to their husbands at the office. At work the wives were assigned to the firm's less visible and less prestigious cases, and often were stuck with nonlegal administrative tasks. Among the psychology pairs studied by the Brysons and Lichts in the mid-1970s, the responsibility for the home and child care also rested mostly on the wives' shoulders. In many ways the women's careers took second place to those of their husbands, leading to lower productivity. Similarly, in a 1978 study of ten couples with continuous careers, Donald St. John-Parsons found that although the wives enjoyed considerable support from their husbands for pursuing careers, the care of the home nevertheless remained almost entirely theirs. When scheduling conflicts occurred in the two careers, "almost without exception, it was the woman who made the accommodation."[30]

These early studies of white dual-career couples did not find that the employment of wives led to egalitarian marriages. In their 1971 study, Poloma and Garland could classify only one couple out of fifty-three as truly egalitarian, prompting them to suggest that these career wives had a "tolerance of domestication." Statements from the women they interviewed clearly support this conclusion. These wives saw their careers as "really and truly secondary," or admitted that they would not have pursued careers without their husbands' approval:

> I know I wouldn't do it if my husband didn't want me to work. You'd have to have a pretty darn good reason for working if your husband didn't want you to. I can't imagine being married to someone who didn't want me to do what I wanted to do. Even though my career is clearly secondary, I don't feel cheated in any way because I want it this way. If I didn't want it this way, I think the marriage institution as we know it, and as we say it is in fact, in our society would be disrupted and that my marriage wouldn't be a successful one.[31]

Poloma and Garland classified about half of these families as "neo-traditional" families in which the wife's income was needed to maintain the standard of living, though it typically was used for luxuries such as expensive vacations, private school for the children, or special purchases, rather than pooled with the husband's income for daily maintenance. While granting the wife's contribution some importance, this practice nevertheless marginalized it.

The other half of the families were what Poloma and Garland termed "traditional" dual-career families. For these families, the wife's career was more or less a hobby and her income was not missed if she stopped working. These families were barely one step removed from the kind of traditional family another writer characterized as the "two-person single career" family in which the husband alone was employed and looked to his wife for the support needed to facilitate his career development and advancement.[32] As Martha Fowlkes reports in "The Myth of Merit and Male Professional Careers: The Role of Wives," her own study of the wives of doctors and academics reveals the indebtedness of married male professionals to their wives.[33] Her research explodes the myth that males' success stemmed solely from their own hard work and dedication and demonstrates persuasively how much the husbands' careers were advanced by the wives' supporting roles. This support went well beyond taking care of the home and children to include typing and editing manuscripts, providing research assistance, and—in the case of physicians' wives—working as office managers, receptionists, hospital auxiliaries, and community volunteers to promote their husbands' practices.

Poloma and Garland do point out one major difference between the traditional and the neo-traditional dual-career families they studied. Although in both groups the wife remained responsible for home and children, in neo-traditional families the wife's career assumed some importance in family decisions such as a possible move. This was no doubt due to the significance of her income for the family. These wives had taken at least a small step toward equal roles.

All these early studies of dual-career families give the impression that white wives moved only very slowly away from their traditional roles in the late 1960s and early 1970s. Most of these women appeared content to allow their careers to play second fiddle to their husbands' and to their own domestic responsibilities—a testament to the power of socialization. These early studies suggest that the wives' tendency to accommodate their husbands' careers prevented them from developing continuous careers for themselves and increasing their own power in their marriages.

Still, to characterize these wives as "tolerating domestication" may be too harsh an assessment. These women had been socialized in the traditional norms of the family, and when they attempted to move beyond the boundaries of these norms, they found scant support from society, especially when small children were involved. There is no evidence that even supportive husbands were inclined to substantially lighten their wives' domestic load by actively participating at home. In virtually all cases these wives had to resort to the use of domestic help to ease their burden and enable them to pursue careers. Although this generation of white upper-middle-class women moved away from the traditional paradigm of the family by entering the labor force, they were not able to achieve egalitarian marriages, and few were able to fashion continuous careers. To their credit, in spite of these obstacles they continued to enter the work world and by the late 1970s were becoming less accommodating to their husbands.

Redefining Roles in the 1980s and 1990s

A large influx of college-educated women into the labor force during the 1970s brought the percentage of employed white middle-class wives aged twenty-five to forty-four to about 62 percent by 1980. Many of these women had, by this time, experienced several years in and out of the labor force, but perhaps as many as 22 percent had managed to maintain continuous careers. For all these women, the 1970s were a time of enduring the frustration of inadequate support both in the workplace and at home. Still, a large number were also strongly influenced by the feminist movement, which urged them to jettison the traditional model of the family and seek fulfillment in the workplace. Many women aged thirty in 1980 had been college students in the late 1960s and early 1970s, when both the student movement and the feminist movement were prominent. Those aged twenty-five in 1980 may have just been entering high school in 1970, but they reached young adulthood at the height of the feminist movement. These women had witnessed demonstrations, and many had participated in consciousness-raising activities. Together, their employment and the feminist movement would strongly affect how they approached and negotiated their roles of wife, mother, and worker. In 1980 these women faced two alternatives: they could continue to tolerate domestication and experience the frustration of stymied careers, or they could reconceptualize their lives as women.

Researchers in the early 1980s soon discovered signs of such a reconceptualization among white dual-career wives. Whereas Poloma and

Garland saw little evidence of career commitment in 1971, several studies of dual-career couples in the early and mid-1980s found that employment was just as salient to the wives as to the husbands.[34] Like their husbands, these wives perceived their careers as an integral and satisfying
part of their lives. One study of 1,712 career female managers and professionals in the mid-1980s found them bullish on combining career and
motherhood.[35] The majority of these women (86.7 percent) had children,
and 41.4 percent had a child under two years old. Yet, though most
(69.1 percent) acknowledged the difficulty of pursuing a career while
raising a child, they nevertheless were determined to do so and did not
believe that it would jeopardize future progress in their careers.

These wives had rejected the traditional admonition that a woman's
complete happiness lay in the home, caring for her husband and children. It seems, from these studies, that more and more white wives in the
1980s were seeing a career as integral to their personal happiness. For increasing numbers this translated into continuous careers: 44.9 percent in
1994 worked full time while caring for a child under six years old — compared with only 22.4 percent fourteen years earlier.

Nothing less than a redefinition of both womanhood and motherhood
was taking place, mirroring the redefinition pioneered by black women
earlier in the century. Increasingly, women were looking for more than
marriage and motherhood. Already this new reality was apparent in the
early 1980s in a study by the Wellesley Center for Research on Women,
which found that a high-prestige job ranked above a husband as a pre-
dictor of these women's well-being.[36] Indeed, this study found that the
women who scored highest in well-being not only held high-prestige
jobs but were also married with children. Uma Sekaran's study of 127
dual-career couples in the early 1980s found that—with one exception
discussed below—career salience for wives and husbands was influenced by identical factors: the degree to which they derived self-esteem
from their work, their job involvement, their sense of competence, and
their level of education.[37]

Still, there were signs that the pursuit of a career and the happiness it
brought remained more conditional for these wives than for their husbands. Sekaran also discovered that for wives, but not husbands, career

salience depended on the extent to which the couple had planned on a dual-career family before getting married. As Sekaran suggests, women seemingly still looked for legitimization of this new lifestyle in a kind of verbalized agreement with their spouses. This tendency should not be surprising, given that society has traditionally disapproved of the employment of married women and mothers but approved and supported careers for men regardless of marital or parental status. Sekaran also found that although careers appeared to be equally salient for wives and husbands, the wives perceived themselves as less involved in their jobs, perhaps because of their heavy family responsibilities. Baron's study of married career women supports this interpretation. Noting that these women were married to a great variety of men, from those who did "practically nothing" at home to those who were full partners, she concluded that women whose husbands did not help out at home were the "most pessimistic" about combining a successful career with a family.

During the 1980s and early 1990s a growing literature reported on the stress experienced by dual-career couples, especially wives.[38] Indeed, in this period stress became a dominant theme. Much of this stress can be linked to the determination of a new generation of women to combine career and family without sacrificing either. Whereas in the 1960s and 1970s women may have given priority to family and sacrificed a career, in the 1980s they were more likely to attempt to be "superwomen" and do it all.[39] In the absence of job flexibility and husbands who shared substantially in housework and child care, the price these women paid was often a stressful lifestyle with little time for personal leisure activities. The frustration resulting when a husband fails to pitch in at home is evident in the words of one woman interviewed by sociologist Arlie Hochschild in the late 1990s:

> My husband's a great help watching our baby. But as far as doing housework or even taking the baby when I'm at home, no. He figures he works five days a week; *he's* not going to come home and clean. But he doesn't stop to think that I work *seven* days a week. Why should I have to come home and do the housework without help from anybody else? My husband and I have been through this over and over again. Even if he would just pick up from the kitchen table and stack the dishes for me, that would

make a big difference. He does nothing. On his weekends off, I have to provide a sitter for the baby so he can go fishing. When I have a day off, I have the baby all day long without a break. He'll help out if I'm not here, but the minute I am, all the work at home is mine.[40]

Some studies in the 1980s showed that even when husband and wife both subscribed to egalitarian values, the husband did not back up his avowed values in practice or expressed ambivalent feelings about surrendering his traditional superiority. At the same time the wife often struggled with feelings of guilt about neglecting her traditional family responsibilities, especially toward her children.[41]

Family studies now began to examine a new concern, "work-family conflict." and the challenges posed to wives and husbands in meshing the demands of these two spheres.[42] Attempts to provide couples with new coping strategies proliferated.[43] One study by Gloria and Gerald Bird investigated the effectiveness of eight different stress reduction strategies: legitimate excuse, stalling, compartmentalization, barriers against intrusion, reducing responsibilities, delegation, organization, and empathy.[44] Their conclusion: couples in their sample of 183 dual-career husbands and wives tended to employ the strategies of organization, empathy, and stalling, but not reduction of responsibilities. Other researchers focused on the degree to which individuals used "cognitive restructuring coping strategies" such as overlooking difficulties or "role reduction strategies" such as reducing leisure activities or job involvement.[45] Still other researchers examined the strategies of "reframing," using "spiritual support," and using "social support."[46] Despite the diversity of stress reduction strategies uncovered by researchers, some common themes emerge in these studies. One is that wives experience greater stress than husbands, which is understandable given the addition of full-time employment to their traditional roles of housework and child care. For their part, husbands with flexible job schedules experience lower stress than those with rigid schedules. Not surprisingly, wives whose husbands are willing to assist with housework and child care have less stress and are happier than those whose husbands do not. Yet whatever the stress accompanying career and motherhood, women appeared to find greater happiness when juggling the demands of home and work than when confined to the domestic role of housewife. One woman in the late 1980s expressed the importance of work to sociologist Rosanna Hertz. "I'm . . . a person whose career is of primary importance. It's not just a means to an end. I get satisfaction if I do a good job and I'm promoted. I'd go crazy at home. I could never, never stay at home. Work is a fundamental part of my identity. . . ."[47]

DIFFERENCES IN BLACKS' AND WHITES' ATTITUDES TOWARD WIVES' EMPLOYMENT

How did black wives manage to walk this gender tightrope, balancing domestic responsibilities and career demands? Were they more or less accommodating of their husbands' careers than white wives? Were they more or less successful in forging continuous careers? And what were the implications for the balance of power in their marriages?

Unfortunately, most of the research on dual-career marriages has focused exclusively on white couples. The few studies of black couples, however, suggest striking differences between blacks and whites. In the late 1960s one researcher found a greater preference for the regular employment of wives among recent black male college graduates than among their white counterparts.[48] The same study showed that black female college graduates also were more likely than white female graduates to perceive their husbands as wanting them to work. A 1967 study of 565 white and 67 black males in Florida found that 68.7 percent of black males, compared with 48.1 percent of white males, believed that their wives should work if they so desired.[49]

Still another study found that black female and male college students in 1960 and 1970 held considerably more liberal views of the female role than their white counterparts.[50] In both 1960 and 1970, black female college students were "more self-achieving in orientation than white women" and they perceived the males' ideal woman as more independent than did white women. Correspondingly, for black males the ideal woman was more self-achieving than for white males. Although all four groups developed more liberal views of female roles over the decade, in both 1960 and 1970 black males and females conceived the ideal woman as more self-achieving and independent than did whites.

These early findings of racial differences in gender attitudes among college students and young adults appeared in later studies of older married couples. In our analysis of data from a national survey in 1975, Margaret Jendrek and I found not only that black middle-class and working-class husbands were more likely to support their wives' employment, but also that they were less likely to prevail when they opposed it. Over two-thirds (68.3 percent) of black middle-class husbands either preferred their wives to work (24.3 percent) or expressed no preference (44.0 percent), while just over half (55.6 percent) of white middle-class husbands either preferred (17.9 percent) their wives to work or expressed no preference (37.7 percent). Among those families in which the husbands preferred that the wife remain in her traditional housewife role, only 10.6 percent of white middle-class wives were employed full time, compared with 43.8 percent of black wives. Among working-class families in which husbands preferred their wives to remain at home, 13.6 percent of white wives, versus 25.3 percent of black wives, were employed full time.[51] Clearly, black females and males have for some time held more egalitarian views than whites of a wife's role in marriage. But have these differences in attitudes been realized in more egalitarian relationships in black families?

Black and White Differences in Marital Power

In recent decades sociologists have devoted a great deal of effort to developing theories and valid measures of marital power. Relationship power is frequently assessed by investigating decision making among couples. If we think of power as the ability to "get one's way" even over the objections of another, then the person who manages to prevail exercises power in that situation. The fact that Jendrek's and my 1975 study found far more black than white wives to work when their husbands opposed their decision suggests that black wives had more power than white wives. It does not, however, mean that black wives had more power than their husbands, as sociologists Robert Blood and Donald Wolfe have suggested.[52]

It is not difficult to understand how black wives might have more power than white wives yet still have less power than their husbands. Simply put, it is a question of both race and gender differences. Like white women, black women are handicapped by gender discrimination in the workplace, yet have higher and more continuous employment than white women. In the resource theory of power, sociologists argue, an individual may appeal either overtly or covertly to certain characteristics or factors to prevail over another. Within a marriage these include societal norms, socialization, and personal attributes such as job or income. Certainly, societal norms and socialization have supported a husband's authority and power by assigning him the role of head of the family, but equally important is his traditional role as breadwinner. Through his breadwinner role, a husband gains the personal resources of an occupation, income, and status. When he is the sole breadwinner, he alone can insert these factors into decision making in a manner that contributes to his desired outcome.

A wife also can utilize these resources to increase her power in marriage—if she can acquire them. Becoming employed is the quickest and most direct route to increasing a woman's marital power. One white middle-class wife described the greater sense of equality resulting from her employment. "Working has increased my status in terms of equality within the marriage, and it also has decreased my dependence, both my own sense of dependence and my husband's sense that I am dependent on him. That makes it into much more of a voluntary relationship. . . ."[53] Husbands, too, recognize the change that comes to the relationship when a wife is employed, and many welcome it. One white middle-class husband in Hertz's study of dual-career couples spoke proudly of his wife's employment. "She has a sense of a full partnership and she should. . . . I think the partnership would be less equal if she didn't work, because she would sense herself as being far less equal if she were not working and having that self-esteem."[54] When a wife is employed and contributes to the family's living standard she has a greater voice in decision making, as Poloma and Garland observed among their "neo-traditional" families, in which the wife did indeed have a say in decisions such as a contemplated move. A wife's entry into the labor force, therefore, changes the balance of power in marriage in a way that is unaccessible to wives in traditional families.

A job or even a career, however, does not automatically confer *equal* power on wives. Resources such as a job and income are acquired outside of the home and brought into the marriage. In their struggle to acquire these resources, wives are handicapped relative to their husbands because they are women. That is, the structural barriers of discrimination and social norms prevent most women from acquiring resources equal to those of men. In 1990 college-educated women aged twenty-five to thirty-four who were employed full time, year-round, still earned only 76 percent of their male counterparts' incomes. As we will see in the next chapter, most wives continued to trail their husbands in earnings in the late 1990s, even with an equal work effort. The discriminatory barriers faced by women and minorities in climbing the corporate ladder were considered serious enough for Congress to establish a Glass Ceiling Commission within the United States Department of Labor in 1991.[55] Also, the tradition of sex-typing occupations begun in the nineteenth century still results in women's being disproportionately concentrated in lower-paid, service-type occupations such as elementary school teachers, nurses, and librarians. The structural theory of power suggests that so long as women are handicapped relative to men in their struggle for resources outside the family, they will not be able to achieve equal power within the marriage.[56]

This inequity, of course, applies to both black and white women. But how does these factors' overall effect on the balance of power compare in black and white families? Black wives have not only historically worked at a higher rate than white wives but are also likely to have worked for a longer time and are more likely to have maintained continuous careers. Again, if we use as a rough measure of continuous employment the percentage of wives employed full time who have preschool children, we find that by 1960 20 percent of black middle-class wives and only 10 percent of white middle-class wives had continuous careers. Over the next two decades the proportion of black middle-class wives maintaining continuous careers increased rapidly to three out of four wives with preschool children by 1980, then rose more slowly to 80.4 percent in 1990. White middle-class wives did not reach the black wives' 1960 level until the mid-1970s, and they were only slightly more than half as likely to pursue continuous careers in 1994.[57]

Black wives as a group have historically commanded greater resources than white wives through higher rates of employment and a longer and more continuous presence in the labor force. In this way they have contributed more than white wives to their families' income and have consequently held more power in their marriages. Since power sharing contributes to egalitarianism in marriage, it is not surprising that researchers have tended to find black families more egalitarian than white families.[58] Black women have also benefited more than white women from community support for their expanded role in employment and, consequently, for more egalitarian marriages. Nevertheless, as we will see in the next chapter, black husbands still hold more power in their marriages since—like white husbands—they generally earn higher incomes than their wives.

6 The Economic Contribution of Wives

The expansion of wives' role to shared breadwinning gradually led to the demise of the traditional family. Instead of rigidly separate breadwinner and homemaker roles, spouses in the "new family" now pursued permeable and flexible—if not entirely interchangeable—roles. In a way this was a return to the preindustrial pattern of the family as an economic unit, with both spouses exercising economically productive roles. What distinguishes this new family from the preindustrial one is that these productive roles were now performed away from the home, rather than in it. In addition to the social and psychological benefits for wives and husbands, this change had a major impact on the family economy, in terms of income.

WIVES' CONTRIBUTIONS TO THE FAMILY INCOME

Today it has become commonplace to think of families relying on two incomes, but this was not always so. In the post-Second-World-War period until the mid-1970s, a booming economy and high wages enabled most two-parent families to manage well on the husband's income. With the increasingly severe economic downturn of the 1970s and 1980s, however, many families found it difficult or even impossible to manage on only one income. Although the desire to expand their roles beyond the home motivated many wives to enter the labor force during the 1970s, economic conditions provided an added incentive in the 1980s. Whatever the reason for a wife's employment, her earnings added significantly to the family's income, especially in the later 1970s, 1980s, and 1990s.[1]

In 1960 employed middle-class white wives, aged twenty-five to forty-four, contributed a median of 24.6 percent of the family income, compared with 28.6 percent by middle-class black wives (figure 11). Over the next three and a half decades women's contributions to family income continued to rise. The increase was especially sharp in the 1980s, as many more wives entered the labor force or went from part- to full-time work in order to maintain their family's living standard during a period of stagnating or declining male incomes and growing income inequality in the society.[2] By 1990 black and white middle-class wives were making median contributions of 42.9 and 34.7 percent, respectively, to their families' incomes. These contributions did not vary greatly between upper- and lower-middle-class wives among either blacks or whites.

Though not as great as that of middle-class wives, the income contributions of black and white working-class wives also increased impressively during these decades, reaching levels of 36.2 and 26.5 percent, respectively, by 1990. The economic well-being and living standards of most American families were now closely tied to the employment of both husbands and wives. For some of these families a wife's exit from the labor force might cause only minor inconvenience, but for others it could lead to a lower standard of living or even a serious economic crisis. The economy as a whole was now equally dependent on the continued presence of these women in the labor force.

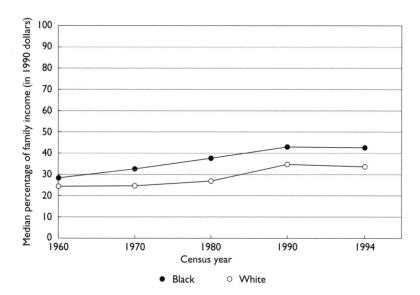

FIGURE 11.   Median Percent Contribution to Family Income by All Employed Middle-Class Wives, Aged 25 to 44

Increase in Families with Two Full-time Employed Spouses

The above figures include all employed wives, whether they worked full or part time. Between 1960 and 1980 the percentage of families in which both spouses were employed full-time grew by an average of 10 percentage points each decade among both black and white middle-class families (figure 12). This rate of increase more than doubled during the economic turbulence of the 1980s, before declining slightly in the early 1990s. By 1990 over two-thirds of black (69 percent) and more than half of white (52.6 percent) middle-class families had both spouses employed full time.

Families with two full-time employed spouses also increased impressively among both black and white working-class families after 1960, reaching levels of 42.8 and 29.7 percent, respectively, by 1980. In contrast to the middle class, however, in the working class the percentage of black and white families with both spouses employed full time declined between 1980 and 1990, and continued to decrease in the early 1990s. This decline suggests the greater vulnerability of working-class families to de-

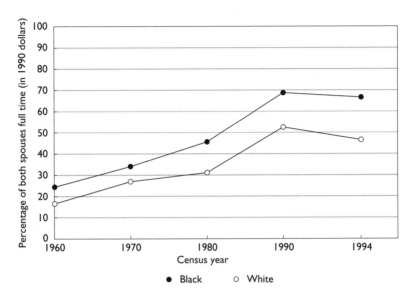

FIGURE 12. Percentage of Middle-Class Families with Both Spouses Employed Full Time

industrialization in the 1980s, which led to higher unemployment in the working class than in the middle class.

Just how much of a difference did it make to the family's economy if a wife worked full time? In 1960 middle-class black and white wives employed full time contributed medians of 38.1 and 34.9 percent, respectively, to their families' incomes, contributions that were 10 percentage points higher than those of the combined categories of full- and part-time workers. In subsequent decades, their contributions continued to be larger. By 1994 black and white middle-class wives in families in which both spouses were employed full time claimed median income contributions of slightly over 40 percent. Similarly, among working-class families, wives contributed significantly more when they worked full time. By 1990 these black and white working-class wives contributed medians of 38.9 and 36.3 percent, respectively, of their families' incomes.

Whether we consider all families in which both spouses are employed at least part time or only those families in which husbands and wives both work full time, today a wife's contribution to her family's income is substantial. Over the decades her economic role has reached proportions unimaginable just a generation ago, and many families' living standards now depend on her employment as well as on the husband's. This is especially true of those in the working class, as one white male's complaint in the early 1990s shows. "I know she doesn't mind working, but it shouldn't have to be that way. A guy should be able to support his wife and kids. But that's not the way it is these days, is it? I don't know anybody who can support a family anymore, do you? Well, I guess those rich guys can, but not some ordinary Joe like me."[3] In upper-middle-class families, a wife's employment often has a different meaning, liberation of the husband from the burden that comes with being the sole breadwinner. "I'm not a workaholic. I'm pretty comfortable with what I'm doing. I probably could make more money if I was interested in working a lot harder, but I would have to sacrifice a lot of things for that—like time with my family, personal time, a lot of things. I'm just not willing to do that, and in part, I don't have to do that because my wife works."[4]

With the growth of their income contribution has presumably come an increase in wives' power in family decisions. Median contributions of 35 to 40 percent to a family's income are no longer pin money or spare cash for special purchases or luxury items. And since it is median income, 50 percent of these wives have contributed more than the median, some of them even earning more than their husbands. Many of these wives, therefore, can now negotiate from positions of financial strength. For black wives, this seems all the more true, as they are more likely than white wives to be employed full time, and thus to contribute more. In 1994, while close to half (47.3 percent) of middle-class white families with wives aged twenty-five to forty-four had two full-time employed spouses, two-thirds (67 percent) of similar middle-class black families had dual full-time earners (figure 12). According to the resource theory of power, higher employment rates and greater income contribution to the family should translate to more marital power among black than white wives and, therefore, to more egalitarian marriages. It is clear, however, that among both black and white families, wives are gaining power. And as the following remark by a white wife emphasizes, like middle-class wives, many working-class wives enjoy employment's liberating experience. "I couldn't believe what a difference it made when I went to work. I feel like I've got my own life. I never felt like I really ruled my life before. You know, I went from my parents' house to my husband's. He's a good man, but he's bossy. Now I'm working just like him, so he can't just boss me around so much anymore. I mean, he still tries, but I don't have to let him."[5]

Nevertheless, neither black nor white wives as a group have attained equal power with their husbands. The structural theory of power offers a reason. Even when employed full time, both black and white middle-class wives contributed a median of less than 50 percent of their families' incomes in 1994. As a group, therefore, both black and white wives have a long way to go before reaching resource parity with their husbands.

Wives' Percentage of Husbands' Income

The greater resources—and therefore power—of husbands become even clearer when we compare the wife's and the husband's incomes. In 1960 employed black middle-class wives (full and part time) earned a median of less than half (44.4 percent) of their husbands' incomes; white wives had median incomes of only slightly more than one-third (35.7 percent) of their husbands'. Over the next thirty years, although both black and white middle-class wives made impressive gains of 77 and 52 percent, respectively, they still fell far short of income parity with their husbands. In 1990 black wives' incomes had reached a median of 78.6 percent of their husbands'; white wives had a median of only 54.6 percent of their husbands'. Both groups of wives experienced slight declines in income relative to their husbands in the early 1990s.

Wives in families where both spouses worked full time fared far better (figure 13). In these families black and white middle-class wives had median incomes that were 65 and 58 percent, respectively, of their husbands' incomes in 1960. By 1990 the median for black wives reached 80 percent of the husband's income; for white wives, 66.7 percent. In the early 1990s black wives maintained their income position, and white wives improved theirs significantly. Thus in 1994, half of black middle-

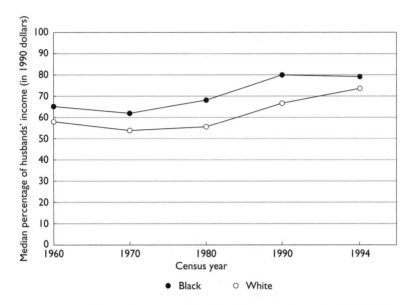

FIGURE 13.   Median Percentage of Husbands' Income Earned by Middle-Class
Wives, Aged 25 to 44 (Both Spouses Employed Full Time)

class wives in these families earned an income that was over 80 percent
of the husband's income. Among similar white families, the figures are
lower but still significant, with half earning incomes over the median of
73.8 percent. Between 1960 and 1994, from 2 to 3 percent of white and
from 3 to 4 percent of black middle-class wives were actually at parity,
earning incomes equal to their husbands'. In terms of income, at least,
these wives had reached parity with their husbands and, theoretically,
the potential for equal power in their relationships. In such marriages,
couples frequently opt for two individual accounts and one joint account
for family expenses. Hertz noted that dual-career couples discover that
this arrangement eliminates money arguments and gives both spouses
freedom to pursue their own whims without interference. The high income of one wife made it possible for the couple to begin marriage with
this agreement. "When we decided to get married, we had a very, very
financial-type discussion. You know, where neither of us wanted to give
up the right to go out—like I'll go out and spend $400 on a suit and I

don't want to hear about it; and Bill the same thing—he'll go to Florida and spend $1,000 on golf and he doesn't want to hear about it. So we both knew that we had to have enough money on our own, and this seemed like the fair way to do it."[6] Another white dual-career couple came to this decision only after many years of marriage and much dissatisfaction for the wife:

> [The money] was all in one joint account, and I found that I was always coming up short. And I figured that I was busting my tail at work and at home and that I should have money left for me. I didn't at all. . . . Over the years my discretionary income was subsidizing his expense account at his office, and I finally decided, "Nope, you can sink on your own." Now it is wonderful I have *that* income. And now he says, "How am I going to pay my half of the Marshall Field's bill?" and I say, "It's your problem. Here's a check for my half of the bill."[7]

As noted earlier, employed black working-class wives also improved their relative power position between 1960 and 1980, but unlike middle-class wives, they did not make gains during the 1980s. Moreover, their incomes actually declined relative to their husbands' in the early 1990s. Employed white working-class wives made only a slight gain relative to their husbands in the 1970s and did not improve their position thereafter. In working-class families with two full-time employed spouses, both black and white wives enjoyed far stronger positions relative to their husbands, yet remained far from parity (see appendix figure B9). In 1980 these black and white working-class wives had median incomes that were 66.7 and 58 percent, respectively, of their husbands' incomes. A decade later their medians had increased to only 68 and 60 percent, respectively. Again, although the 1980s saw significant income gains among middle-class wives, there was little among working-class wives.

Wives with Higher Incomes Than Their Husbands

Among those wives with incomes above the median, a small percentage have not only reached parity with their husbands but actually exceeded it. In 1960, in the middle class, 15.2 percent of all employed black and 11 percent of all employed white wives had higher incomes than their husbands. The number of wives with higher incomes than their husbands increased modestly in the 1970s, then more rapidly during the 1980s, when the income of males stagnated. By 1990, 31 percent of black and 19 percent of white middle-class wives had higher incomes than their husbands. The percentage of black wives with incomes greater than their husbands remained about the same in the early 1990s, while increasing slightly to 21.2 percent among white wives by 1994. In families with both spouses employed full time, similar percentages of wives earned higher incomes than their husbands.[8]

Among dual-career families, the proportion of wives earning more than their husbands was even higher in 1980: 26.3 and 15 percent, respectively, for black and white wives. By 1990 the figures had risen to 28.5 percent of black and 21.4 percent of white dual-career families. By 1994 the proportion of black dual-career wives with higher earnings had declined to 18.1 percent, while that of white dual-career wives had climbed to 26.8 percent. This appears to have resulted from opposite income trends among black and white college graduates in the 1990s. Between 1989 and 1997 the wages of white female college graduates increased more rapidly (8.9 percent) than those of white male college graduates (1.3 percent); while the opposite was true among their black counterparts. Wages of black female college graduates grew by only 1 percent; while those of black college-educated males increased by 2.6 percent.[9]

The specter of wives with higher incomes than their husbands seems to always raise questions of marital discord. While husbands earning more than their wives is taken as normative, the reverse is viewed with alarm. The issue generally is seen as one involving the male ego. Will husbands whose wives earn higher incomes perceive this as a challenge to their traditional superior position in the family, even their masculinity? Will they feel inadequate? Will they feel emasculated? Unfortunately there has been more speculation about the effects of a wife's employment and earnings on her husband's happiness than systematic empirical research. The anecdotes gleaned from the studies of Hertz and Rubin of middle- and working-class families suggest that husbands and wives of both classes sometimes experience ambivalence when wives go to work and earn a high income. In general, this appears to be truer in working-class than middle-class families. Working-class men were the most likely to maintain a belief in the traditional family and to see themselves as the breadwinners even when their wives worked full time. Their self-concepts were still strongly tied to their ability to single-handedly provide for the family, and they tended to view their wives' employment as a temporary expediency. A wife earning a higher income would therefore be more likely to be perceived as a threat by these husbands.

One white working-class wife interviewed by Rubin was torn between the traditional notion of making her husband "feel like a king" and the conviction that she is "as equal as him." [10] A working-class husband often has to face the reality that his job may be less secure than his wife's. Larry Meecham summarized the feelings of many working-class males after losing his job through downsizing. "One day you got a job; the next day you're out of work, just like that." [11] Interviewed in the 1980s, Hertz's middle-class husbands also struggled with traditional gender notions, although they appeared more supportive and even encouraging of their wives' employment. Faced with the question of income parity, however, one white middle-class husband reflected, "I don't feel competitive with my wife, but that's qualified to the extent that if she were making $100,000 a year and I were making $30,000, I can't say that I would not in that circumstance feel differently. . . . There were periods in our marriage where she made $3,000 more than I did, and it didn't bother me because essentially, as I view it, we are exactly even. I think in that circumstance it's rather difficult to feel like a lace is untied. If she earned significantly more, it just might come untied." [12] Age also affects these couples' gender attitudes. Older males (over forty) in both the middle and working class tend to hold more conservative attitudes and appear more reluctant to yield their traditional provider role. Sociologist Jean Potuchek recounts the following exchange with a husband in a dual-career marriage. Both spouses were in their fifties and the wife earned a higher income:

> Keith, however, reveals some attachment to breadwinning as a gender boundary, regardless of circumstances. His responses suggest some discomfort with his wife's higher earnings. . . . When I ask whose job is considered more important, he answers that both are considered equally important and then adds, "I would honestly say so; I'd have

to at this point. I mean, dollar-wise, she's still ahead of me. I'm catching up a little, but. . . . That might change in the future." He says that he can imagine her leaving the labor force if his income improves: "I wouldn't need Roseanne working," he explains. "She might go into a substituting or part-time thing, or something like that."[13]

Yet in one rare empirical study of the effect of a wife's occupational superiority on marital happiness conducted in the late 1970s, sociologist John Richardson found no significant negative effect on a couple's marital happiness when the wife occupied the superior occupational position.[14] He suggests that since couples learn a great deal about each other during courtship, such couples presumably accepted this kind of superiority before entering into marriage. It seems plausible, then, that men who might have difficulty with a wife's superior occupational position would be likely to avoid marrying such a woman.

Occupational superiority and income superiority may not be perceived similarly, however. While the former may already exist before marriage, the latter can occur unexpectedly, years later and shift the balance of power to some husbands' discomfort. Still, Hertz found that many middle-class husbands understand the advantages of a second high income and are even relieved to share the breadwinner role. A number of these husbands took advantage of their wives' high earnings to strike out in new directions—to try a new career, or start a business—something they acknowledged would not have been possible without the career wife's substantial income. One husband mused, "One of the things I've thought about is I would love to own an antique shop or a bookstore and just do that. . . . Sometimes I think I don't like being in the rat race. I don't want to have pressures, but to be able to do something I really enjoy that's relaxing. . . . I can seriously think about these things, not just fantasize, because there is always a fallback position—my wife's working."[15] For another husband, having an employed wife with high earnings eliminates the pressure of the traditional breadwinner. "The woman who works and makes as much as the man gives the man flexibility and freedom in his job. He doesn't have to worry incessantly: 'What if something happens—what if I die or what if I get fired or what if I hate this career and I'd rather refinish furniture and start my own business?' He has more flexibility because of the economic freedom."[16]

Middle-class husbands, as a group, may be more able to take such a position because they are more secure in their own occupational achievements than are working-class men. Unlike college educated middle-class males, those in the working class have been more likely to experience a decline in income, unemployment, or the threat of unemployment during the 1980s and 1990s. Between 1989 and 1997 men of all groups (white, black, Latino and Asian) with only a high-school diploma experienced a decline in average hourly wages.[17]

Analysis of recent data from the 1991–94 National Survey of Families and Households reveals continuing racial and class differences in husbands' attitudes toward their wives' employment.[18] Respondents were asked to express their agreement or disagreement with the statement, "It is better for everyone if the man earns the main living and the woman takes care of the home and family." White working-class husbands were the most likely to agree with this statement (47.4 percent), followed by black working-class husbands (43.6 percent). Middle-class black (32.9 percent) and white (34.5 percent) husbands were the least likely to agree.

Obviously, not all working-class husbands feel threatened by a wife with a higher income, and conversely, some middle-class husbands do feel threatened by a wife with higher earnings. Indeed, over half of working-class husbands did support their wives' employment. Nevertheless, the existing evidence—sparse as it is—suggests that working-class husbands as a group remain more attached to the traditional family paradigm and are more threatened than middle-class husbands by their wives' income superiority, although not necessarily by their occupational superiority. Income, being more tangible than occupation, may be more readily perceived as a measure of a man's—and increasingly an employed woman's—self-worth.

7 Husbands and Housework: A Stalled Revolution?

With the majority of both white and black wives now sharing the bread-winner role, there is no doubt that a revolution in the family has occurred. In 1994 only 17.5 percent of black and 22.1 percent of white families still conformed to the traditional family model of a breadwinner father and a homemaker mother. In the upper middle class their proportions were even lower: 11 percent of black and 22 percent of white families. The actual percentages may be even lower than these statistics suggest, as the U.S. decennial census takes only a snapshot of American families at a particular point in time and thus fails to capture the dynamic nature of family life. It seems likely that some families may have only appeared tra-ditional for the moment in 1994 in that the wives had been employed at some time in the past.

But the entrance of wives into the workforce and shared breadwinning alters only one part of the equation. To complete the revolution in family functioning, husbands need to enter the domestic sphere and share the homemaker role. Numerous studies, however, indicate that husbands' participation in household labor seriously lags behind wives' expansion into breadwinning. Rather, there appears to be what sociologist Arlie Hochschild has called "a stalled revolution."[1]

WIVES' "DOUBLE DUTY" IN THE 1960S AND 1970S

As we saw in chapter 5, early studies of white dual-career families found that primary responsibility for the home and children remained in the wives' hands. Those in demanding professions such as law and academia were often forced to compromise their careers in order to maintain their domestic responsibilities. Husbands who verbally supported their wives' careers assumed that their own careers would remain primary and provided little assistance in the home. Poloma and Garland dubbed wives' acquiescence to this state of domestic affairs a "tolerance of domestication." This picture, however, was based on small qualitative studies that were more interested in the phenomenon of the dual-career family than in any accurate measure of the allocation of household tasks. It was left to other researchers to focus on this issue.

Such studies began appearing in the late 1970s and continued in the 1980s and 1990s. One of the earliest was a study of how Americans use time by sociologist John Robinson, who rightly pointed out the inherent difficulty in determining which activities such research should include.[2] Indeed, many of the studies since the late 1970s are difficult to compare since the researchers used different data and approaches. Some studies draw on representative national samples;[3] others are limited to data collected by the researchers themselves. Most have relied on surveys in which wives, husbands, or both responded to questions about time spent on individual household tasks; a few have had respondents keep diaries of their activities.[4] With few exceptions these researchers utilized only samples of whites. Findings from these varied investigations have yielded surprisingly similar results: as white wives entered the labor force in growing numbers, their efforts were not matched by a similar increase in the hours their husbands spent on household chores.

Three surveys of dual-worker families conducted in the 1960s and 1970s found that men spent an average of only 11 hours per week on housework.[5] Another study, using a representative national sample collected in 1977, calculated weekly housework hours at 12.8 for husbands and 29.8 for wives. Combined with time devoted to child care, husbands spent an average of 25 hours per week on domestic chores—still a far cry from the 47 hours spent by wives.[6] Although the husbands in this study devoted an average of 11 hours more to paid work than wives, when hours of domestic and paid work were combined wives nevertheless exceeded the husbands' total by about 11 hours: 87.4 hours to 76.5.

Other studies using data collected in the 1970s revealed that husbands with employed wives did not significantly increase their hours of housework compared with husbands married to full-time housewives. Nor did husbands in dual-career marriages contribute more hours of housework than those in dual-worker families, leading one research team to conclude, "Dual-career wives, while devoting less than half the number of hours that full-time housewives devote [to housework] . . . still spent nearly three times as many hours doing housework each week as their husbands."[7]

Researchers also found little or no change in husbands' hours of housework between the 1960s and the 1970s. In view of this, one pair of researchers commented that as of 1976 "men's involvement in the traditional 'woman's sphere,' if occurring at all, is lagging considerably behind women's entry into the traditional 'man's sphere.'"[8] Husbands who did help their wives at home were more likely to engage in the more pleasant task of child care or the less demanding tasks of washing dishes and light housecleaning. Two-thirds of employed wives remained stuck with the more onerous, time-consuming, and inflexible chores of cooking, grocery shopping, and washing clothes.[9] The findings of these social scientists confirmed the suspicions of many that employed wives in the 1960s and 1970s were often forced to do "double duty"—a full day's work at the office or factory and a full day's work at home. As more wives entered the labor force in the 1970s, the only strategy available to them to make life manageable was to reduce the time spent on housework, and this they did, decreasing their hours of domestic labor by 19 percent.[10]

As we saw in chapter 5, by the end of the 1970s signs indicated that employed white middle-class wives were beginning to exhibit the same commitment to careers as their husbands. Their reduced hours of housework were one consequence of this change. If the 1950s witnessed the "last ditch" stand of the traditional family, the 1960s and 1970s represented a transitional stage during which more and more wives subscribed to a new family paradigm. These wives, as I have suggested, were going against the grain, pushing aside the increasingly intolerable constraints of their socially assigned domestic role. But, as they discovered, their husbands had not yet fully signed on to change. As wives became more committed to work outside the home, how could they manage both paid and domestic work if their husbands were reluctant to expand their own roles in the home?

HOUSEWORK IN THE 1980S AND 1990S

By 1980, 79.6 percent of black and 59.2 percent of white middle class wives were employed, with at least 75 and 22 percent, respectively, maintaining continuous careers. Over the next decade the percentage of middle-class wives who remained continuously employed would more than double to 43 percent among whites, while increasing to 80 percent among blacks. Moreover, by 1990, these wives' median incomes were over half (55 percent) their husbands' among whites and more than three-fourths (79 percent) their husbands' among blacks. Even more to the point, when both spouses were employed full time, the wife's median contributions among both blacks and whites equaled about 42 percent of the family income. Clearly wives now substantially shared the breadwinner role, but had their husbands correspondingly increased their contribution to housework and child care?

The National Survey of Families and Households, which was first conducted in 1987–88 (NSFH1) and repeated about five years later in 1991–94 (NSFH2), provided more recent data on the hours husbands and wives spent on housework.[11] Since the study oversamples black households, it affords the best survey data to date with which to compare the house-work contributions of black and white husbands.[12] This survey asked couples to indicate the amount of time spent during the previous week on each of nine household tasks: cooking meals, washing dishes, clean-ing house, washing and ironing clothes, shopping for groceries, paying bills, caring for the car(s), working outdoors, and driving the children.

The first five tasks—cooking, dishwashing, housecleaning, washing and ironing, and grocery shopping—are traditionally performed by women. Auto upkeep and outdoor work are typically male activities, while driving children and paying bills are more neutral tasks, which either the wife or the husband might be expected to perform. As many researchers have pointed out, not only are the traditionally female house-hold tasks more numerous than male tasks, they are also far more time-consuming and less flexible. Cooking and washing dishes are daily activities. True, frozen dinners and microwaves have altered the pattern of meal preparation somewhat—but not a great deal. And they have not eliminated the tasks of planning meals, shopping for ingredients, or stor-ing and keeping stock of supplies. Even when other family members "take turns" in preparing meals, it is still the wives who typically coor-dinate and supervise this activity. In contrast, outdoor tasks are seldom performed more than once a week, typically on the weekend rather than after a stressful day on the job. Moreover, many of these tasks are sea-sonal, and some, such as mowing the lawn, may even serve as a source of relaxation after a hectic week at the office. The real equity issue, then, is whether husbands have increased their share of the traditionally female household tasks.

The Kitchen or the TV Couch: Did Husbands Increase
Their Hours of Housework in the 1980s?

Drawing on NSFH1 data, a number of studies have concluded that even in the late 1980s white wives in dual-income families continued to per-form the bulk of the housework. These studies found that husbands spent from 14.4 to 17 hours per week on all household tasks. Although this was about a 17 percent increase over the 12.8 hours devoted to housework in the mid-1970s, it nevertheless represented only about a third of the total housework hours (between 31 and 35 percent).[13] Wives, however, devoted from 29 to 33 hours of their week to these tasks. Furthermore, a high percentage of husbands did not contribute any hours to certain tasks. One study revealed that only 48 percent of husbands did any housecleaning; just 52 percent cooked meals or did dishes; and only 25 percent did laundry.[14]

These studies also found that household labor remained highly segregated by gender. Wives did most of the cooking, cleaning, laundry, dishes, and shopping; husbands did the bulk of outdoor work and car maintenance. In one study, this translated into 52 percent of wives' total housework hours being spent cooking and cleaning, with 41 percent of husbands' hours given to auto maintenance and outdoor work.[15] In the most gender-segregated families (50 percent of all families in that study), husbands spent 58 percent of their homework hours on the two male tasks, with only 15 hours being given to meal preparation and housecleaning. Only among the least gender-segregated families (21 percent of the total) did husbands devote more hours to meal preparation and housecleaning (38) than to outdoor tasks and auto maintenance (23).[16] In another study, restricted to households in which both spouses were employed, the husbands devoted 69.1 percent of their total hours to the two traditionally male tasks, while wives spent 78.1 percent of their hours on the five traditionally female tasks.[17] The conclusion of these studies is clear: as recently as 1988 wives continued to do the bulk of housework, even when they were employed full time. Husbands increased their hours of housework by only about 17 percent in the 1970s and 1980s, and almost half did not assist in some of the individual female tasks. Did this change in the 1990s?

Any Change in the 1990s?

Among whites, the five-year gap between the NSFH1 and NSFH2 surveys brought little or no change in the distribution of housework. My analysis of the 1994 data indicates that white husbands spent about 18 hours on housework a week, doing about 34 percent of total housework—virtually the same as five years earlier.[18] Wives devoted about 35 hours to these same chores. As in the late 1980s, although less than one percent of white husbands had failed to do *any* housework during the previous week, many had not participated in particular tasks. For example, 26 percent contributed no time to preparing meals, 22.9 percent did no dishes, and 62.7 percent did no laundry. In 1994 household tasks remained highly gendered, with wives devoting 87 percent of their housework hours to the five traditionally female tasks and husbands spending 40.8 percent of their hours on the two traditionally male tasks. But were there any racial differences in this household division of labor? Clearly, the majority of white households had not changed, but had the traditionally more egalitarian attitudes of black families translated into a more equitable division of labor within black households?

A COMPARISON OF BLACK AND WHITE HUSBANDS' HOUSEWORK

Although research points to more egalitarian attitudes among black than white couples, attitudes do not necessarily translate into corresponding behavior.[19] Given the historically different ideologies of womanhood in black and white communities, however, one might expect that just as black wives took the lead in expanding their role into shared breadwinning, black husbands would be more assertive in moving into the private sphere of housework. Indeed, various comparative measures reveal that black husbands do contribute more time to housework than do white husbands. This is not to say that most black husbands perform half the housework. Both black and white husbands—as a group—continued to fall far short of equity in household labor in the early 1990s. Still, a moderate but consistent gap favored black husbands.

Black husbands, for instance, spent about 22.2 hours on all eight household tasks in the early 1990s; white husbands spent 18.4 hours, or 17.1 percent less. These hours represented 36.9 percent of the total of 60.2 hours black husbands and wives spent on household labor, and

34.4 percent of the 53.4 hours white couples devoted to housework. Black husbands performed a larger share of a *greater number* of total household hours reported. More tellingly, about a third of black husbands (32.3 percent) compared with about a fourth of white husbands (24.2 percent) performed 50 percent or more of the total household work in their families. Thus the egalitarian group included a significantly higher percentage of black than white husbands.

Husbands' Share of "Woman's" Work

Given that the five traditionally female tasks consume the bulk of household labor, the true test of a husband's expansion beyond his traditional breadwinner role is his participation in these duties. How did black and white husbands measure up to this test? In the early 1990s, both black and white husbands contributed less than a third of the total hours spent by couples on traditionally female tasks. Black husbands performed 28.6 percent of an average total of 46.1 hours a week that black couples devoted to cooking, washing dishes, cleaning house, shopping, and doing laundry. White husbands contributed 25.4 percent of an average total of 40.9 hours a week that white couples devoted to these five tasks. In absolute terms, black husbands put in an average of 13.2 hours a week on "female" tasks and white husbands 10.4 hours, or about 21 percent fewer hours than black husbands.

If—as the criterion of a truly egalitarian division of labor—we use a husband's equal sharing of the traditionally female household tasks, we discover that while this group is pitifully small among both blacks and whites, it is 46 percent larger among black husbands. About 20.5 percent of black husbands compared to 14 percent of whites contributed 50 percent or more to the five female chores. Thus, whether measured in relative terms (percentage of all five tasks) or in absolute terms (actual number of hours), black husbands' contributions to traditionally female household labor exceed those of white husbands.

The two "male" tasks of auto maintenance and outdoor chores required far fewer hours on average than "female's" work. Both black and white couples spent an average of only 10 hours per week on auto maintenance and outdoor work, less than one-fourth the time devoted to traditionally female tasks. There was not much difference in the average number of hours devoted to these chores by black (8.7 hours) and white (7.5 hours) husbands. Both black and white husbands performed the bulk of these two activities, 84.5 and 75 percent, respectively. Paying bills, the "neutral" task, consumed a total of about 5.4 hours a week on average among blacks and 3.6 hours among whites. In both groups, husbands gave slightly more time to this task than wives: black husbands 57.4 percent, white husbands 61.1 percent.

A Closer Look at Individual Household Tasks

Combining household activities into types, however, conceals a wide variation in patterns of husbands' housework. While 98 percent of both black and white husbands performed some housework, some devoted all their household labor time to traditionally male tasks, some participated in only one or two traditionally female chores but not others, and still others gave a bit of time to each task.

In general (with the exception of washing clothes) a slightly higher percentage of black husbands did not participate in specific individual tasks, but among those who did participate in a specific task black husbands gave more hours on average than white husbands. Almost a third of black and more than a fourth of white husbands did not share in the two most demanding household chores: cooking and housecleaning. Doing laundry, however, was the chore most avoided by husbands: 62.7 percent of whites and 42.9 percent of blacks. Whether this results from husbands' particular distaste for this task, wives' distrust of their husbands' ability to distinguish light from dark clothes, or some other factor is not known. Surprisingly, a substantial group of husbands avoided even those traditionally female tasks that husbands are most often thought to share: doing dishes and shopping. The stereotype of the wife cooking the meal and the husband washing the dishes afterward was not supported in 28.8 percent of black families and 22.9 of whites. Similarly, the image of a couple going to the supermarket together was not realized in 30.3 percent of black and 24.8 percent of white families. The smallest percentage of non-participants was not surprisingly found in the traditionally male task of outdoor work: 19.7 percent of black and 9.7 percent of white husbands. This large difference in the percentage of black and white nonparticipants in outdoor activities may result from a higher proportion of renters among blacks than whites, as well as from a higher percentage of whites residing in suburbs.

Among those husbands—and they were the majority—who participated in at least some housework, blacks spent somewhat more hours on these chores than whites and, with the exception of shopping, performed a higher proportion of the total hours a couple devoted to each task. The traditionally female task receiving the greatest input from husbands per week was cooking: 5.1 hours by black husbands and 3.7 hours by white husbands (figure 14). Next highest was housecleaning (3.8 to 2.8 hours), followed by dishes (3.5 to 3.1 hours). Husbands spent the least time grocery shopping (3.1 to 2.4 hours) and washing clothes (2.7 to 2.3 hours). They made their greatest input in the traditional male activity of outdoor chores: 6.6 and 6.1 hours, respectively, for blacks and whites.

While the absolute number of hours husbands contributed to housework provides a useful yardstick for comparing the efforts of black and white husbands, it is not necessarily a useful measure for comparisons between spouses. For this, researchers often turn to the *relative* contribution of husbands to housework. Those husbands *who did participate* in a traditionally female task made their highest relative contributions to two activities that tend to be performed once a week: grocery shopping and washing clothes; however, only 37.3 percent of white and 57.1 percent of black husbands did any laundry (figure 15). Still, those who did laundry supplied over a third of the time this task required weekly. Grocery-shopping husbands did even better, devoting over 40 percent of the couple's total hours spent on this task. Black husbands were responsible for a little over a third of the hours devoted to cooking and dishes; white husbands slightly over a fourth. About a third of housecleaning hours came from black husbands, compared with slightly over a fourth from white husbands. In contrast to their moderate contribution to traditionally female tasks, black and white husbands monopolized auto upkeep and outdoor work and contributed more than half of the total time spent on finances.

If we define husbands' egalitarian behavior as contributing at least

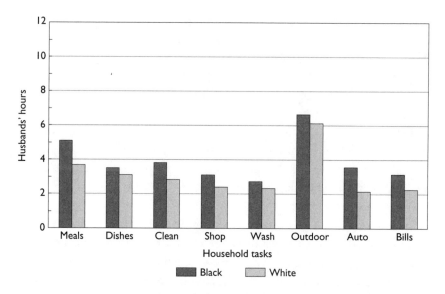

FIGURE 14. Husbands' Hours on Household Tasks, for Those Reporting at Least One Hour

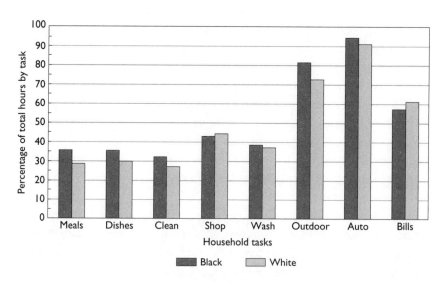

FIGURE 15. Husbands' Percentage of Household Tasks, for Those Reporting at Least One Hour

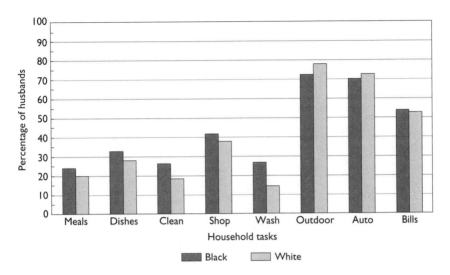

F I G U R E   1 6.   Percentage of Husbands Contributing 50 Percent or More to
Individual Tasks

half of the time spent on traditionally female tasks, then we find that black
and white husbands were most egalitarian in sharing grocery shopping
and washing dishes, and in both cases, a higher percentage of black than
white husbands were egalitarian (figure 16). Black husbands were the
least egalitarian in sharing cooking, though even there 24 percent of
black husbands cooked at least half the time compared to 19.8 percent
of whites. White husbands were the least egalitarian at doing laundry,
with only about 14.5 percent participating at least half the time in contrast to 26.8 percent of blacks. Only in outdoor work and auto upkeep did
the percentage of white husbands exceed that of black husbands.

These comparisons support earlier researchers' findings that black
families are more egalitarian than white families. Since researchers have
generally found that husbands do not significantly increase their hours
of housework in response to their wives' employment, we cannot simply
attribute the greater contribution of black husbands to the traditionally
higher employment rate of black wives.[20] As I have already suggested,
the more plausible explanation lies in different ideologies about women's
and men's roles. Holding a more egalitarian view of gender roles, black

wives are probably more forceful in persuading their husbands to participate in housework, and in turn the general support for egalitarianism in
the black community may make it easier for black than white husbands
to engage in housework.

The responses of blacks and whites to two questions in the NSFH2
survey support this interpretation. One question asked them to indicate
their degree of agreement with the statement, "Both the husband and
wife should contribute to family income." Seventy-eight percent of black
husbands compared with 48.9 percent of white husbands agreed with
this statement. Furthermore, 23.0 percent of black husbands expressed
strong agreement compared with only 8.9 percent of whites. An even larger
percentage of black wives, 82.4 percent, agreed with the statement, compared with 51.6 percent of white wives. Thus there appears to be far more
support among blacks than whites for dual-worker families.

In chapter 4 we saw that although both black and white wives steadily
increased their participation in the workforce in the twentieth century,
the group with the lowest participation rate remains white wives with
preschool-age children. In 1994, when 68.3 percent of these mothers had
jobs, the employment rate of all other groups exceeded 80 percent. The
NSFH2 survey found attitudinal support for this behavior in the contrasting views of blacks and whites. When asked to respond to the statement, "It is all right for mothers to work full time when their youngest
child is under age 5," 43.5 percent of black husbands and 50.4 percent
of black wives agreed. In contrast, only 30.3 percent of white husbands
and 38.4 percent of white wives agreed. Not only do we find a higher percentage of black than white mothers employed, but as these data reveal,
behind this contrasting behavior lie more liberal gender attitudes among
black couples.

CLASS DIFFERENCES IN HUSBANDS' HOUSEWORK

If black middle-class wives were the first to develop an egalitarian ideology of womanhood and family roles, then this is the group where we
should find the highest participation by husbands in household labor.

Logically, we might expect these wives to be either more likely to choose men with egalitarian attitudes or more successful in persuading their mates to share the burden of housework. A comparison of middle-class and working-class husbands reveals that black middle-class husbands did indeed contribute more hours to housework than white middle-class husbands or working-class husbands of either race. Moreover, black working-class husbands frequently did more hours of housework than white middle-class husbands. This, too, should be expected, given that middle-class ideologies spread to the working class.

Since middle-class and working-class families, as well as blacks and whites, apparently devoted different total hours to domestic duties, the relative contributions of husbands offers the most accurate comparison. In 1994 middle-class black husbands performed 42.5 percent of a total of 60.3 hours a couple spent weekly on all eight household tasks. This is substantially more than middle-class white husbands, who contributed 35.7 percent of the 51.3 hours white middle-class couples committed to housework. Black and white working-class husbands were responsible for 36.4 and 32.3 percent, respectively, of the 62.4 hours each group devoted to domestic chores. In rank order, black middle-class husbands contributed most to housework, followed by working-class black husbands, middle-class white husbands, and then working-class white husbands.

Almost the same rank order was found in these husbands' shares of traditionally female tasks. In the middle class, black husbands contributed one-third (33 percent) of 41.8 total hours, and white husbands about one-fourth (26.5 percent) of 37.4 hours; in the working class, black husbands performed about one-fourth (26.3 percent) of 45.2 hours and white husbands somewhat over one-fifth (22.4 percent) of 45.1 total hours.

The gap among race and class groups is even larger for those husbands who contributed 50 percent or more to total housework: in the middle class, over one-third (36.2 percent) of black, versus one-fourth (24.9 percent) of white husbands; in the working class, one-third (33.3 percent) of black, versus one-fifth (20.5 percent) of white husbands. Turning to the litmus test of egalitarian relationships—sharing 50 percent or more of traditionally female chores—we find 23 percent of black middle-class husbands in this group but only 14.7 percent of white middle-class husbands. In the working class, we find 17.4 percent of black and 11.1 percent of white husbands. Also, both middle- and working-class black husbands contributed a higher percentage of hours to individual tasks per week than white husbands, with differences ranging from 3.1 to 9.5 percentage points. These findings are supported by Lillian Rubin's study of families in the early 1990s, which showed that black husbands participated more in housework than white, Latino, or Asian husbands. She writes, "The commonly held stereotype about black men abandoning women and children . . . doesn't square with the families in this study. In fact, black men are the most likely to be real participants in the daily life of the family and are more intimately involved in raising their children than any of the others. True, the men's family work load doesn't always match their wives', and the women are articulate in their complaints about this. Nevertheless, compared to their white, Asian, or Latino counterparts, the black families look like models of egalitarianism." Rubin notes three-quarters of the African American males whom she studied did "a substantial amount of the cooking, cleaning, and child care, sometimes even more than their wives," and that they responded to her queries with some version of, "I just figure it's my job, too."[21]

What about gender role attitudes in the different classes? Using the two statements from NSFH2 cited above, we find that 80.2 percent of black middle-class husbands agreed that both the husband and the wife should contribute to family income, while only 47.3 percent of white middle-class husbands did. A similarly large gap existed among middle-class wives, with 78.6 percent of blacks compared to 49.9 percent of whites supporting dual employment.[22] Though the differences are not as great, substantially larger percentages of black middle- and working-class couples also supported a mother's employment with a child under age five in the home.[23] It would appear, then, that both the actual division of household labor and attitudes toward wives' employment support the notion that blacks hold a more egalitarian ideology of gender roles.

This analysis leads to two major conclusions. First, the more egalitarian ideology of womanhood and family developed by black middle-class wives in the late nineteenth and early twentieth centuries apparently has had some impact on their husbands' attitudes and behavior. Black husbands seem to be more supportive of their wives' movement into the labor force, and—just as important—are more forthcoming than white husbands in extending their own role into the home. Second, the extension of the husband's role into the domestic sphere still lags far behind the movement of wives into the breadwinning arena. The revolution in the family has indeed stalled. The question that now faces our society is, can the dual-worker family thrive, or are wives doomed to continue their struggle to fulfill the demands of home and work with a minimum of societal support?

Conclusion:
The Future of
Dual-Worker Families

Now that dual-earner families have become the norm, how are they managing? Are they basking in the warmth of newfound egalitarianism? Are they finding new stresses and strains? Are they longing for the "good old days" with the traditional division of labor? Perhaps all of the above. New terminology has invaded the writings of social scientists and journalists writing on the family. We hear about "the work-family connection," "balancing home and work," "the family-friendly workplace," "day care," and "the time bind." The last phrase comes from one of the titles of a pair of recent books that arrived at vastly different conclusions about the lives of today's dual-worker couples. Arlie Russell Hochschild in *The Time Bind*, a study of workers at Fortune 500 Amerco, finds men and women fleeing the stresses of home life and becoming more invested in their jobs.[1] In contrast, in *She Works, He Works*, Rosalind C. Barnett and

164

Caryl River, who studied three hundred randomly selected dual-earner couples in the greater Boston area, conclude, "The new American family is alive and well. Both partners are employed full time, and according to the latest research, the family they create is one in which all members are thriving: often happier, healthier, and more well-rounded than the family of the 1950s."[2]

Can both conclusions be accurate? That is altogether possible since the studies examined different populations. The more important question is the extent to which their findings represent dual-worker couples nationally. Statistically, neither can make that claim. But has either nevertheless managed to capture the reality of the lives of dual-earner families at the end of the twentieth century?

Perhaps a 1998 national survey of four thousand men and women, conducted by the *Washington Post* jointly with the Henry J. Kaiser Family Foundation and Harvard University, more accurately portrays the lot of today's modern family. Based on the survey, the *Post* reported that "after nearly a generation of sharing the workplace and renegotiating domestic duties, most men and women agree that increased gender equity has enriched" their lives. Yet at the same time these writers pointed out that "both also believe that the strains of this relatively new world have made building successful marriages, raising children and leading satisfying lives ever more difficult."[3] Most surprising of all, two-thirds of both men and women in the survey said that although it may be necessary for mothers to work, it would be better if they could "stay home and just take care of the house and children."

AMBIVALENCE AND LACK OF SUPPORT

That women and men in dual-income families should feel ambivalent in the late 1990s seems natural. In a very real sense, these men and women are poised between two worlds, each trying in different ways to adjust to the transition from the traditional to the modern family. Although dual-worker families are now the statistical majority, this new family form is not yet fully institutionalized and does not always function smoothly.

Granted, many employed wives today receive more support at home from their husbands than they did in the 1960s and 1970s. Moreover, wives no longer seem willing to be superwomen and are demanding more help. Still, many husbands do not always "get it," as one thirty-four-year-old woman in the *Post*-Kaiser-Harvard survey complained: "My husband just doesn't seem to get it when I tell him that I feel I'm always on duty. When we're at home, I'm the one who always has an eye out for our son, making sure he's eating on time, things like that."[4] Another woman in Rubin's study protested, "He'll give the kids a bath or help with the dishes. But only when I ask him. He doesn't have to *ask* me to go to work every day, does he? Why should I have to ask him."[5] Like my own findings in chapter 7, the *Post*-Kaiser-Harvard survey concluded, "Most men in the polls said they were happy to share child care and domestic chores with wives who work outside the home. Yet household duties remain sharply divided along gender lines. Working mothers still do twice as much housework as their husbands, and more than half of all women questioned expressed at least some dissatisfaction with the amount of help their husbands provide around the house."[6]

In 1998 the operative word was still *help* around the house. As we saw in chapter 7, racial differences notwithstanding, most husbands are far from being as invested in the home as their wives are in the workplace. Herein lies one of the biggest problems that continue to plague today's families and the lives of working wives. But uncooperative husbands are not the only "culprits." Another is the workplace, and still another is society itself. Family sociologist Andrew Cherlin suggests that "neither employers nor government nor many men recognize the inescapable consequence: working mothers need support if they are to balance their double burden."[7]

At the epicenter of the controversy is still the mother's role. Being a mother, whether employed or not, has been problematic ever since industrialization created the role of housewife. "Experts" have fretted over the possibility that children could easily be ruined by the least misstep in parenting—not by fathers, of course, but by mothers. In a special 1998 issue of the *New York Times Magazine* on motherhood, writer Jane Smiley discusses how she discovered that "motherhood is the most public of personal conditions": "Everyone has an opinion about a mother and her behavior, and lots of those opinions are infuriating. Opinions about motherhood in our culture aren't just specific, they are also general. Mothers should stay home, mothers should work, mothers should not hire nannies, mothers should enlist fathers in child care, mothers should stop telling fathers what to do, mothers should be satisfied with being good enough, mothers are never good enough to prevent their own dysfunctions (read 'humanity') from infecting their children."[8]

This sentiment echoes the *Post*-Kaiser-Harvard survey, which reveals how many mothers are torn between staying at home with their children and going out to work. Even at the point where traditional families have all but disappeared and most mothers have joined the workforce, a mother's role remains mired in controversy. And while we talk about "the new fatherhood," about more involved dads, it is clear that men and women use different measuring rods to judge the extent of men's involvement in parenting and household labor. Wives tend to assess their husbands' participation in terms of the share of total housework and child care performed, whereas husbands often measure their efforts against those of their fathers. As a result a husband may feel proud that he is doing more than his father, while his wife continues to feel burdened because his participation is still far from equal.

THE FAMILY AS PUBLIC GOOD: THE EUROPEAN MODEL

Everyone may have an opinion about a mother's role, but the family as a whole remains a low priority in United States public policy debates. Indeed, the only family issue likely to be discussed is the alternative between a woman's staying at home with her children or going out to work. Not so in Europe. There the family rather than the mother's role holds center stage, and the welfare of children is not measured by the extent to which mothers remain at home or are employed. Although the role of parents is considered important in children's well-being, so, too, are what the government and the community do. The family is not a "private matter" as in the United States; it is a public good.

The Lessons of the Family and Medical Leave Act

In spite of the controversies that have surrounded the family in the postindustrial United States, in spite of the high profile political debates give to "family values" in the United States, not until February 5, 1993, did Congress pass and the president (in this case, Bill Clinton) sign a bill granting parents some kind of protected leave surrounding the birth of a child. Although Congress had passed similar bills before, President George Bush had vetoed them at least thirty-two times.[9]

The reason President Bush gave for vetoing the Family and Medical Leave Act offers a clue to why the United States took so long to provide working mothers with the kind of protection that has been common for years in all European countries. Bush said he "objected to mandating how businesses should conduct themselves," proposing instead that Congress adopt a family leave tax credit for businesses that "voluntarily" adopt leave policies.[10] This opposition to a policy that would infringe on "free market" business decisions is typical of the conservative approach to family policy in the United States. Behind it lies the view that a good family is one in which the wife remains home with her children without inconveniencing society in any way. It should *not* take a village to raise a child; a mother should do it all on her own—without even making demands on her husband. A married woman with children who joins the workforce is behaving selfishly if she does not need to work. Never mind that in a large percentage of families a wife's employment is an economic necessity. Many United States lawmakers still perceive the family as women's work and thus give it a back seat to business interests.

But just how extensive—how threatening—are the benefits of the Family and Medical Leave Act? As enacted in 1993 the law applies only to businesses with fifty or more workers, in effect exempting over 90 percent of all private-sector employers. In addition, to be eligible, an employee must have worked for the employer for at least twelve months and have "rendered at least 1,250 hours of service" in the previous twelve months.[11] In other words, the application of the law is far from universal. Employees in firms with fewer than fifty employees continue to be at the mercy of their boss. For one out of every twenty new mothers, having a child resulted in her being fired or laid off, according to a 1990 study by the United States Census Bureau. For countless others, pregnancy and motherhood led to suspicion about their work commitment, hostility, or outright discrimination.[12]

Another limitation of the law is that employees are entitled to only twelve weeks of leave and this is without pay. It seems stingy compared with the average European country's sixteen weeks of *fully paid* maternity leave.

Finally, it is a Family *and* Medical Leave Act, covering not only parental leave for the birth or adoption of a child, but also leave for serious illness of the employee or a relative. By including events other than the birth of a child, the bill deemphasizes a central issue faced by working women—support for motherhood. Mothers are entitled to *unpaid* leave as part of a larger group of employees sharing some need for leave from employment.[13] This is not to suggest that the provision including leave for personal illness or a relative's illness is not important. Indeed, that has been the most heavily used provision. Maternity, however, needs to be recognized as a legitimate claim for special benefits apart from all other conditions.

Maternity as Illness

In an odd twist, because the United States has been reluctant to grant protected leave from work to care for newborns, women have had to rely upon a legal definition of maternity as an illness—officially, a "disability." Even this approach has been difficult. The Supreme Court twice rejected arguments to extend benefits to mothers under state disability laws. In *Geduldig v. Aiello* (1974) the justices held that "denial of benefits for work loss resulting from normal pregnancy did not violate the Equal Protection Clause of the U.S. Constitution."[14] In *General Electric v. Gilbert* (1976) the court ruled that GE's disability plan excluding pregnancy did not violate Title VII of the Civil Rights Act. In both cases, first Justice Potter Stewart and then Justice William Rehnquist wrote majority opinions that the exclusion of pregnant women from disability benefits "does not exclude anyone from benefit eligibility because of gender but merely removes one physical condition—pregnancy—from the list of compensable disabilities."[15]

In both cases Justice William Brennan dissented, contending that "by singling out for less favorable treatment a gender-linked disability peculiar to women, the State has created a double standard for disability compensation. . . . Such dissimilar treatment of men and women, on the basis of physical characteristics inextricably linked to one sex, inevitably constitutes sex discrimination."[16] Brennan's argument provided the reasoning for the 1980 passage of the Pregnancy Discrimination Act, which amended Section 701 of the Civil Rights Act so that the outlawed discrimination "because of sex," encompassed "pregnancy, childbirth, or related medical conditions." No one commented on how viewing pregnancy and childbirth as disabilities had become the only approach to maternity leave in the United States.

In contrast to the United States, both Canada and Europe have approached maternity leave by focusing on procreation as a societal benefit rather than merely an individual matter. Although the Canadian Supreme Court at first took the same approach as in the United States, arguing that pregnant women were being treated differently from other workers because they were pregnant rather than because they were women, it later reversed itself and emphasized the inseparability of pregnancy from womanhood. In *Andrews v. Law Society of British Columbia* (1989), the justices underscored the "unfair disadvantage [that] may result when the costs of an activity from which *all of society benefits* are placed upon a single group of persons."[17] Justice Dickson writing for the majority stated explicitly, "It cannot be disputed that everyone in society benefits from procreation."[18] In *Brooks, Allen and Dixon et al. v. Canada Safeway Ltd.* (1989), the justices noted, "Combining paid work with motherhood and accommodating the childbearing needs of working women are ever-increasing imperatives. That those who bear children and benefit society as a whole thereby should not be economically or socially disadvantaged seems to bespeak the obvious."[19]

The importance of the different philosophies underlying these two approaches to childbearing cannot be overemphasized. On the one hand, an individualistic approach absolves the larger society from any responsibility or involvement; on the other hand, a recognition that childbearing is part of the fabric of society mandates society's concern and support. The social approach realizes that it does "take a village to raise a child."[20] It also shifts the issue from a narrow focus on pregnancy to the larger one of procreation, in which everyone in society has a stake.

Support for Childbearing in Europe

In Europe we find a number of philosophical approaches to the family and childbearing, but the tendency is for countries in northwestern Europe in particular to encourage the employment of mothers and support the reconciliation of work and family life. The most progressive position is represented by Sweden, Denmark, and Norway, whose approaches are based on promoting equality between men and women in the home and in the labor force. Since 1970, for example, Sweden has promoted an "equal status contract," whereby men and women should share "not only the same opportunities but also the same responsibilities and duties."[21] French family policy also includes strong support for working mothers, a position firmly backed by public opinion.[22] All four countries support their family policies with a variety of social programs that I will discuss below. As a result of these government-supported approaches, the employment rates of mothers in these countries are among the highest in Europe.

The approach to child care, too, in these northwestern European countries is radically different from that in the United States. In the United States there is a strong emphasis on mothers as caregivers. It might even be said that the mother is seen as the only legitimate caregiver, especially for small children. Many countries of northwestern Europe tend to focus on promoting either gender equality (as in Sweden, Denmark, and Norway) or opportunities for mothers' employment (as in France). Far from neglecting the welfare of children, these approaches lead to active government involvement in financing a national system of quality day care for children and providing other economic support for working mothers and dual-earner families. In contrast, by focusing on individual mothering, the United States removes consideration of a national day care system from the public policy agenda. Although local governments are active in regulating private day care facilities, they are seldom involved as providers. When governmental bodies do become involved in supporting child care, it is often only in support of the employment of poor single mothers. This approach effectively forestalls the discussion and development of a national system of quality day care, and it leaves working mothers—single or married—with punitively expensive "choices" for child care. It has also made it impossible even to mount a serious discussion of a national policy of paid maternity leave such as exists universally in Europe.

THE CHILD CARE DILEMMA: WHAT'S A (WORKING) MOTHER TO DO?

In 1972 we appeared for a moment to be on the threshold of a new era for families and for gender equality. Both houses of Congress had passed legislation to establish a national day care system. When it reached President Richard Nixon's desk, however, he vetoed the bill, following the conservative argument that day care would "weaken" the family. Such an opportunity has not occurred since.

By all accounts the day care system in the United States—if it can be called a system—is a hodgepodge of centers that vary wildly in quality, cost, and accessibility. Choosing a day care facility is a time-consuming, emotionally stressful effort rivaled only by a job search. And most often, the task falls to mothers.

The first consideration parents face in choosing day care is cost. This factor alone can stop parents in their tracks or force them to settle for a poor quality facility. In 1993 the United States Census Bureau estimated that 8.1 million families had preschoolers who required care while their mothers worked. The cost to families with children in day care facilities (56 percent of the 8.1 million) averaged $110 per week for those with two or more preschoolers and $66 for those with one preschooler.[23] This expense consumed an average of 7 percent of nonpoor families' annual income and a whopping 18 percent of poor families' income. On a yearly basis, the Children's Defense Fund estimates, full-day child care costs between $4,000 and $10,000.[24] The same source reports that a parent with a three-year-old in day care spent $8,840 annually for child care in Boston, $6,030 in Minneapolis, and $4,210 in Dallas.

Hardest hit by the high cost of day care are working-class families, particularly the poor among them. And "poor" does not necessarily mean welfare or single mothers. The Children's Defense Fund calculated that in 1998 a family with both parents working full time at minimum wage earned only $21,400. The burden of poor families can be measured in part by the high portion of their income that goes to financing day care—18 percent. In spite of the large share of their income devoted to child care, the poor still spend significantly less for day care than do the nonpoor, averaging $50 to $76 per week nationally, and lower expenditure generally translates into lower quality.[25] United States Census Bureau data document a direct correlation between a family's class and the amount spent on day care, with college-educated mothers averaging $93 a week. Even when states and local governments offer subsidies to assist poor families with child care, there is often a long waiting list.[26] A 1998 nationwide survey by the Children's Defense Fund disclosed that nine out of ten children from low-income working families failed to receive these subsidies because of inadequate federal and state funding.[27]

It is not just the working poor who are faced with hard choices. Psychologist Lillian Rubin found that about 20 percent of the working-class families in her study were forced to take on shift work to ensure the presence of one parent at all times for child care. With barely an hour together during the week, this arrangement took a toll on their marriages. To Rubin's question about their opportunity to talk, one respondent quipped, "'Talk? How can we talk when we hardly see each other?' 'Talk? What's that?' 'Talk? Ha, that's a joke.'"[28] Another working-class woman who was employed days while her husband worked a night shift was resigned: "I don't mean to complain; we're lucky in a lot of ways. We've got two great kids, and we're a pretty good team, Daryl and me. But I worry sometimes. When you live on this kind of schedule, communication's not so good."[29]

Middle-class families fare much better, of course. When combined incomes reach six figures, they can often afford the most expensive day care or employ a nanny or au pair. Those with less income may not be so lucky. In August 1998, the *San Diego Union-Tribune* ran a story about a middle-class dual-career couple's decision to become a one-income family.[30] Their combined incomes from her job as a middle-school math teacher ($27,500) and his work at an insurance company ($28,000) had brought in $55,500. But they were spending $300 to $400 a month on child care, and after deducting other assorted, mostly work-related expenses, they found they had only about $6,000 remaining from the wife's paycheck. As a result the couple decided that she would quit her job to remain home with their daughter. In this family's case, the wife's ability to earn $10 an hour as a math tutor and $15 teaching violin lessons—all in her home—would bring sufficient additional income to meet their needs. Without her ability to earn income working part-time at home, however, their choice would have been far more difficult.[31] This family's story underscores the dilemma that millions face in combining work and family responsibilities in the United States.

DAY CARE AVAILABILITY AND QUALITY

A system of privately owned and operated day care facilities must be fee driven. As with any fee-driven service, both availability and quality depend on the users' ability to pay. Although the availability of child care has grown with demand, that does not mean day care slots are always available where needed. A study by the United States Department of Education in 1991 found that there were no vacancies in two-thirds to three-fourths of all day care centers, as well as in more than half of all regulated family day care homes.[32]

Especially troublesome to families seeking day care is the acute shortage of high-quality facilities. Several studies have produced strong indictments of day care quality in the United States. A 1995 study of four states by the University of Colorado, Denver, identified only 14 percent of child care centers as providing "good quality" care.[33] A 1994 study by the New York-based Families and Work Institute claimed 13 percent of regulated and 50 percent of unregulated family day care providers offered "inadequate" care.[34] These studies agreed that the problem is most acute for poor families. Given the higher rate of poverty among African American and Latino families, these groups suffer disproportionately from the lack of affordable quality day care.[35] But even black middle-class and working-class families face greater difficulties than white families because of the higher percentage of dual-worker families among blacks.

Quality depends upon a clear definition of the term as well as vigorous enforcement by local governmental regulators. Although there is some debate about what constitutes quality day care, a consensus appears to be emerging about the most important elements, as well as about the most troublesome problems. The American Academy of Pediatrics (AAP) and the American Public Health Association (APHA) have pinpointed certain "measurable" basic standards for ensuring children's health and safety, such as regulations for hand washing, preemployment staff health evaluation, staff training, and infant-to-staff ratio.[36] In a 1988 national study of state licensing requirements for child care services in out-of-home settings, the AAP and APHA found that 25 to 50 percent of states lacked basic, important standards for insuring children's health and safety.[37] Furthermore, the study found that state regulations were weaker for group and family care facilities, the very settings that provided the majority of day care.

Stressing the importance of adequate licensing requirements and enforcement, the AAP-APHA developed guidelines that states could use. Commenting on these guidelines, Dr. George Sterne, a clinical professor of pediatrics at Tulane University School of Medicine in New Orleans, has emphasized, "Federal legislation is desperately needed to provide states with first, a blueprint of what quality child care is, and second, with the financial support to ensure that attaining that quality is possible."[38] High turnover of day care teachers, inadequate training, and low pay continue to plague United States day care facilities. Congress has yet to act on President Clinton's initiative to provide increased federal funding to meet the country's day care needs.

Quality child care, however, is not limited to basic health and safety standards. Professionals in the field stress that care must foster children's cognitive and emotional development. Early brain development, most researchers agree, is augmented by enriching, stimulating environments and attentive, warm, and loving caregivers. Recent research has documented not only that the first three years of life are the critical ones for brain development, but also that quality day care can promote this development.

Industry and Child Care

Because of the difficulty finding quality child care convenient to the workplace, many workers have placed their hopes on industry provided day care. Parents whose work sites are distant from children's day care centers are justifiably concerned. What if a child becomes ill during the workday, necessitating a drive of forty-five minutes to an hour to pick up the child? Distance can make late afternoon pickups an exasperating experience with rush hour delays and the specter of steep fees for being even a minute late. These and other concerns have goaded President Clinton to call for the private sector to participate in providing child care to employees. At the historic White House Conference on Child Care on October 23, 1997, he announced "the appointment of a Child Care Working Group that will report to Treasury Secretary Robert Rubin on the role that business can play in providing child care."[39]

What has industry done to date? There are some notable examples of corporate involvement. But before I discuss them, it is important to describe the extent of industry's present involvement. Admittedly, it is difficult to find solid figures on corporate involvement in child care because of the many different programs and services offered, both direct and indirect. In addition, while some surveys report the number of employees served in a city or nationwide, others cite the number of businesses offering services. *Working Woman* reported in its June 1993 issue that only "one-tenth of 1 percent" of all United States companies (about 5,600 businesses) offered "formal programs" of direct assistance such as on-site child care, emergency child care, or day care subsidies to their employees.[40] A 1994 survey of 1,035 large companies by Hewitt Associates, a Chicago benefits consulting firm, found only 12 percent offered emergency child care, up from 5 percent the previous year.[41] Companies fared better in offering indirect assistance such as free access to child-care information services or tax breaks through special pretax spending accounts. Here industry involvement swelled to 60 percent of major corporations, but only 10 percent of smaller firms. It should be noted that the indirect benefits frequently cost these corporations little or nothing, though the benefits to employees may be important.

Nationally, according to the Bureau of Labor Statistics (BLS), only 7 percent of employees of large- and medium-size firms and 2 percent of small firms received the more costly child care services, such as on-site child care centers, in 1993. Moreover, the better-paid professional and technical workers benefited most. For instance, BLS found that 12 percent of professional and technical workers received child care benefits, compared with only 4 percent of blue-collar and low-skilled service workers. According to a Bureau of National Affairs special report on Work and Family, "Few companies have systematically determined their employees' needs and fewer have developed comprehensive plans to meet those needs. Even fewer companies have considered changing their culture and practices so they help meet their employees' changing needs."[42]

A few corporations have gone beyond lip service to offer a wide variety of services that exceed on-site child care. They have moved to what experts call "stage two," with "something going on in every area, where work and family is not just seen as child care."[43] In their special report on Corporate Work and Family Programs, the BNA also quotes Fran Rodgers, president of Massachusetts-based Work/Family Directions, who defines a stage-two company as one that is "actively involved" in child care and elder care assistance. This includes "actively" reexamining work hours and getting "more active in a public stance to solve the related societal problems."[44] Procter and Gamble, for instance, surveys its employees to learn their needs, then designs services to meet them. *Working Woman* has documented four ways in which this "elite group" of companies departs from the mainstream. "They are developing programs that benefit the *communities* in which they operate as well as their own employees. They are leveraging their resources by teaming up on projects with local businesses and public agencies. They are extending their efforts to new groups, such as school-age children and mildly ill kids. They are helping to bridge the gap between what good care costs and what parents can afford."[45]

So far it appears that only large Fortune 500 corporations—such as Procter and Gamble, IBM, NationsBank, Xerox, Hallmark, Campbell Soup, Stride Rite, Apple Computer, and Levi-Strauss—have had the resources or the will to join the small group of stage two companies. Or at least those are the companies one hears and reads about developing family-friendly workplaces. Many of these companies have established multi-million-dollar development funds to improve and expand child care facilities in cities where they have a large number of employees. Examples of the services provided include recruiting and training day care providers, adding space to local day care center facilities for infants and toddlers, and creating before- and after-school programs for older children. Lancaster Labs has received national acclaim for its innovative intergenerational on-site family center. The center provides care for up to 25 elderly or handicapped relatives of employees plus day care for 151 children. Its family center also houses a fitness center open to the community, with employees paying a discounted rate.[46]

To meet the need for child care when a parent's usual arrangement falls through, 5 percent of large corporations now provide and subsidize emergency backup services. These backup services typically take the form of sick-child centers or sponsoring a service that sends trained child care providers into an employee's home. The latter can be so expensive as to be out of the reach of all but highly paid professionals. While corporations may make the institutional arrangements for a service such as emergency care or summer camps for older children, usually parents must pay all or at least a large share of the cost. Levi-Strauss, however, has experimented with a $100-a-month voucher for workers earning less than $32,000 a year. NationsBank is spending $25 million to extend a program to all employees that began with a $35 a week child care subsidy to its low-income employees.[47]

Among the most promising developments in child care services is the emergence of public-private partnerships with local governments, private industry, and nonprofit organizations pooling resources to offer a variety of services to working parents.[48] One such collaboration produced the Connecticut Consortium for Child Care in Hartford, which offers parents active assistance in locating quality day care services. In Michigan the collaborative Family to Family Program has trained 4,400 child care providers and recruited 1,600 more. In Colorado, the Downtown Denver Child Care Consortium, a state-of-the-art day care center was built to accommodate 110 children with combined funding from the state and private corporations. A unique feature of this collaboration was Governor Roy Romer's leadership in reaching out to 120 senior managers and CEOs in Denver.[49] While the result of this collaborative effort was impressive, culminating in a high-quality downtown day care center, it is sobering to learn that a study revealed that at the project's inception, 1,200 parents working in downtown Denver were still looking for day care for their children.[50]

Parents certainly highly prize on-site day care centers. They are not only physically close to their children but can often visit with them during their lunch hour. But since this is not yet available to most, some parents have turned to a new, creative alternative that allows "virtual visits" to their child's day care center. A few day care centers have installed cameras that parents can access over the Internet by using a unique password. The device, dubbed a "kiddie cam," allows parents to actually see their child in a day care center for a monthly fee of about twenty dollars. To some parents, the feeling of being in touch and the reduced anxiety are well worth the fee.[51]

Child Care and the Corporate Bottom Line

Corporate executives readily admit that the economic bottom line rather than altruism drives their involvement in family-friendly programs such as day care. In a tight labor market recruitment has become difficult for many companies, and the high cost of replacing even low-skilled workers is forcing companies to focus on creative ways to find and keep employees. While firms are experimenting with a variety of benefits that might attract and keep workers, many are discovering that day care and other family-related benefits are among the highest on workers' lists.[52] After a recent business conference in New York City, David Lawrence, chairman and CEO of the Kaiser Foundation Health Plan, emphasized the connection. "Let's put it in crass economic terms. It costs our organization a lot to hire people and train them, and [losing valued employees] has a terrible impact."[53] In some companies the cost of recruiting and training salaried employees can run as high as $30,000 to $40,000.

At the Manhattan meeting, some executives also voiced concern that without attention to day care the United States' future economic competitiveness may be at stake. Citing new brain research emphasizing the critical nature of the first three years for a child's intellectual development, they worried that the United States might fail to keep up with countries that more actively nurture the brain development of infants and toddlers. Such informed executives, however, are probably a small minority.

For most corporations, the immediate problems of recruitment and retention drive their efforts. The results are tangible for those progressive companies that have taken the step. With unemployment below 4 percent in the Indianapolis area, RCI International discovered that subsidizing child care for workers at a new $1.1 million day care center paid off in lower employee turnover. NationsBank, which pays half the cost of day care for bank tellers and back-room operations employees with household incomes below $35,000, has found that the turnover rate for those receiving subsidies is less than half that for those at the same grade and pay who do not receive subsidies.[54]

There are ample signs of satisfaction and even enthusiasm from employees receiving these benefits. One worker at RCI International in Indianapolis with a five-year-old son at its subsidized day care center remarked, "RCI is saying, 'I care about you and your family.' I feel like they are helping me raise my kid."[55] Of employees' response to emergency back-up child care services, Karol Rose, Time Warner's director of work/family programs, commented, "They talk about how they were able to concentrate on their work, and that translates to productivity. That's the bottom line."[56]

It may be well to emphasize again that only a small minority of companies offer these attractive child care benefits. A 1998 survey of 1,057 firms by the Families and Work Institute revealed that only 9 percent of them provided child care centers, 5 percent offered child care subsidies,

4 percent provided backup or emergency care, and 36 percent offered referral services to help workers locate child care.[57] The corporate view of the employee as merely a producer, of value only to generate profits, remains dominant.

Child Care in Europe

In comparison to the United States, European countries as a group support child care far more generously.[58] A number of countries have a system of paid benefits to families for each child, and these benefits are not tied to means or a mother's employment status. Rather, these benefits are seen as assistance to families in the care and raising of their children. Also, most European countries have systems of state-funded day care. Often, as in Sweden, the combined contributions of the national and local governments fund high-quality centers. Day care workers tend to be well paid, typically at the same level as elementary school teachers. By contrast, United States day care workers are in the lowest 10 percent of all wage workers, earning on average less than $200 a week. As a result, many day care centers are plagued by staff turnover as high as 85 percent annually.[59]

What are the reasons for greater state intervention in child care in Europe? As we have seen, there is perhaps more of a tendency to view early childhood development as a social concern and children as a societal good. As one writer indicates, "In all the Scandinavian countries the provision of high-quality day-care is commonly regarded as a national concern and is incorporated as a part of the welfare state service system. Access to publicly funded day-care is often presented as part of children's democratic rights."[60]

A more controversial issue, even in the progressive Scandinavian countries, is the relationship of day care to the employment of wives. As we have seen, Sweden has taken the lead with its "equal status contract," but Denmark, France, and Norway also support mothers' employment by providing state-funded day care. In 1993 in Sweden 77 percent of children ages three to six were in publicly funded child care; in Denmark the figure was 74 percent, and in Norway 63 percent. Although facilities exist for younger children, far fewer children under age three were in day care in 1993: Sweden, 32 percent; Denmark, 47 percent; Norway, 20 percent; France, Belgium, and Iceland, 20–29 percent. This difference is probably due in part to the generous paid maternity leave enjoyed by European mothers and in part to the large numbers of mothers with less than a college degree who in the past did not return to work after the birth of a child.[61] In Europe, though, unlike in the United States, parents do not generally have to worry about either the cost or the quality of day care.

Effects of Day Care on Children

Perhaps because of the high quality of day care in European countries, there does not appear to be the same concern about its effects on children as in the United States. In addition to feelings of guilt over leaving their children in the care of "strangers," American parents worry about the long-term effects of day care on their children. Some mothers also worry about the possibility of a decrease in their infants' attachment to them. According to some research, children in high-quality day care fare very well, even when placed there as infants,[62] and are not less attached to their mothers.[63] They may even experience special benefits over children who do not have that experience. A number of studies have found that children who spent the most time in high-quality day care from infancy on had more friends in elementary school, were more assertive and better adjusted, and performed well academically.[64] The operative word, of course, is *high-quality.* Still, these findings should motivate parents to demand more resources for day care from both government and industry.

MATERNITY LEAVE

Maternity leave is a child care benefit in a class by itself. While all other benefits, such as flex time and on-site day care, help employees on the job balance work and family responsibilities, maternity (and paternity) leave allows a parent to suspend her (or his) actual work activity for a time to care for infants. For women, it has pluses and minuses. In Europe, as mentioned above, women typically receive sixteen weeks of maternity leave at full pay. In France and Sweden maternity leave can be extended to twenty-six and twenty-four weeks, respectively, at somewhat less than full pay. Payment is funded through a combination of state and employer contributions.

In addition to universal paid maternity leave, some countries include a few days of paid paternity leave (ten days each in Sweden and Denmark). Additional forms of parental leave exist in most countries, though the benefits included here vary widely. In France, during the first three years of a child's life, unpaid parental leave is available to all employees, regardless of the number of employees in a firm. Not surprisingly, 99 percent of takers are mothers, so the plan is widely viewed as reinforcing the traditional model of the family.[65]

In contrast to France, Norway designed its parental leave policy, which went into effect in 1993, to ensure the participation of fathers—at least on a limited basis. Of the twelve months allowed, six weeks are reserved for the mother following birth, but four weeks of parental leave (a "father's quota") are also reserved for the father. The couple can share the remaining weeks in whatever way they wish. This policy of "enforcing fatherhood" appears to be working, as the majority of fathers included in the scheme have taken their quota.[66] In 1998 Norway modified its plan to provide a second year of paid leave. The first year is supported at 80 percent of the mother's normal salary; the second year (which the father can take) pays a little less than $5,000 per year. Discussing the rationale behind this new policy, Valgard Haugland, the minister of Children and Family Affairs, explained, "We have decided that raising a child is real work. And that this work provides value for the whole society. And that the society as a whole should pay for this valuable service."[67]

In the United States, as we have seen, parental leave continues to follow a tortured path. While paid maternity leave is available to all employed women in Europe, access to maternity leave in the United States depends on the woman's place of employment. In 1993, when the Family and Medical Leave Act (FMLA) was passed, only thirty-four states, Puerto Rico, and the District of Columbia had some form of job-guaranteed, mandatory maternity or paternity leave legislation for at least some employees. In several states the laws applied to both the public and the private sectors, in others only to state employees. Leaves ranged from a low of sixteen hours to one year. Very few of these states mandated coverage as comprehensive as that in the FMLA, and only five states—New York, New Jersey, Rhode Island, Hawaii, and California—required any pay during leave. In these states, paid leave was covered under temporary disability laws that provided only a portion of typical earnings, ranging from an average of $169 per week in California to $196 in New Jersey in 1990.[68]

The policies in the private sector were hardly any better. According to a survey commissioned by the Department of Labor in 1994–95, only "a quarter to a third of formal employer policies matched FMLA requirements in the protections they offered."[69] In many instances leaves were handled on a case-by-case basis, without benefits and without a job guarantee. Among the notable exceptions were "stage two" companies like Procter and Gamble and Johnson and Johnson that provided paid maternity leave along with other family benefits. Overall, workers in the private sector were more likely to find maternity and other family leave coverage in large than in medium-size or small firms. Nationally some 37 percent of large firms (over 100 employees), compared with 18 percent of smaller companies, offered unpaid maternity leave in 1992. Far fewer companies—just 2 percent—of either type offered paid maternity leave. In addition some companies offered better benefits to their highly paid professional staff than to their hourly wage employees or none to part-timers. Wage workers had to use vacation or accumulated sick pay in order to receive any income while on leave.

The Family and Medical Leave Act in Practice

To what extent has the passage of the Family and Medical Leave Act increased family-related benefits? Survey data collected in 1995 indicate a much improved situation that nevertheless left many workers uncovered.[70] Nationally, only slightly more than half (55.6 percent) of women were covered and eligible for benefits in 1995 in both the public and private sectors combined. About the same percentage of men (54.2 percent) were covered and eligible. An additional 10 percent of men and 14 percent of women worked at sites protected by the FMLA but were not eligible because they did not meet the conditions of at least twelve months' employment and at least 1,250 work hours during the year preceding the start of the desired leave. Even fewer employees (46.5 percent) met eligibility requirements in the private sector. The surveys also found that among noncovered work sites only 32.3 percent offered parental leave and only 41.7 percent offered leave to care for a seriously ill child, spouse, or parent. These data clearly suggest that the FMLA benefits fell far short of universal coverage.

Utilization of leave provided under the FMLA was also hindered by lack of employee awareness and the absence of salary replacement during leave. Although 86.5 percent of employers were aware that they were covered by the FMLA, only 58.2 percent of their employees had heard of the law. Apparently, many employers have failed in their responsibility to inform workers about their rights under the FMLA.

More important, though, is the lack of any mandated salary replacement during the leave period. This factor inherently injects a class and race bias into the legislation. Working-class women (and men), poor women, women moving off welfare, and single mothers are the least likely to be able to take advantage of their right to twelve weeks of unpaid maternity leave, just as they are the least likely to be able to afford quality day care. In fact the surveys found that 63.9 percent of the surveyed employees who needed but did not take leave were hourly workers, African Americans, or employees with at most only some college education. Moreover, the better-positioned employees—salaried workers, union members, those with a higher education, men, and higher income workers—were the most likely both to know about the legislation and to receive full or partial wage replacement during their leave. The Bureau of Labor Statistics report concludes, "Not surprisingly, then, employees who fare best in covering for lost income during leave-taking are employees with high family incomes, salaried employees, union members, highly educated employees and white employees."

Certainly, the FMLA has increased the availability of protected leave for parents and other workers in the United States, but it is important to remember that only about half of all workers are covered and eligible. Furthermore, those least likely to benefit from the legislation are those workers most in need of it: the poor and minorities.

RECONNECTING THE PUBLIC
AND PRIVATE SPHERES

American families have traversed several systems over the past two hundred years, from the preindustrial economy in which husbands and wives shared both breadwinning and homemaking roles, through the cult of domesticity and the rigid separation of these roles, to once more reuniting work and family roles. The two most important factors contributing to the reunion of the two spheres were first, the new ideology of womanhood and family pioneered by the black middle class and later adopted by whites through the feminist movement, and second a changing economy that made two incomes a necessity in many families. Although this reunion in many ways may still be a "virtual reality," movement toward it seems unstoppable. Only the final shape of this union remains uncertain. At some point in the future, the FMLA may be seen as the significant first step in that direction, since it marks the beginning of legislating a national superstructure needed to enable a harmonious union of family and work.

Three major obstacles to this union must still be overcome. The first is our outdated philosophical approach to children and their care. The second is a corporate culture that has historically viewed work as the domain of married males whose wives free them from any concern beyond the office door or plant gate. The third is the reluctance of husbands and fathers to match their wives' movement into the workforce with a comparable shift into the arena of housework and child care.

Our Outdated Family Philosophy

Although the governments and citizens of most European countries have long viewed children as a societal good whose care and development the entire society must support, Americans have considered child rearing (aside from education) as a private family matter. Indeed, in the United States, the family itself has been considered a private domain, shielded from government "interference." Government has even been reluctant to intervene in cases of domestic violence involving acts that would be seen as criminal behavior if they occurred between unrelated individuals.

Given this outlook, it is no surprise that it took so long to pass legislation as mild as the Family and Medical Leave Act, that no government-funded national day care system has been established, and that even today no politician is willing to propose paid maternity leave. The earliest maternity benefits had to be couched in universal terms—as *short-term disability coverage*—rather than relating specifically to maternity. Even then the Supreme Court twice rejected the idea that failure to include pregnancy under short-term disability coverage constituted gender discrimination. In spite of the facts that women now comprise 45 percent of the workforce and that 62 percent of mothers of preschoolers are employed, many people still view women as wives and mothers only and contend that mothers are the only legitimate caretakers of their children (except when it comes to welfare mothers). Conservatives even decried the Family and Medical Leave Act as a step toward creating a "nanny state."[71] This kind of thinking seems totally out of step with the realities of the industrialized world, the demand for workers, and women's rights. The passage of the FMLA marks a small departure from this deep-seated reactionary view.

A Punishing Corporate Culture

The corporate culture has legitimately come under scrutiny as a major obstacle to the reconciliation of the home and the workplace. Unlike men, women do not leave behind the responsibilities of the home and child care when they move into the workplace. Female employees are expected to act as males on the job and as women (wives/mothers) at home. The result is not a reconciliation of home and workplace but double duty, added to which is the guilt these mothers have been made to feel by the stay-at-home-mothers-only philosophy of child care. The corporate culture must change to see employees as complete persons with ties to both work and family, rather than just as worker bees. The present myopia creates the "time bind" described by Hochschild and helps to explain why two-thirds of the men and women in the *Washington Post*-Harvard-Kaiser poll said it was better if mothers remained at home to care for children. The more in-depth interviews conducted along with the survey revealed the reason for this view. In these interviews respondents voiced their fear that families are ill served by the demands of today's business world, where men and women must work increasingly long hours without the support of reliable and affordable child care. "Seeing little hope that their workloads could lessen," a *Post* article comments, "many respondents simply harkened to an earlier era and fondly described the ideal of women at home caring for children in an arrangement that seemed simpler and easier on families."[72]

The Time Bind vividly describes the time demands of the American workplace, which are augmented by corporate worries about profits and global competition. As one Americo manager Hochschild interviewed explained, "Here in the plant, we have a macho thing about hours. Guys say, 'I'm an eighty-hour man!' as if describing their hairy chests."[73] Expressing just how trapped many workers feel, this manager explained, "You have the high-risers grabbing all they can. Then you have the discontent of the lower-downs. Then you have confused people in the middle like me. A day doesn't go by where I don't talk about overload. It's an underground conversation here. You don't want to say it too loud. We're in this whirlwind; we work ourselves to death. Then when we die: What purpose did we serve? Is it worth it? But we're afraid to get off the roller coaster for fear we won't be able to get back on."[74] Surveys of workers in other companies indicate that such time binds are typical, at least in large corporations. In one survey, only 9 percent of 1,446 respondents said they were able to balance the demands of work and family "very well."[75] These responses make the term "family-friendly workplace" an oxymoron. This corporate culture is only reinforced by conservative politicians who are philosophically opposed to "interfering" with business practices and put up barriers to legislation. This was the attitude that led President Bush to veto the Family and Medical Leave Act thirty-two times.

Fortunately, this too is beginning to change, albeit glacially. Some companies are beginning to understand the financial benefits of truly family-friendly policies. Good salaried employees can be costly to replace and—in a tight labor market—difficult to find. But companies with a reputation for good family benefits often have more applicants than they can use and are also more successful in retaining their workers. Women are more likely to return to work—and sooner—when they have been assisted by maternity leave, especially if paid. A 1993 evaluation of work-life programs at Johnson and Johnson found that seventy-one percent of employees who used these services rated them very important in their decision to remain with the company.[76]

There are additional signs of attitudinal changes in the more progressive companies. Donna Klein, director of work-life programs at Marriott International in Bethesda, Maryland, speaks of "a new paradigm, a new way of looking at the worker."[77] "It's a new face corporations are wearing," she continues. "It's a new role, and I think corporations are doing it willingly. Employees are not a unit of labor. They come with a lot of baggage. Once we believed they left it at the door, but now we realize it's never left at the door. We're getting increasingly less hesitant to get involved."[78]

Employer involvement may entail offering such benefits as paid maternity leave, subsidized day care, flex time, assistance with college expenses, emergency day care centers, support for high school equivalency diplomas on company time—and the list goes on. Once employee workshops were only job related. Increasingly they now offer assistance with family-related issues, and in some companies managers are expected to act, to a certain extent, as "social workers."

Executives in some major corporations are also becoming concerned about meeting our future manpower needs. Some have become aware of recent research conducted by such solid organizations as Carnegie, the Families and Work Institute, and the National Institute of Child Health and Human Development—research that has confirmed the importance of the first three years of life for brain development and highlighted the intellectual, social, and behavioral benefits children derive from high-quality day care. Eager not to be outdone by countries with better preschool day care systems, they are turning their attention to expanding family benefits to employees. Recently two dozen firms representing 2.5 million workers and calling themselves the Employer Group began holding brainstorming meetings on how to increase benefits to low-wage workers.[79] This is especially important in light of findings that the children of the poor have the lowest-quality day care. But such "postmodern" attitudes are, unfortunately, far from typical.

Nonparticipant Fathers

Finally, regardless of how family friendly the workplace becomes, employed mothers will need help at home with housework and child care. Indeed, until the division of household labor and child care is more nearly equalized, the revolution in the family will remain unfinished. The problem lies both in employers' negative reaction and in husbands' reluctance to take on tasks that as males they have not been socialized to value and that society fails to reward in any tangible way. At present male employees' requests for time off to attend to family responsibilities are more likely to be greeted by raised eyebrows than by understanding. Until employers begin to value and respect male workers as individuals with family responsibilities as well as contributors to profit, male workers will continue to give priority to paid work over family responsibilities. Until employers send out the message that they regard a "family man" as one who is involved in housework and child care rather than just bringing home a pay check, wives will continue to experience difficulty winning husbands' cooperation. Researchers have found that even in progressive countries such as those in Scandinavia, husbands are reluctant to share available family leave for fear of the possible negative effect on their careers—loss of advancements, loss of wages, and the stigma of not being strongly "committed" to the company. Although a number of companies have become more open to male employees' family responsibilities, these companies are still a small minority. Finally, our socialization of boys needs to become less gendered. They should learn "domestic" skills early by performing their share of household chores, and should be led to expect to share both market work and housework in marriage.

THREE SCENARIOS FOR THE FUTURE

The work-family *reconnection* is still in a very fluid state. In the early 1980s, sociologists Janet and Larry Hunt argued that because careers were historically structured around the male role, a female career was becoming incompatible with family life. They predicted that future families would polarize around two types, an often childless, "career-centered" family and a "family-centered" one, with consequent differences in resources and life styles.[80] Recent calls for a "mommy track" suggest some basis for their view. However, there are also signs of growing flexibility among even the most demanding employers, large corporate law firms.[81] It is now possible in some law firms for female lawyers to receive extra time to make partner because of childbearing. Similarly, some universities, such as my own institution, the University of Maryland, offer untenured female faculty who give birth extra time to make tenure. These accommodations signal movement toward environments where women can combine career and family.

Such flexibility, however, can be a two-edged sword. Women may be allowed to pursue high-powered, rewarding careers while meeting the responsibilities of motherhood, but this flexibility may come with a price in lost wages. Economist Nancy Folbre's work suggests that the amount of income lost by working mothers depends on the amount of institutional investment in child care facilities. In countries with heavy public investment in child care, such as France and Sweden, Folbre estimates the loss in lifetime income to working women is relatively small: 12 percent and 6 percent, respectively. By contrast, in countries with relatively low public investment in child care like Germany and England, their sacrifice of lifetime earnings rises to 49 and 57 percent, respectively.[82] While I have not seen comparable figures for the United States, the meager public investment in child care suggests an even larger income penalty for working mothers.

Given all of this, I envision three different possible futures for the dual-worker family in the United States. In the first model, we will more or less continue as we are. Primarily mothers will take time off around the birth of a child, although increasingly they will be able to replace some, or most of their income for a maternity leave period of twelve weeks, maybe more. To some extent, this first model will continue to have a class and race bias. Working-class and poor mothers (among whom the number of minorities is disproportionately large) will be less likely to avail themselves of maternity leave because they will be less likely to receive pay. Child care will continue to be costly, so poor and minority children will not have access to the same quality day care as those in the middle class. Overall, mothers will be penalized economically for taking time off while the fathers do not.

In the second scenario, neither spouse will take time off around the birth of a child, except for a few days or weeks by the mother. To achieve equality in the workplace, women will experience pressure to pursue continuous careers and to place even infants in day care, or to remain childless. By pursuing continuous careers, women will make progress toward income and occupational parity with men. But they will continue to bear the principal burdens of housework and child care. Their marriages will not be truly egalitarian. Since the corporate culture will remain male centered, women will experience a serious time bind.

In the third scenario federal and state government and private corporate programs will support and encourage both mothers and fathers to take some time off to care for newborns. Day care will be either free or subsidized according to income. Quality will be ensured by government support for well-trained and well-paid providers, compensated at the level of elementary school teachers. In addition, employers—either individually or collectively—will offer a wide variety of benefits to enable workers to meet their families' varied needs. Stage two corporations will take the lead and create models for cooperative family-friendly benefit packages throughout the economy. This model assumes a commitment to gender equality as well as family care and therefore involves changing to a corporate culture that recognizes workers as whole persons with work *and* family responsibilities. In such a climate, husband and wife will share equally in the responsibilities of home and work, making their marriage truly egalitarian. Avoiding race and class bias, this model will provide quality day care for all children, not just the more affluent middle-class families. To further guarantee freedom from class and race bias, maternity leave will be *paid* leave. The cost of paid maternity leave will be shared by federal and state government and employers, as it is in Europe. Only such a model, I believe, will make maximum use of the country's human resources, regardless of race, gender, or class.

Ending the Conspiracy of Silence

Felice Schwartz, founder of Catalyst, a nonprofit organization that works with corporations to promote women in the workplace, has complained about "a terrible conspiracy of silence."[83] It is a complaint voiced by other women involved in changing the male-centered culture of the workplace. Women are often afraid to request benefits that meet their unique needs for fear of not being taken as "serious" players in the corporate world or for fear of jeopardizing their chances at mobility. Schwartz advises these women to share their experiences with each other and collectively make demands on top management. If only because of sheer numbers, women have become indispensable to the corporate bottom line, a situation that gives them bargaining power. Companies with many women in top management positions are about six times as likely to provide on-site child care as companies dominated by men only.[84] This implies that what is often lacking is sensitivity and awareness of the special needs of female employees. According to Schwartz, "It's because employers are afraid of litigation, and women don't want to appear different from men. But women are different from men in the childbirth period. Pregnancy and motherhood can be planned for and managed. But the cost of failing to manage it is enormous."[85] In the brave new world of my third scenario, women will be accepted and respected as different "in the childbirth period" yet nonetheless valuable in the workplace. Men will be accepted as parents as well as workers. Family and work will be reunited. If progressive countries like Sweden, Norway, and Denmark can move in this direction, why can't we?

Appendix A Statistics on Family Households

Table A1 presents the raw statistics for a thirty-six-year period, 1960 to 1996, for all family households—those with couples, just a male or female head, and "others."[1] The categories of male and female-headed families in table A1 include only households headed solely by an adult male or female with their own children under eighteen, since this definition coincides most closely with the general notion of single-parent families.[2] The category of "other" encompasses a variety of situations, including male or female heads living with a relative under eighteen who is not their own child, single parents living with children over eighteen, and groups of related individuals living together, such as a grandparent and a grandchild or a brother and a sister.

Looking at table A1, we see that there were roughly 3.1 million black and 36.2 million white couple families in 1960. By 1996 there were 3.8 million black and 47.9 million white couple families. When we examine the rate

Table A1 Family Households, by Type and Race of Householder: 1960–1996

TYPE OF FAMILY	NUMBER (IN THOUSANDS)					AVERAGE ANNUAL PERCENTAGE CHANGE			
	1995–96	1990–91	1980	1970	1960	1990–96	1980–90	1970–80	1960–70
BLACK									
All Family Households	8,074	7,471	6,184	4,887	4,234	1.3	2.1	2.7	1.5
Couples	3,776	3,660	3,433	3,323	3,118	0.5	0.7	0.3	0.7
Male Heads	273	188	99	73	593*	7.5	9.0	3.6	6.6*
Female Heads	2,447	2,264	1,794	912		1.3	2.6	9.7	
Other	1,576	1,359	858	579	523	2.7	5.8	4.8	1.1
WHITE									
All Family Households	58,653	56,697	52,243	46,261	40,828	0.6	0.9	1.3	1.3
Couples	47,886	46,998	44,751	41,049	36,217	0.3	0.5	0.9	1.3
Male Heads	1,191	933	500	271	1,736*	4.6	8.7	8.5	3.1*
Female Heads	4,908	4,269	3,559	1,995		2.5	2.0	7.8	
Other	4,669	4,497	3,433	2,946	2,875	1.6	3.1	1.7	0.2

*In 1960 male-headed and female-headed families are combined. In 1960, also, census data are available only for all "nonwhites" combined.
SOURCE: U.S. Census, P-20, No.106; P-20-480, adapted from Table F; P-20, No.458; 1995–96 from unpublished data.

of growth over these years, though, certain racial differences emerge. White couple families grew most rapidly in the 1960s, at a rate of 1.3 percent per year, and that growth rate declined steadily to 0.3 percent annually in the 1990s. Black couple families show their highest growth rate not only in the 1960s but also in the 1980s (0.7 percent per year), with their lowest rate in the 1970s.

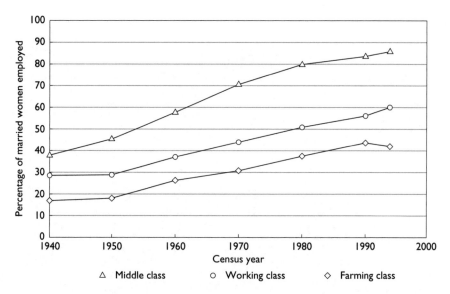

FIGURE B1. Percentage of Black Married Women in the Labor Force, by Class, 1940–1994

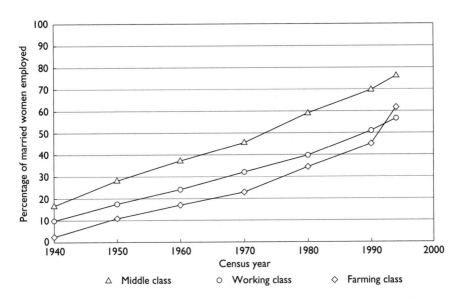

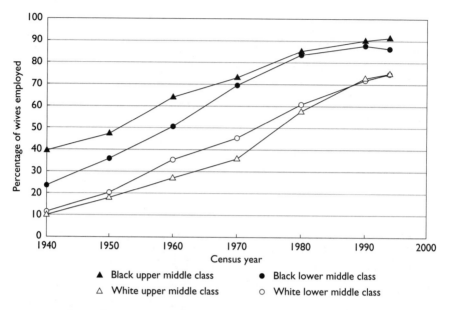

FIGURE B3. Percentage of Employed Upper- and Lower-Middle-Class Wives, Aged 25 to 44, with Children under 18

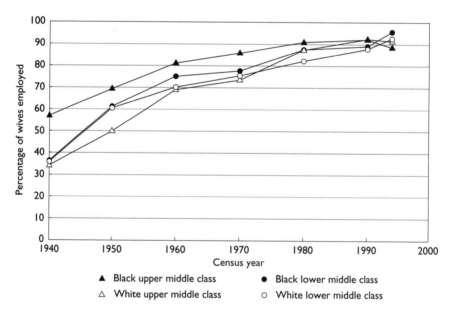

FIGURE B4. Percentage of Employed Upper- and Lower-Middle-Class Wives, Aged 25 to 44, without Children under 18

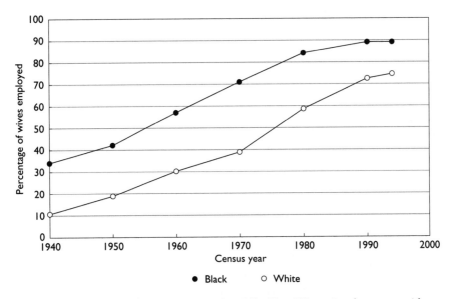

FIGURE B5. Percentage of Employed Middle-Class Wives, Aged 25 to 44, with Children under 18

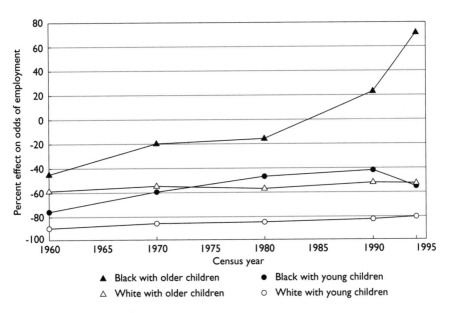

FIGURE B6. The Effects of Older and Younger Children on the Odds of Employment of Middle-Class Wives, Aged 25 to 44, by Race

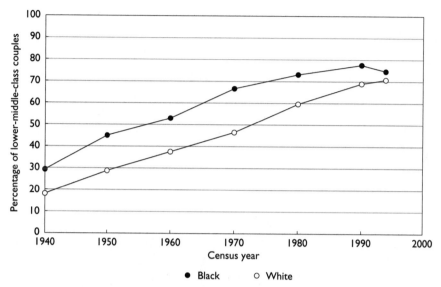

FIGURE B7.   Growth of Lower-Middle-Class Dual-Worker Families, with Wives Aged 25 to 44, by Race, 1940–1994

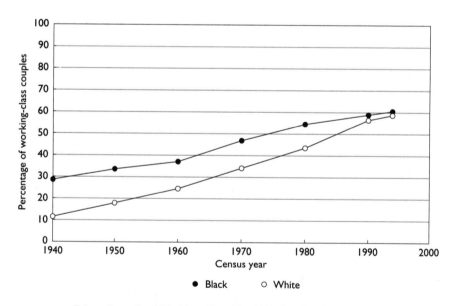

FIGURE B8.   Growth of Working-Class Dual-Worker Families, with Wives Aged 25 to 44, by Race, 1940–1994

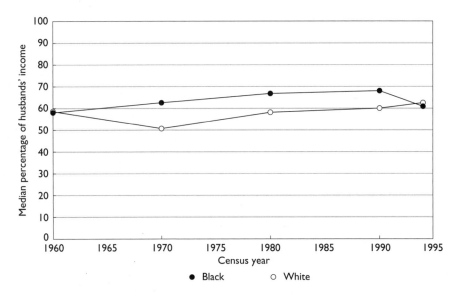

FIGURE B9.   Median Percentage of Husbands' Income Earned by Working-Class Wives, Aged 25 to 44 (Both Spouses Employed Full Time)

Appendix C Logistic Regression Models

Table C1 Logistic Regression Model of the Effects of Children on the Odds of Middle-Class Wives' Employment, by Race, Aged 25 to 44

Variable	1960			1970			1980
	b	antilog	%	b	antilog	%	b
BLACKS							
und18	−1.0854***	0.3378	−66.22	−.6054***	0.5459	−45.41	−.4045***
	(.1214)			(.1056)			(.1029)
edwife	.1977***	1.2186	21.86	.1893***	1.2080	20.84	.1684***
	(.0171)			(.0148)			(.0152)
loghinc	−.4030***	0.6683	−33.17	−.4275***	0.6521	−34.79	−.0863**
	(.0793)			(.0648)			(.0282)
constant	.0404			.6350*			.3898
	(.3355)			(.3107)			(.3376)
WHITES							
und18	−1.6277***	0.1964	−80.36	−1.3776***	0.2522	−74.78	−1.3468***
	(.0736)			(.0607)			(.0578)
edwife	.0436***	1.0446	4.46	.0414***	1.0423	4.23	.0874***
	(.0116)			(.0089)			(.0083)
loghinc	−.7765***	0.4600	−53.99	−.8499***	0.4275	−57.25	−.5482***
	(.0465)			(.0373)			(.0328)
constant	3.3633***			4.2840***			5.7905***
	(.2318)			(.2002)			(.3321)

*p < .05   **p < .01   ***p < .001
df = 3 in all instances.
Standard errors in parentheses.

1980		1990			1994		
antilog	%	b	antilog	%	b	antilog	%
0.6673	−33.27	−.1893* (.0909)	0.8275	−17.25	−.2364** (.0924)	0.7895	−21.05
1.1830	18.34	.1798*** (.0163)	1.1970	19.70	.4731*** (.0271)	1.6050	60.50
0.9173	−8.27	−.0432 (.0234) .7144** (.2870)	0.9577	−4.23	−.6080*** (.0600) 1.3321** (.6634)	0.5444	−45.56
0.2601	−73.99	−1.3005*** (.0611)	0.2724	−72.76	−1.2377*** (.0225)	0.2900	−70.99
1.0910	9.13	.0979*** (.0099)	1.1029	10.29	.1516*** (.0043)	1.1640	16.37
0.5779	−42.20	−.5450*** (.0311) 6.8325*** (.3220)	0.5798	−42.02	−.7892*** (.0129) 8.3425*** (.1361)	0.0129	−54.58

Table C2 Logistic Regression Model of the Effects of Big and Little Children on the Odds of Middle-Class Wives' Employment, by Race, Aged 25 to 44

variable	1960			1970			1980
	b	antilog	%	b	antilog	%	b
BLACKS							
loghinc	−.3925*** (.0807)	0.6754	−32.463	−.4503*** (.0656)	0.6374	−36.256	−.0910*** (.0287)
edwife	.2049*** (.0173)	1.2274	22.740	.1971*** (.0151)	1.2179	21.787	.1774*** (.0154)
bgkid	−.5940*** (.1420)	0.5521	−44.789	−.2185 (.1163)	0.8037	−19.628	−0.1680 (.1110)
bgLtl	−1.4095*** (.1291)	0.2443	−75.573	−.9108*** (.1110)	0.4022	−59.780	−.6384*** (.1088)
constant	−.0678 (.3413)	0.9344		.6237* (.3143)	1.8658		.2996 (.3410)
WHITES							
loghinc	−.8753*** (.0486)	0.4167	−58.326	−.9827*** (.0393)	0.3743	−62.570	−.6780*** (.0353)
edwife	.0794*** (0.122)	1.0826	8.264	.0716*** (.0093)	1.0742	7.423	.1238*** (.0087)
bgkid	−.8974*** (.0797)	0.4076	−59.237	−.7931*** (.0646)	0.4524	−54.756	−.8490*** (.0620)
bgLtl	−2.3065*** (.0814)	0.0996	−90.039	−1.9702*** (.0655)	0.1394	−86.057	−1.8861*** (.0622)
constant	3.2716*** (.2395)	26.3535		4.4479*** (.2073)	85.4473		6.5032*** (.3525)

$*p < .05$ $**p < .01$ $***p < .001$
df = 3 in all instances
Standard errors in parentheses.

| 1980 | | 1990 | | | 1994 | | |
antilog	%	b	antilog	%	b	antilog	%
0.9130	−8.698	−.0504* (.0239)	0.9509	−4.915	−.6907*** (.0619)	0.5012	−49.877
1.1941	19.411	.1918*** (.0165)	1.2114	21.143	.3830*** (.0215)	1.4667	46.668
0.8453	−15.465	.2116* (.1036)	1.2357	23.565	.5410*** (.1122)	1.7177	71.772
0.5281	−47.186	−.5371*** (.0966)	0.5844	−41.556	−.7852*** (.0976)	0.4562	−54.397
1.3493		.6520* (.2906)	1.9194		−6.1325*** (.9534)	0.0022	
0.5076	−49.237	−.6086*** (.0323)	0.5441	−45.589	−.8157*** (.0131)	0.4423	−55.767
1.1318	13.179	.1346*** (.0103)	1.1441	14.408	.1402*** (.0037)	1.1505	15.050
0.4284	−57.216	−.7274*** (.0675)	0.4832	−51.684	−.7315*** (.0247)	0.4812	−51.881
0.1517	−84.834	−1.7511*** (.0639)	0.1736	−82.642	−1.6201*** (.0234)	0.1979	−80.212
0.5032		7.0629*** (.3316)	1167.83		5.2325*** (.1748)	187.2604	

Notes

INTRODUCTION

1.   In no way is this to be taken as a criticism of single-parent families. Rather, it is simply a statement of fact. The sharp increase in single-parent families since 1970 is largely a consequence of societal changes that have resulted in a high divorce rate and a rise in out-of-wedlock births. A poorly performing economy, resulting in high unemployment and increased family poverty during the 1970s and 1980s, has also impeded family formation. While a large percentage of single-parent families are poor, however, many others manage well financially. Whether poor or well-off, many mothers heading these families perform well, even heroically against heavy odds (see Nancy E. Dowd, *In Defense of Single-Parent Families* [New York: New York University Press, 1997]).

2.   Theodore Caplow et al., *Middletown Families: Fifty Years of Change and Continuity* (Minneapolis: University of Minnesota Press, 1982), p. 116.

3.   Mary P. Ryan, *Womanhood in America: From Colonial Times to the Present* (New York: New Viewpoints, 1975), p. 224.

4.   Alice Kessler, "Stratifying by Sex: Understanding the History of Working Women," pp. 217–242 in Richard C. Edwards et al., eds., *Labor Market Segmentation* (Lexington, Mass.: D. C. Heath).

5.   Ryan, *Womanhood in America*, p. 226.

6.   Daniel P. Moynihan, *The Negro Family: The Case for National Action* (Washington, D.C.: U.S. Government Printing Office, March 1965).

7.   See Herbert G. Gutman, *The Black Family in Slavery and Freedom 1750–1925* (New York: Vintage Books, 1976); Jacqueline Jones, *Labor of Love, Labor of Sorrow: Black Women, Work and the Family, From Slavery to the Present* (New York: Vintage Books, 1985). This point will be discussed at greater length in chapter 2.

8.   Census data for 1960 are for all nonwhites combined. Also, in 1960 female and male heads could not be separated, so the category "female head" includes male heads.

9.   Census data for single-parent families by sex of head are not available for the 1960s.

10.   The percentages of female heads in 1980, 1990, and 1996 were 29.0, 29.9 and 30.3 among blacks, and 6.8, 7.4, and 8.4 among whites.

11.   Bart Landry, *The New Black Middle Class* (Berkeley: University of California Press, 1987).

12.   I do not mean to imply that there are only 400 members of the upper class. In both the Weberian and Marxian traditions, the upper class (capitalists) are defined as the propertied class. They are distinct in their controlling ownership of income producing property (large corporations, real estate, and financial capital such as banks). Determining their exact number is difficult, but studies of wealth holdings find that about 1 percent of the population owns over half of all stocks and bonds (see Frank Ackerman and Andrew Zimbalist, "The Distribution of Income and Wealth," pp. 217–227 in Richard C. Edwards, Michael Reich, and Thomas E. Weisskopf, eds. *The Capitalist System*, 3rd ed., [Englewood Cliffs, N.J.: Prentice-Hall, 1986]). Owners of small businesses form a separate class from both capitalists and those without "property" (wealth) who must therefore work for others.

13.   Lower white-collar workers are sometimes referred to as "pink collar" occupations. These are female dominated occupations in the service sector. For an extensive study of these occupations see Ronica Nicole Rooks, *The Effects of Working in Pink-Collar Occupations on Upward Occupational Mobility*, Ph.D. Dissertation, the University of Maryland, 1999.

14.   See Marcus Felson and David Knoke, "Social Status and the Married Woman," *Journal of Marriage and the Family* 36, no. 3 (August 1974): 516–521; Linda Burzotta Nilson, "The Social Standing of a Married Woman," *Social Problems* 23, no. 5 (1976): 581–592.

15.   Traditionally more black than white families have owed their class position to wives. See chapter 5 of Charles Vert Willie, *A New Look at Black Families*, 2nd ed. (Bayside, N.Y.: General Halls, 1981), for a number of vignettes of such families.

CHAPTER I. THE RISE AND FALL OF THE
TRADITIONAL FAMILY

1.   Stephanie Coontz, *The Way We Never Were: American Families and the Nostal-gia Trap* (New York: Basic Books, 1992), p. 29.

2.   Ibid., p. 29.

3.   Ibid., pp. 37, 34.

4.   Ibid., p. 37.

5.   Ibid., p. 32.

6.   Quoted in Lynn Y. Weiner, *From Working Girl to Working Mother: The Female Labor Force in the United States, 1820–1980* (Chapel Hill, N.C.: University of North Carolina Press, 1985), p. 113.

7.   Morton Hunt, "The Future of Marriage," pp. 506–521 in John F. Crosby, ed., *Reply to Myth: Perspectives on Intimacy* (New York: John Wiley, 1984); Suzanne Keller, "Does the Family Have a Future?" pp. 137–150 in Arlene S. Skolnick and Jerome H. Skolnick, eds., *Family in Transition*, 4th ed. (Boston: Scott, Foresman, 1983); Marvin B. Sussman, "The Family Today," pp. 17–23 in Leonard Cargan, ed., *Marriage and Family: Coping with Change* (Belmont, Calif.: Wadsworth, 1985); A. Etzioni, "The Family: Is It Obsolete?" *Journal of Current Social Issues* 14, no. 1 (Winter 1977): pp. 4–9.

8.   Hunt, "The Future of Marriage," p. 517.

9.   Sussman, "The Family Today," p. 17.

10.   Edward Cornish, "The Future of the Family," pp. 508–516 in Skolnick and Skolnick, eds., *Family in Transition*, 4th ed. (Boston: Scott, Foresman, 1983), p. 515.

11.   Keller, "Does the Family Have a Future?" p. 150.

12.   A number of scholars made important contributions to this debate in the years following its publication, among them most prominently Andrew Billings-ley, Robert Hill, Harriette Pipes McAdoo, and Robert Staples. See especially Andrew Billingsley's pathbreaking book, *Black Families in White America* (Englewood Cliffs, N.J.: Prentice-Hall, 1968), and his more recent work, *Climbing Jacob's Ladder* (New York: Touchstone, 1992). Robert Hill's *Strengths of Black Families* (New York: Emerson Hall, 1971) has been recently revised as *The Strengths of African American Families: Twenty-Five Years Later* (Washington, D.C.: R & B Publishers, 1997). Robert Staples and Harriette McAdoo have both published influential edited works that have taken up this and other issues over the years: McAdoo, *Black Families* (Thousand Oaks, Calif.: Sage); Staples, *The Black Family: Essays and Studies* (Belmont, Calif.: Wadsworth). John H. Scanzoni, *The Black Family in Modern Society: Patterns of Stability and Security* (Chicago: University of Chicago Press, 1971), offered sound empirical analysis of the diversity among African American families.

13.   Moynihan et al., *The Negro Family*, pp. 5–6.

14.   For the nineteenth and early twentieth centuries see, for instance, Herbert G. Gutman, *The Black Family in Slavery and Freedom 1750–1925* (New York: Random House, 1976); Tamara K. Hareven, *Family Time and Industrial Time: The Relationship Between the Family and Work in a New England Industrial Community* (New York: Cambridge University Press, 1982); also S. J. Kleinberg, *The Shadow of the Mills: Working-Class Families in Pittsburgh, 1870–1907* (Pittsburgh: University of Pittsburgh Press, 1989) and Jacqueline Jones, *Labor of Love, Labor of Sorrow: Black Women, Work and the Family, from Slavery to the Present* (New York: Vintage Books, 1985). For the contemporary period see Rosanna Hertz, *More Equal Than Others: Women and Men in Dual-Career Marriages* (Berkeley: University of California Press, 1986) and Lillian B. Rubin, *Families on the Fault Line: America's Working Class Speaks about the Family, the Economy, Race, and Ethnicity* (New York: Harper Collins, 1994).

15.   Current Population Reports, Population Characteristics: Marital Status and Living Arrangements, 1991, Series P-20, no. 461, p. 5. The median age at first marriage continues to increase, reaching 26.3 years for men in 1991 and 24.1 years for women. In 1998 the census bureau reported that the median age at first marriage for women rose to 25.0 years and 26.8 years for men (Barbara Vobejda, "Unwed Pairs Make Up 4 Million Households: Number Has Grown Eightfold Since 1970," *Washington Post*, July 27, 1998, pp. A10–11).

16.   Mary Ann Schwartz and Barbara Marliene Scott, *Marriages and Families: Diversity and Change* (Englewood Cliffs, N.J.: Prentice-Hall, 1994), p. 193.

17.   Thomas S. Kuhn, *The Structure of Scientific Revolutions*, paperback ed. (Chicago: University of Chicago Press, 1962), p. 91. Italics added.

18.   U.S. Bureau of the Census, *Current Population Reports*, Series P-20, No. 467, March 1996.

19.   Lenore J. Weitzman and Ruth B. Dixon, "The Transformation of Legal Marriage Through No-Fault Divorce," pp. 338–351 in Arlene S. Skolnick and Jerome H. Skolnick, eds., *Family in Transition*, 5th ed. (Boston: Little Brown, 1986).

20.   Ibid., p. 339. See also Homer Harrison Clark, *The Law of Domestic Relations in the United States* (St. Paul: West, 1968), p.181.

21.   Louise A. Tilly, Joan W. Scott, and Miriam Cohen, "Women's Work and European Fertility Patterns," pp. 289–312 in Michael Gordon, ed., *The American Family in Socio-Historical Perspective*, 2nd ed. (New York: St. Martin's Press, 1978).

22.   Mary Frank Fox and Sharlene Hesse-Biber, *Women at Work* (Palo Alto, Calif.: Mayfield, 1984), pp. 15–16.

23.   Lewis Corey, *The Crisis of the Middle Class* (New York: Covici, Friede, 1935).

24.   C. Wright Mills, *White Collar: The American Middle Classes* (New York: Oxford University Press, 1951), p. 63.

25.   Glenn Porter, *The Rise of Big Business, 1860–1920.* (Wheeling, Ill.: Harlan Davidson, 1992).

26.   The middle-class that emerged with industrialization in the nineteenth century is often called the new middle class to distinguish it from the middle class of independent farmers and artisans of the preindustrial period prior to the 1840s (C. Wright Mills, *White Collar*). Some historians refer to it as the "middling class" or "middling classes" (Stuart M. Blumin, *The Emergence of the Middle Class: Social Experience in the American City, 1760–1900* [New York: Cambridge University Press, 1989]).

27.   Jessie Bernard, "The Good-Provider Role: Its Rise and Fall," *American Psychologist* 36, no. 1 (January 1981): pp. 1–12.

28.   Mary P. Ryan, *Cradle of the Middle Class: The Family in Oneida County, New York: 1790–1865* (New York: Cambridge University Press, 1981).

29.   Quoted in Barbara Easton, "Industrialization and Femininity: A Case Study of Nineteenth Century New England," *Social Problems* 23, no. 4, (1976): 393.

30.   Barbara Welter, "The Cult of True Womanhood, 1820–1860," *American Quarterly* 18, no. 2 (Summer 1966): pp. 151–174.

31.   Easton, "Industrialization and Femininity," p. 396.

32.   Ibid., p. 391.

33.   Welter, "The Cult of True Womanhood," p. 326.

34.   Ibid., p. 325.

35.   Quoted in Easton, "Industrialization and Femininity," p. 394.

36.   Quoted in Welter, "The Cult of True Womanhood," p. 319.

37.   Ibid., p. 319.

38.   Ibid., p. 318.

39.   Blumin, *The Emergence of the Middle Class.*

40.   Easton, "Industrialization and Femininity," p. 395.

41.   Eleanor Flexner, *Century of Struggle: The Woman's Rights Movement in the United States* (Cambridge: Harvard University Press, 1975), pp. 71–77.

42.   Mary P. Ryan, *Womanhood in America: From Colonial Times to the Present* (New York: New Viewpoints, 1975), p. 195.

43.   Martha May, "The Historical Problem of the Family Wage: The Ford Motor Company and the Five Dollar Day," pp. 111–131 in Naomi Gerstel and Harriet Engel Gross, eds., *Families and Work* (Philadelphia: Temple University Press, 1987), pp. 118–123.

44.   Ibid., p. 117.

45.   Ryan, *Womanhood in America*, p. 207.

46.   Hareven, *Family Time and Industrial Time,* chapter 8, pp. 189–217.

47.   Daniel E. Sutherland, *The Expansion of Everyday Life, 1860–1876* (New York: Harper and Row, 1989), pp. 168–172.

48.   Hareven, *Family Time and Industrial Time,* p. 215.

49.   Ibid., p. 215.

50.   Ibid., p. 214.

51.   Jeannie Oakes, *Keeping Track: How Schools Structure Inequality* (New Haven, Conn.: Yale University Press, 1985), p. 17.

52.   Ibid., p. 92.

53.   Ryan, *Womanhood in America,* p. 206.

54.   Kleinberg, *The Shadow of the Mills,* p. 209.

55.   Weiner, *From Working Girl to Working Mother,* p. 88.

56.   Landry, *The New Black Middle Class,* p. 21.

57.   Weiner, *From Working Girl to Working Mother,* p. 89.

58.   Ibid., p. 89.

59.   Elizabeth H. Pleck, "A Mother's Wages: Income Earning Among Married Italian and Black Women, 1896–1911," pp. 490–510 in Michael Gordon, ed., *The American Family in Social-Historical Perspective,* 2nd ed. (New York: St. Martin's Press, 1978), p. 496.

CHAPTER 2. BLACK FAMILIES: A CHALLENGE
TO THE TRADITIONAL FAMILY PARADIGM

1.   Herbert G. Gutman, *The Black Family in Slavery and Freedom, 1750–1925* (New York: Random House, 1976), p. 633, n. 10.

2.   Daniel P. Moynihan et al., *The Negro Family: The Case for National Action* (Washington, D.C.: U.S. Government Printing Office, 1965).

3.   For a discussion of the extent to which slaves preserved elements of African culture in the United States see Melville J. Herskovits, *Myth of the Negro Past* (Gloucester, Mass.: P. Smith, 1958).

4.   Gutman, *The Black Family in Slavery and Freedom,* p. 89.

5.   Ibid., p. 190. Antonio McDaniel in "The Power of Culture: A Review of the Idea of Africa's Influence on Family Structure in Antebellum America" (*Journal of Family History* 15, no. 2 [1990]: 225–238), while not disputing Gutman's findings, argues that Gutman begins his analysis of black families with the "slave plantation" rather than with Africa. McDaniel suggests that for an accurate understanding of slave families, greater weight should be given to culture and to African influences. For that reason, he stresses the point made by some scholars that the extended kin group was more important than the conjugal family in West Africa, the region from which slaves originated, and argues that this should be the proper starting point for an accurate understanding of the slave community and slave families. While the point has considerable merit, he overstates the case when he writes that "the ideal of the nuclear family was not practical for most slaves, or for most of the post-slave period Africans" (p. 232). Certainly the distinction should be made between the conjugal family *household* and the extended family *kin network,* the latter being the relationships maintained between related

conjugal family households. Even among whites, who are thought of as adhering closely to the ideal of the "nuclear family," contacts between nuclear households within the kin network are frequent. It is certainly plausible that these contacts may have been more frequent and of a more "helping" nature than merely social among poor blacks. But this was certainly also true among immigrants earlier in this century. The point is not to argue that there were not cultural differences between blacks and whites, but that we must be careful not to speculate beyond what is warranted by available information.

6.   Gutman, *The Black Family in Slavery and Freedom*, pp. 273–274. Although slave marriages were not legally recognized by the state they did in fact get married in a variety of public ceremonies ranging from "jumping the broomstick" or lying under a blanket to ceremonies presided over by a minister or the slave owner himself.

7.   Ibid., p. 36.

8.   Ibid., p. 6.

9.   Ibid., pp. 15, 150.

10.   Ibid., p. 32.

11.   Ibid., p. 190.

12.   Ibid., pp. 72–73.

13.   Ibid., p. 371.

14.   Ibid., p. 24.

15.   Ibid.

16.   Ibid., p. 384.

17.   Ibid., p. 388.

18.   Ibid.

19.   Ibid., p. 400.

20.   Ibid., p. 410.

21.   Jacqueline Jones, *Labor of Love, Labor of Sorrow: Black Women, Work and the Family, from Slavery to the Present* (New York: Vintage Books, 1985), p. 51.

22.   Gutman, *The Black Family in Slavery and Freedom*, p. 415.

23.   Ibid., p. 417.

24.   Ibid., p. 21.

25.   Ibid., p. 426.

26.   Herbert G. Gutman, "Persistent Myths about the Afro-American Family," pp. 467–489 in Michael Gordon, ed., *The American Family in Social-Historical Perspective* (New York: St. Martin's Press, 1978), p. 476.

27.   Jones, *Labor of Love, Labor of Sorrow*, p. 62. The terminology of "headship" has changed over the years. In historical writings, terms specific to the traditional family are often used ("male head and his wife"). In the second half of the twentieth century one is likely to find terms like *dual-headed* or *two-parent*, the latter in contrast to *single-headed*, *female-headed*, or *single-parent* family. Until 1980, the cen-

sus bureau used the term *head of household,* referring to the husband/father in a two parent family. In response to complaints by feminists, the terminology was changed to *householder* for the 1980 census, and could refer to either the husband or wife. Occasionally *male headed* is used in contrast to *female headed.*

28.   Ibid., p. 84. There is currently a debate among scholars over the extent to which black and white families have differed historically, which some see as a "revision" of Gutman's *Black Families in Slavery and Freedom.* See Antonio Mc-Daniel, "Historical Racial Differences in Living Arrangements of Children," *Journal of Family History* 19, no. 1 (1994): 57–77; S. Philip Morgan et al., "Racial Differences in Household and Family Structure at the Turn of the Century," *American Journal of Sociology* 98, no. 4 (January 1993): 798–828; Deanna L. Pagnini and S. Philip Morgan, "Racial Differences in Marriage and Childbearing: Oral History Evidence from the South in the Early Twentieth Century," *American Journal of Sociology* 101, no. 6 (May 1996): 1694–1718; Samuel H. Preston, Suet Lim, and S. Philip Morgan, "African-American Marriage in 1910: Beneath the Surface of Census Data," *Demography* 29, no. 1 (February 1992): 1–15; Steven Ruggles, "The Origins of African-American Family Structure," *American Sociological Review* 59, no. 1 (Februrary 1994): 136–151. While these scholars do not question Gutman's basic finding that most black families during slavery and afterward were headed by two parents, they do address what they perceive as a misreading of Gutman's work by those who have interpreted him as saying that there were no differences between black and white families historically. These researchers point especially to the higher percentage of "fostering"(the placing of own children to live with relatives) among black than white families that can be traced at least to the late nineteenth century. They also address the issue of the extent of racial cultural differences in family structure and functioning, as well as the reasons for the historically higher incidence of female-headed families among blacks.

Perhaps the major point is that contemporary differences in black and white family structure are "not new" but can be traced at least to the late nineteenth century—though the extent of these differences may be greater today. The more controversial part of this "revision" focuses on explanations of these differences. While acknowledging the impact of economic and demographic factors in creating racial differences in family structure and practice, there appears to be a tendency to give considerable weight to possible "normative" or culture differences. It is here that the discussion becomes speculative. Even the use of oral history (Pagnini and Morgan, 1996) fails to provide conclusive support for the cultural difference argument, since the analysis is based on a very small unrepresentative sample. It should be acknowledged, however, that together these articles make a strong case for the possibility of a degree of racial difference in family structure and functioning resulting from possible cultural differences. Having said this, it should still be emphasized that we are still very far from untangling the relative influences of "demographic, socioeconomic, and cultural/historical factors" (Morgan et al., 1993). It should also be added that none of this research has attempted to examine racial class differences. A careful comparison, controlling for class, and across white ethnic groups as Furstenberg, Hershberg, and Modell, have done, might provide additional insights into the effects of "cultural" differences (Frank F. Furstenberg, Jr., Theodore Hershberg, and John Modell, "The Origins of the Female-Headed Black Family: The Impact of the Urban Experience," *Journal of Interdisciplinary History* 6 [1975]: 211–233). Finally, the racial "differences" in family structure and functioning are historically relatively small, and the largest differences have appeared in the post-1970s. Given the relatively small racial differences in the postbellum period and early twentieth century, does that mean that those black and white families with similar structures were culturally alike? The point is, how much does this debate rest on major differences or on a focus on small differences; that is, on perspective and interpretation?

29.   Paul J. Lammermeier, "The Urban Black Family of the Nineteenth Century: A Study of Black Family Structure in the Ohio Valley, 1850–1880," *Journal of Marriage and the Family* 35, no. 3 (August 1973): 443, Table 2.

30.   Furstenberg, Hershberg, and Modell, "The Origins of the Female-Headed Black Family," pp. 211–233.

31.   While this factor was certainly important, analysis of the 1910 census by Preston, Lim, and Morgan has shown that reported widowhood was exaggerated ("African-American Marriage in 1910," pp. 1–15). See also note 29 above.

32.   Kenneth L. Kusmer, *A Ghetto Takes Shape: Black Cleveland, 1870–1930* (Urbana: University of Illinois Press, 1976), p. 226.

33.   Ibid., p. 433.

34.   I have emphasized the historical fact of the predominance of couple-headed families among blacks both during slavery and in the decades following to counterbalance the prevalent myth of a black matriarchy that has had such an influence on the way black families have been viewed in recent decades. The predominance of two-parent black families continued until 1970 when the percentage of female-headed families increased to 28.3. Thereafter, their proportion of all black families continued growing and in 1993 had reached an alarming 46.7 percent. Still, as I argued in the introduction, dual-headed black families have continued to increase and remain normative.

35.   Gutman, *The Black Family in Slavery and Freedom*, p. 167.

36.   Ibid., p. 168. Italics added.

37.   John W. Blassingame, *Black New Orleans: 1860–1880* (Chicago: University of Chicago Press, 1973), p. 55; Jones, *Labor of Love, Labor of Sorrow*, p. 55.

38.   Quoted in Stephen Steinberg, *The Ethnic Myth: Race, Ethnicity, and Class in America* (Boston: Beacon Press, 1981), pp. 193–194.

39.   Blassingame, *Black New Orleans: 1860–1880*, pp. 195–196.

40.   Jones, *Labor of Love, Labor of Sorrow,* p. 53.

41.   Gutman, *The Black Family in Slavery and Freedom,* pp. 167–168.

42.   Steinberg, *The Ethnic Myth: Race, Ethnicity, and Class in America,* p. 192.

43.   Blassingame, *Black New Orleans: 1860–1880,* pp. 57–58.

44.   Steinberg, *The Ethnic Myth: Race, Ethnicity, and Class in America,* 2nd ed. (Boston: Beacon Press, 1989), pp. 27–28.

45.   Jones, *Labor of Love, Labor of Sorrow,* p. 52.

46.   Ibid., p. 64.

47.   Ibid., p. 63.

48.   Ibid.

49.   Ibid., p. 112.

50.   Florette Henri, *Black Migration: Movement North, 1900–1920* (New York: Doubleday, 1976), p.50.

51.   Leslie H. Fishel and Benjamin Quarles, *The Negro American: A Documentary History* (Glenview, Ill.: Scott, Foresman and William Morrow, 1967), pp. 290–292.

52.   Gutman, *The Black Family in Slavery and Freedom,* p. 435.

53.   Ibid.

54.   Ibid., p. 438.

55.   Ibid., p. 435.

56.   Henri, *Black Migration,* p. 51.

57.   Ibid.

58.   Tamara K. Hareven, *Family Time and Industrial Time: The Relationship Between the Family and Work in a New England Industrial Community* (New York: Cambridge University Press, 1982), p. 216.

59.   Ibid., pp. 195, 197. The overall percentage of employed married women was elevated by the higher employment rate of those "who lived in other household arrangements, such as married daughters who lived in the households of their parents or extended kin, or as married boarders" (p. 198).

60.   Gutman notes that black artisans were disproportionally clustered in a few crafts such as carpentry, bricklaying, barbering, and cigar making, rather than evenly distributed among all crafts (*The Black Family in Slavery and Freedom,* pp. 626–627).

61.   Benjamin Quarles, *The Negro in the Making of America* (New York: Macmillan, 1969), p. 151.

62.   Jones, *Labor of Love, Labor of Sorrow,* p. 124; Landry, *The New Black Middle Class,* p. 52.

63.   Landry, ibid., p. 53.

64.   Blassingame, *Black New Orleans: 1860–1880,* pp. 63, 238; Gutman, *The Black Family in Slavery and Freedom,* pp. 479, 488.

65.   David M. Katzman, *Before the Ghetto: Black Detroit in the Nineteenth Century* (Urbana: University of Illinois Press, 1973), p. 105.
66.   Gutman, *The Black Family in Slavery and Freedom,* p. 512; see also Kusmer, *A Ghetto Takes Shape,* pp. 67–73, chapters 4 and 9.
67.   Kusmer, *A Ghetto Takes Shape,* pp. 67–73.
68.   Jones, p. 161.
69.   See Elizabeth H. Pleck, "A Mother's Wages: Income Earning Among Married Italian and Black Women, 1896–1911," pp. 490–510 in Michael Gordon, ed., *The American Family in Social-Historical Perspective,* 2nd ed. (New York: St. Martin's Press, 1978), p. 496, Table 1.
70.   Jones, *Labor of Love, Labor of Sorrow,* p. 128.
71.   Ibid., p. 129.
72.   Pleck, "A Mother's Wages," p. 496.
73.   Jones, *Labor of Love, Labor of Sorrow,* p. 164.
74.   Ibid., pp. 166, 168.
75.   Ibid., p. 154.
76.   Kusmer, *A Ghetto Takes Shape,* p. 196; Allen H. Spear, *Black Chicago: The Making of a Negro Ghetto, 1890–1920* (Chicago: University of Chicago Press, 1967), p. 33.
77.   Gutman, *The Black Family in Slavery and Freedom,* p. 443; Jones, *Labor of Love, Labor of Sorrow,* p. 125.
78.   Quoted in Jones, *Labor of Love, Labor of Sorrow,* p. 188.
79.   Ibid.
80.   Ibid., p. 162.
81.   S. J. Kleinberg, *The Shadow of the Mills: Working-Class Families in Pittsburgh, 1870–1907* (Pittsburgh: University of Pittsburgh Press, 1989), p. 200.
82.   Quoted in Kleinberg, ibid., p. 200.
83.   Kleinberg, p. 214.
84.   Quoted in Kleinberg, ibid., p. 223.
85.   Kleinberg, p. 211.
86.   Ibid., p. 223.
87.   Ibid., p. 199.
88.   Jones, *Labor of Love, Labor of Sorrow,* p. 164.
89.   Pleck, "A Mother's Wages," pp. 497–499.
90.   Ibid., p. 87.
91.   Ibid.
92.   Jones, *Labor of Love, Labor of Sorrow,* p. 84.
93.   Ibid., pp. 96–98, 222.
94.   Hareven, *Family Time and Industrial Time,* p. 208.

CHAPTER 3. BLACK WOMEN AND A NEW DEFINITION OF WOMANHOOD

1.   Quoted in Hazel V. Carby, *Reconstructing Womanhood: The Emergence of the Afro-American Woman Novelist* (New York: Oxford University Press, 1987), p. 26.
2.   Ibid.
3.   Quoted in Paula Giddings, *When and Where I Enter: The Impact of Black Women on Race and Sex in America* (New York: Bantam Books, 1985), p. 82.
4.   Ibid., p. 82.
5.   Carby, *Reconstructing Womanhood*, p. 20.
6.   Harriet Jacobs, *Incidents in the Life of a Slave Girl*, L. Baria Child, ed. (1861; paperback reprint, New York: Harcourt Brace Javanovich, 1973), p. 29.
7.   Carby, *Reconstructing Womanhood*, pp. 58−59.
8.   Ibid., p. 60.
9.   Jacobs, *Incidents in the Life of a Slave Girl*, p. 93.
10.   Ibid., p. 207.
11.   Quoted in Giddings, *When and Where I Enter*, p. 82.
12.   Quoted in Giddings, ibid., p. 86.
13.   Quoted in Giddings, ibid., p. 87.
14.   Quoted in Giddings, ibid., pp. 86−87.
15.   Quoted in Giddings, ibid., p. 87.
16.   Quoted in Sharon Harley, "Black Women in a Southern City: Washington, D.C., 1890−1920," pp. 59−78 in Joanne V. Hawks and Shiela L. Skemp, eds., *Sex, Race, and the Role of Women in the South* (Jackson, Miss.: University Press of Mississippi, 1983), p. 72.
17.   Eleanor Flexner, *Century of Struggle: The Woman's Rights Movement in the United States* (Cambridge: Harvard University Press, 1959), p. 194.
18.   Giddings, *When and Where I Enter*, p. 93.
19.   Ibid., p. 95. For a discussion of elitism in the "uplift" movement and organizations, see Kevin K. Gaines, *Uplifting the Race: Black Leadership, Politics, and Culture in the Twentieth Century* (Chapel Hill, N.C.: University of North Carolina Press, 1996). Black reformers, enlightened as they were, could not entirely escape being influenced by Social Darwinist currents of the time.
20.   Deborah Gray White, *Too Heavy a Load: Black Women in Defense of Themselves, 1894−1994* (New York: W. W. Norton & Company, 1999), p. 36.
21.   Quoted in Giddings, *When and Where I Enter*, p. 75.
22.   Ibid.
23.   Quoted in Giddings, ibid., p. 75.
24.   Ibid., p. 59.
25.   Ibid.
26.   Evelyn Brooks Higginbotham, *Righteous Discontent: The Women's Movement*

in the Black Baptist Church, 1880–1920 (Cambridge: Harvard University Press, 1993).

27.   Ibid., p. 20.

28.   Cynthia Neverdon-Morton, "Self-Help Programs as Educative Activities of Black Women in the South, 1895–1925: Focus on Four Key Areas," *Journal of Negro Education* 51, no. 3 (1982): 209.

29.   Gerda Lerner, "Early Community Work of Black Club Women," *Journal of Negro History* 59, no. 2: 161; Sharon Harley, "Black Women in a Southern City," p. 72.

30.   Cynthia Neverdon-Morton, "Self-Help Programs as Educative Activities of Black Women in the South," pp. 210–211.

31.   Ibid.

32.   Ibid., p. 215.

33.   Ibid., p. 219.

34.   Ibid.

35.   Rosalyn Terborg-Penn, "Discontented Black Feminists: Prelude and Postscript to the Passage of the Nineteenth Amendment," pp. 261–278 in Lois Scharf and Joan M. Jensen, eds., *Decades of Discontent: The Woman's Movement, 1920–1940* (Westport, Conn.: Greenwood Press, 1983), p. 264.

36.   Ibid., p. 261.

37.   Ibid., p. 264.

38.   Ibid., p. 266.

39.   Ibid., pp. 266–267.

40.   Barbara J. Harris, *Beyond Her Sphere: Women and the Professions in American History* (Westport, Conn.: Greenwood Press, 1978), pp. 85–86.

41.   Giddings, *When and Where I Enter*, p. 81.

42.   Harris, *Beyond Her Sphere*, p. 86.

43.   Estelle Freedman, "Separatism as Strategy: Female Institution Building and American Feminism, 1870–1930," pp. 445–462 in Nancy F. Cott, ed., *Women Together: Organizational Life* (New Providence, R.I.: K. G. Saur, 1994), p. 447.

44.   Nancy Forderhase, "'Limited Only by Earth and Sky': The Louisville Woman's Club and Progressive Reform, 1900–1910," pp. 365–381 in Cott, ed. *Women Together*; Theodora Penny Martin, *The Sound of Our Own Voices: Women's Study Clubs 1860–1910* (Boston: Beacon Press, 1987).

45.   John P. Rousmaniere, "Cultural Hybrid in the Slums: The College Woman and the Settlement House, 1889–1984," *American Quarterly* 22 (Spring 1970): p. 56.

46.   Ibid., p. 55.

47.   Barbara J. Harris, *Beyond Her Sphere*, pp. 101–102.

48.   Ibid., pp. 101–102.

49.   Rousmaniere, "Cultural Hybrid in the Slums," p. 56.

50.   Ibid., p. 61.

51.   Quoted in Linda Gordon, "Black and White Visions of Welfare: Women's Welfare Activism, 1890–1945," *Journal of American History* 78 (September 1991): 583.

52.   Giddings, *When and Where I Enter,* p. 97.

53.   Freedman, "Separatism as Strategy," p. 450; Nancy Forderhase, "Limited Only by Earth and Sky"; Marilyn Dell Brady, "Kansas Federation of Colored Women's Clubs, 1900–1930," pp. 382–408 in Nancy F. Cott, *Women Together.*

54.   Higginbotham, *Righteous Discontent,* pp. 206–207.

55.   Giddings, *When and Where I Enter,* p. 22.

56.   Terborg-Penn, "Discontented Black Feminists," p. 267.

57.   Giddings, *When and Where I Enter,* p. 108.

58.   Ibid., pp. 108–109.

59.   Ibid., p. 113.

60.   Linda Gordon, "Black and White Visions of Welfare," pp. 583.

61.   Ibid., p. 582.

62.   Ibid., p. 585.

63.   Ibid., pp. 568–69.

64.   Ibid., p. 109.

65.   Quoted in Giddings, ibid., p. 110.

66.   Quoted in Giddings, ibid., p. 97.

67.   Elsa Barkley Brown, "Womanist Consciousness: Maggie Lena Walker and the Independent Order of Saint Luke," *Journal of Women in Culture and Society* 14, no. 3 (1989): 188.

68.   Shirley J. Carlson, "Black Ideals of Womanhood in the Late Victorian Era," *Journal of Negro History* 77, no. 2 (Spring 1992): 62. Carlson notes that these black women of the late Victorian era also observed the proprieties of Victorian womanhood in their deportment and appearance but combined them with the expectations of the black community for intelligence, education, and active involvement in racial uplift.

69.   Giddings, *When and Where I Enter,* pp. 110–111.

70.   Brown, "Womanist Consciousness," p. 180.

71.   Ibid., p. 178.

72.   Quoted in Giddings, *When and Where I Enter,* p. 117.

73.   Quoted in Giddings, ibid., p. 119.

74.   See Rosalyn Terborg-Penn, *African American Women in the Struggle for the Vote, 1850–1920* (Bloomington, Ind.: Indiana University Press, 1998).

75.   Rosalyn Terborg-Penn, "Discontented Black Feminists," p. 274.

76.   Stephanie J. Shaw, *What a Woman Ought to Be and to Do: Black Professional Women Workers During the Jim Crow Era* (Chicago: University of Chicago Press, 1996), p. 29. Shaw details the efforts of family and community to socialize these women for both personal achievement and community service. The sacrifices

some families made included sending them to private schools and sometimes re-locating the entire family near a desired school.

77. Ibid., p. 126. Italics added.

78. Giddings, *When and Where I Enter*, p. 108.

79. Brown, "Womanist Consciousness," p. 622.

80. Ibid., p. 623.

81. Carby, *Reconstructing Womanhood*, p. 117.

82. Quoted in Giddings, *When and Where I Enter*, p. 72.

83. Brown, "Womanist Consciousness," p. 182.

84. Quoted in Giddings, *Where and When I Enter*, pp. 196–197.

85. Shaw, *What a Woman Ought to Be and to Do*, p. 113.

86. Ibid., p. 109.

87. Quoted in Giddings, *Where and When I Enter*, p. 109.

88. Betty Friedan, *The Feminine Mystique* (New York: Dell, 1963), p. 68.

89. Quoted in Giddings, *Where and When I Enter*, p. 197.

90. Quoted in Terborg-Penn, "Discontented Black Feminists," p. 274.

91. Ibid., p. 274.

92. Quoted in Giddings, *Where and When I Enter*, p. 138.

93. Quoted in Carby, *Reconstructing Womanhood*, p. 98.

94. B. Berg, *The Remembered Gate* (New York: Oxford University Press, 1978), p. 84.

95. Quoted in Berg, ibid., p. 84.

96. Erlene Stetson, "Black Feminism in Indiana, 1893–1933," *Phylon* 44 (December 1983): 294.

97. Quoted in Barbara Welter, "The Cult of True Womanhood: 1820–1860," p. 318.

98. Carby, *Reconstructing Womanhood*, p. 100.

99. Carby, ibid., p. 99.

100. Carlson, "Black Ideals of Womanhood in the Late Victorian Era," p. 69. This view is supported by historian Evelyn Brooks Higginbotham's analysis of schools for blacks established by northern Baptists in the postbellum period, schools that encouraged the attendance of both girls and boys. Although, as Higginbotham observes, northern Baptists founded these schools in part to spread white middle-class values among blacks, blacks nevertheless came to see higher education as an instrument of their own liberation (*Righteous Discontent*, p. 20).

101. Ibid., p. 67.

102. Quoted in Giddings, *When and Where I Enter*, p. 71.

103. Ibid., p. 101.

104. Quoted in Carlson, "Black Ideals of Womanhood in the Late Victorian Era," p. 65.

105. Quoted in Carlson, ibid., p. 65.

106.   Quoted in Carlson, ibid., p. 69. Italics added.
107.   Carlson, ibid., p. 70.

CHAPTER 4. THE NEW FAMILY PARADIGM TAKES
ROOT AND SPREADS

1.   Martha May, "The Historical Problem of the Family Wage: The Ford Motor Company and the Five Dollar Day," pp. 111–131 in Naomi Gerstel and Harriet Engel Gross, eds., *Families and Work* (Philadelphia: Temple University Press,
1987).
2.   Michael Reich, "The Proletarianization of the Labor Force," pp. 122–131
in Richard C. Edwards, Michael Reich, and Thomas E. Weisskopf, *The Capitalist
System*, 3rd ed. (Englewood Cliffs, N.J.: Prentice-Hall, 1986). Although clerical
work was fast becoming feminized at the turn of the nineteenth century, in 1890
women made up only 16.9 percent of all clerical workers (Evelyn Nakano Glenn
and Roslyn L. Feldberg, "Clerical Work: The Female Occupation," pp. 287–311
in Jo Freeman, ed., *Women: A Feminist Perspective*, 4th ed. [Mountain View, Calif.:
Mayfield Pub., 1989]).
3.   Elizabeth H. Pleck, "A Mother's Wages: Income Earning Among Married
Italian and Black Women, 1896–1911," pp. 490–510 in Michael Gordon, ed., *The
American Family in Social-Historical Perspective*, 2nd ed., (New York: St. Martin's
Press, 1978), p. 497. Italics added.
4.   Ibid., pp. 497–498.
5.   Ibid., p. 500.
6.   Ibid., p. 492.
7.   Kleinberg, *The Shadow of the Mills: Working-Class Families in Pittsburgh,
1870–1907* (Pittsburgh: University of Pittsburgh Press, 1989), p. 200.
8.   Tamara K. Hareven, *Family Time and Industrial Time: The Relationship between the Family and Work in a New England Industrial Community* (New York: Cambridge University Press, 1982), p. 202.
9.   Pleck, "A Mother's Wages," p. 496.
10.   Quoted in Hareven, *Family Time and Industrial Time*, pp. 192–193.
11.   Jacqueline Jones, *Labor of Love, Labor of Sorrow: Black Women, Work and the
Family, from Slavery to the Present* (New York: Vintage Books, 1985), pp. 157–158.
12.   The data for chapters 4 through 6 are from the U.S. Census One Percent
Public Use Microdata Samples (PUMS) for the years 1940, 1950, 1960, 1970, 1980,
and 1990 and from the U.S. Census Current Population Survey Public Use Microdata Sample for March 1994. Since information on individual income and on children was not available for all households in the 1940 and 1950 PUMS, some of the
analysis had to be confined to the years 1960 through 1994. Statistics are for same-

race married couples only. Interracial couples were eliminated to avoid possible problems of interpretation.

13.   Upper-class families are difficult to study. These are the people who hold controlling shares of the largest corporations such as those on the *Fortune 500* list. Their numbers are very small, probably no more than a few million, and they cannot be identified from census data. It appears that wives in these families have historically observed the cult of domesticity, but today sometimes have careers of their own. For an insightful analysis of their lives see G. William Domhoff, *Who Rules America Now?: A View for the '80s,* (Englewood Cliffs, N.J.: Prentice-Hall, 1983).

14.   See Francine D. Blau and Marianne A. Ferber, *The Economics of Women, Men, and Work,* 2nd ed. (Englewood Cliffs, N.J.: Prentice Hall, 1992), pp. 80–99.

15.   Ibid., p. 111.

16.   Quoted in Paula Giddings, *Where and When I Enter: The Impact of Black Women on Race and Sex in America* (New York: Bantam Books, 1985), p. 196.

17.   Robert E. Riegel, *American Feminists* (Lawrence: University Press of Kansas, 1968), pp. 163–173.

18.   Dorothy Sterling, "Terrell, Mary Eliza Church," pp. 678–680 in Barbara Sicherman et al., eds., *Notable American Women: The Modern Period* (Cambridge: Harvard University Press, 1980).

19.   Betty Friedan, *The Feminine Mystique* (New York: Dell, 1963), p. 228.

20.   Quoted in Friedan, ibid., p. 228.

21.   Quoted in Friedan, ibid., p. 229.

22.   Bart Landry and Margaret Platt Jendrek, "The Employment of Wives in Middle-Class Black Families," *Journal of Marriage and the Family* 40, no. 4 (November 1978): 795–796.

23.   Alice Kessler-Harris, "Stratifying by Sex: Understanding the History of Working Women," pp. 217–242 in Richard C. Edwards, et. al., *Labor Market Segmentation* (Lexington, Mass.: D. C. Heath, 1973).

24.   Darlene Clark Hine, *Hine Sight: Black Women and the Re-Construction of American History* (Brooklyn: Carlson Publishing, 1994), p. 159.

25.   Ibid.

26.   Ibid., p. 149.

27.   While focusing primarily on Italian wives, Pleck presents statistics that show similar avoidance of employment by married women in other immigrant groups.

28.   Susan A. Basow, *Gender Stereotypes and Roles,* 3rd ed. (Pacific Grove, Calif.: Brooks/Cole Publishing, 1992), p. 236.

29.   The cult of domesticity originated in the mid-nineteenth century and institutionalized a doctrine of separate spheres for husbands and wives. It made no distinction between wives with or without children. All wives were to remain at home. In the twentieth century, the prohibition against married women's being

employed gradually relaxed, but this did not extend to mothers, especially mothers of preschool children. It is this latter stance that I call the twentieth-century version of the cult of domesticity.

30.   Blau and Ferber, *The Economics of Women, Men, and Work,* pp. 88 ff.

31.   See for instance studies by Glen C. Cain, *Married Women in the Labor Force: An Economic Analysis* (Chicago: University of Chicago Press, 1966); William G. Bowen and T. Aldrich Finegan, *The Economics of Labor Force Participation* (Princeton: Princeton University Press, 1969); Duran Bell, "Why Participation Rates of Black and White Wives Differ," *Journal of Human Resources* 9, no. 4 (Fall 1974): 465–479; and Claudia Dale Goldin, "Female Labor Force Participation: The Origin of Black and White Differences, 1870 and 1980," *Journal of Economic History* 37, no. 1 (March 1977): 87–112.

32.   Iris Krasnow, "It's Time to End the 'Mommy Wars,'" *Washington Post,* May 7, 1999, p. C5.

CHAPTER 5. DUAL-CAREER COUPLES: PROTOTYPES OF THE MODERN FAMILY

1.   Rhona and Robert Rapoport, *Dual-Career Families* (Harmondsworth, Middlesex, England: Penguin, 1971), p. 18.

2.   Arlie Russell Hochschild, *The Time Bind: When Work Becomes Home and Home Becomes Work* (New York: Henry Holt, 1997), p. 89.

3.   Rosanna Hertz, *More Equal Than Others: Women and Men in Dual-Career Marriages* (Berkeley: University of California Press, 1986), p. 75.

4.   Rapoport and Rapoport, *Dual-Career Families,* p. 8.

5.   Rosanna Hertz, "Dual-Career Couples and the American Dream: Self-Sufficiency and Achievement," *Journal of Comparative Family Studies* 22, no. 2 (Summer 1991): 47.

6.   Hochschild, *The Time Bind,* p. 125.

7.   Rosalind C. Barnett and Caryl Rivers, *She Works, He Works: How Two-Income Families are Happy, Healthy, and Thriving* (Cambridge, Mass.: Harvard University Press, 1998), p. 63.

8.   Ibid., p. xi.

9.   Lillian Rubin, *Families on the Fault Line: America's Working Class Speaks about the Family, the Economy, Race and Ethnicity* (New York: Harper Collins, 1994), p. 86.

10.   Ibid., p. 87.

11.   Cynthia Fuchs Epstein, "Law Partners and Marital Partners: Strains and Solutions in the Dual-career Family Enterprise," *Human Relations* 24, no. 6 (1971): 549–564; Margaret M. Poloma and T. Neal Garland, "The Married Professional Woman: A Study in the Tolerance of Domestication," *Journal of Marriage and*

the Family 33 (1971): 531–540; Rebecca B. Bryson et al., "The Professional Pair: Husband and Wife Psychologists," *American Psychologist* 31, no. 1 (January 1976): 10–16.

12.   See for instance, Caroline Bird, *The Two-Paycheck Family* (New York: Rawson, Wade, 1979); F. S. Hall and D. T. Hall, *The Two-Career Couple* (Reading, Mass: Addison-Wesley, 1979); L. L. Holmstrom, *The Two-Career Family* (Cambridge, Mass.: Schenkman, 1972).

13.   If we enlarge the definition of dual-career couples to include those in which one spouse holds a professional or managerial occupation while the other holds a clerical or sales position, then almost 50 percent of both black and white upper-middle-class couples were dual-career by 1980. Although some people may object to the inclusion of white-collar workers other than professionals and managers, Dala Vannoy Hiller and Janice Dyehouse reveal that the term *career* is a bit murky ("A Case for Banishing 'Dual-Career Marriages' from the Research Literature," *Journal of Marriage and the Family* 49 [November 1987]: 787–795). They point to three different definitions in the dual-career literature: a structural one emphasizing objective characteristics of occupations (such as progression through a "patterned job sequence"), a subjective one including attitudes such as job commitment and "high achievement aspirations," and a mixture of structural and subjective components.

Arguing that "commitment is a subjective state that may be attached to any kind of work," Hiller and Dyehouse tested the assumed association between individual job commitment and high-status professional and managerial occupations on a sample of 450 husbands and 344 wives. They found no relationship between job status and commitment. Of the five job characteristics tested for both men and women—job satisfaction, number of jobs, income, occupational status, and education—they found that only "job satisfaction, predicts job commitment for both men and women." Job commitment, they concluded, is not confined to professional and managerial occupations. Moreover, numerous clerical and sales jobs are characterized by a "developmental sequence" similar to that in professional and managerial occupations, although perhaps not as pronounced. This developmental quality is evident in white-collar workers' use of job resumes and the possibility for some horizontal movement within a given occupational field. There are thus several reasons to include these occupations in the category of careers. Blue-collar jobs, on the other hand, are not usually thought of as careers since as a group they generally lack a developmental character or progression through patterned job sequences. I have nevertheless focused my discussion on the narrow definition of dual-career couples for greater comparability with existing literature.

14.   There is yet another category, professional or managerial female breadwinners of couple-headed families. The number of such families is probably

rather small, however. There is also the problem of distinguishing those families in which these "role reversals" are enduring from those that are temporary, due to a husband's unemployment.

15.   In 1960, among white wives age twenty-five to forty-four years, 30.8 percent had no children in the home. Although some women postpone childbearing (or continue it) into their late thirties or even early forties, they are still the exception.

16.   Simone de Beauvoir, *The Second Sex* (New York: Alfred A. Knopf, 1957), p. 480.

17.   Ibid., p. 532.

18.   S. J. Kleinberg, *The Shadow of the Mills: Working-Class Families in Pittsburgh, 1870–1907* (Pittsburgh: University of Pittsburgh Press, 1989), p. 199.

19.   Rapoport, *Dual-Career Families*, p. 20. The Rapoports wrote of three different work patterns among the women in their study: the conventional pattern, the interrupted pattern, and the continuous pattern.

20.   Rhona Rapoport and Robert N. Rapoport, "Further Considerations on the Dual Career Family," *Human Relations* 24, no. 6 (1971): 520.

21.   The Rapoports chose their subsample of eighteen families for indepth analysis from a larger study of college educated women in Britain.

22.   Myra Marx Ferree, "Family and Job for Working-Class Women: Gender and Class Systems Seen from Below," pp. 289–301 in Naomi Gerstel and Harriet Engel Gross, eds., *Families and Work* (Philadelphia: Temple University Press, 1987).

23.   Lillian B. Rubin, *Families on the Fault Line: America's Working Class Speaks About the Family, The Economy, Race and Ethnicity* (New York: Harper Collins, 1994), p. 94.

24.   Ibid., p. 85.

25.   Frank Levy, *Dollars and Dreams: The Changing American Income Distribution* (New York: Russell Sage Foundation, 1987), p. 4. See also Lawrence Mishel, Jared Bernstein, and John Schmitt, *The State of Working America, 1998–99* (Ithaca, N.Y.: Cornell University Press, 1999). In chapter 3 Mishel, Bernstein, and Schmitt document this trend's continuation in the 1990s.

26.   See Robert B. Reich, *The Work of Nations: Preparing Ourselves for Twenty-First Century Capitalism,* chapter 14 (New York: Random House, 1991), for a discussion of this point.

27.   Hertz, *More Equal than Others*, p. 186.

28.   Ibid., p. 170.

29.   Hertz, "Dual-Career Couples and the American Dream," p. 247.

30.   Donald St. John-Parsons, "Continuous Dual-Career Families: A Case Study," *Psychology of Women Quarterly* 3, no. 1 (Fall 1978): 33.

31.   Poloma and Garland, "The Married Professional Woman," p. 533.

32.   Hanna Papanek, "Men, Women, and Work: Reflections on the Two-Person Career," *American Journal of Sociology* 78, no. 4 (1973): 852–871.

33.   Martha R. Fowlkes, "The Myth of Merit and Male Professional Careers: The Roles of Wives," pp. 347–360 in Naomi Gerstel and Harriet Engel Gross, eds., *Families and Work* (Philadelphia: Temple University Press, 1987).

34.   Uma Sekaran, "An Investigation of the Career Salience of Men and Women in Dual-Career Families," *Journal of Vocational Behavior* 20 (1982): 111–119; Uma Sekaran, "How Husbands and Wives in Dual-Career Families Perceive Their Family and Work Worlds," *Journal of Vocational Behavior* 22 (1983): 288–302.

35.   Alma S. Baron, "Working Parents: Shifting Traditional Roles," *Business and Human Resources* 36 (January–March 1987): 36–37; Alma S. Baron, "Working Partners: Career-Committed Mothers and Their Husbands," *Business Horizons* (September–October 1987): 45–50.

36.   Alma S. Baron, "Working Parents," p. 36.

37.   Uma Sekaran, "An Investigation of the Career Salience of Men and Women in Dual-Career Families," p. 117.

38.   See, for instance, Denise A. Skinner, "Dual-Career Family Stress and Coping: A Literature Review," *Family Relations* 29 (October 1980): 473–481; Brian F. Pendleton, Margaret M. Poloma, and T. Neal Garland, "An Approach to Quantifying the Needs of Dual-Career Families," *Human Relations* 35, no. 1 (1982): 69–82; Gloria W. Bird and Gerald A. Bird, "Strategies for Reducing Role Strain Among Dual-Career Couples," *International Journal of Sociology of the Family* 16 (Spring 1986): 83–94; Margaret R. Elman and Lucia A. Gilbert, "Coping Strategies for Role Conflict in Married Professional Women with Children," *Family Relations* 33 (April 1984): 317–327; Elaine A. Anderson and Leigh A. Leslie, "Coping with Employment and Family Stress: Employment Arrangement and Gender Differences," *Sex Roles* 24. nos. 3–4 (1991): 223–237; Maureen G. Guelzow, Gloria W. Bird, and Elizabeth H. Koball, "An Exploratory Path Analysis of the Stress Process for Dual-Career Men and Women," *Journal of Marriage and the Family* 53 (February 1991): 151–164.

39.   Elman and Gilbert, "Coping Strategies for Role Conflict in Married Professional Women with Children," pp. 317–327.

40.   Hochschild, *The Time Bind*, p. 38.

41.   Audrey D. Smith and William J. Reid, "Role Expectations and Attitudes in Dual-Earner Families," *Social Casework: The Journal of Contemporary Social Work* 67, no. 7 (September 1986): 394–402; Julie Connelly, "How Dual-Income Couples Cope," *Fortune* (September 24, 1990): 129–136.

42.   See for instance J. Pleck, G. Staines, and L. Lang, "Conflicts Between Work and Family Life," *Monthly Labor Review* 103, no. 3 (March 1980): 29–32; Richard T. Kinnier, Ellen C. Katz, and Martha A. Berry, "Successful Resolutions to the Career-Versus-Family Conflict," *Journal of Counseling and Development* 69 (May–June 1991): 439–444; Kim A. Burley, "Family-Work Spillover in Dual-Career Couples: A Comparison of Two Time Perspectives," *Psychology Reports* 68 (1991): 471–489;

Christopher Alan Higgins, Linda Elizabeth Duxbury, and Richard Harold Irving, "Work-Family Conflict in the Dual-Career Family," *Organizational Behavior and Human Decision Processes* 51 (1992): 51–75.

43.   Marolyn Parker, Steven Peltier, and Patricia Wolleat, "Understanding Dual Career Couples," *Personnel and Guidance Journal* 103, no. 3 (September 1981): 14–18; Elman and Gilbert, "Coping Strategies"; Bird and Bird, "Strategies for Reducing Role Strain"; Skinner, "Dual-Career Family Stress and Coping"; Anderson and Leslie, "Coping with Employment and Family Stress."

44.   Bird and Bird, "Strategies for Reducing Role Strain," pp. 83–94.

45.   Guelzow, Bird, and Koball, "An Exploratory Path Analysis of the Stress Process for Dual-Career Men and Women," pp. 151–164.

46.   Anderson and Leslie, "Coping with Employment and Family Stress," pp. 223–237.

47.   Rosanna Hertz, *More Equal Than Others: Women and Men in Dual-Career Marriages* (Berkeley: University of California Press, 1986), p. 75.

48.   J. H. Fitchter, *Graduates of Predominantly Negro Colleges: Class of 1964*, Public Health Service Publication No. 1571 (Washington, D.C.: U.S. Government Printing Office, n.d.), quoted in Leland J. Axelson, "The Working Wife: Differences in Perception among Negro and White Males," *Journal of Marriage and the Family* 32, no. 3 (August 1970): 457.

49.   Axelson, ibid., p. 458.

50.   Elaine Crovitz and Anne Steinmann, "A Decade Later: Black-White Attitudes toward Women's Familial Role," *Psychology of Women Quarterly* 5, no. 2 (Winter 1980): 170–176.

51.   Bart Landry and Margaret Platt Jendrek, "The Employment of Wives in Middle-Class Black Families," *Journal of Marriage and the Family* 40, no. 4 (November 1978): 787–797.

52.   Nor—most emphatically—does it mean, as Blood and Wolfe asserted in *Husbands and Wives* ([Glencoe, Ill.: Free Press, 1960], p. 34), that black husbands had "unusually low power." Blood and Wolfe interpreted their findings from the perspective of the 1950s, when women's domestic role was still idealized and husbands' dominance was perceived as socially acceptable and even desirable. Rather than conclude that white wives had "unusually low power," they argued that it was black husbands who had "unusually low power." It would have been more accurate to conclude that since black wives had more power than white wives, black marriages were more egalitarian than white marriages. Indeed, Blood and Wolfe's conclusion underscores the bias of the traditional framework within which they worked, as well as their flawed methodology. See Constantina Safilios-Rothschild, "Family Sociology or Wives' Family Sociology? A Cross-Cultural Examination of Decision-Making," *Journal of Marriage and the Family* 31, no. 2 (May 1969): 290–301, for a perceptive critique of the limitations of Blood and Wolfe's data analysis.

53.   Quoted in Rosanna Hertz, *More Equal Than Others,* p. 75.

54.   Ibid., p. 75.

55   The commission issued detailed reports in 1995 and ceased to exist in March 1995.

56.   For a discussion of the structural theory of power see Dair L. Gillespie, "Who Has the Power? The Marital Struggle," *Journal of Marriage and the Family* 33, no. 3 (August 1971): 445–458.

57.   Black upper-middle-class wives were only slightly more likely to have continuous careers than lower-middle-class wives; white upper-middle-class wives were considerably less likely to maintain continuous careers than lower-middle-class wives until the mid-1980s. Among both blacks and whites, working-class wives were about half as likely to maintain continuous careers as middle-class wives in the 1990s.

58.   Letitia Anne Peplau and Susan Miller Campbell, "The Balance of Power in Dating and Marriage," pp. 121–137 in Jo Freeman, ed., *Women: A Feminist Perspective,* 4th ed. (Mountain View, Calif.: Mayfield, 1989).

CHAPTER 6. THE ECONOMIC CONTRIBUTION OF WIVES

1.   Because of peculiarities in the collection of data for the 1940 and 1950 censuses, this analysis must begin with 1960.

2.   See for instance Frank Levy, *Dollars and Dreams: The Changing American Income Distribution* (New York: Russell Sage Foundation, 1987); and Sheldon Danziger and Peter Gottschalk, *America Unequal* (New York: Russell Sage Foundation, 1995).

3.   Quoted in Lillian Rubin, *Families on the Fault Line: America's Working Class Speaks about the Family, the Economy, Race and Ethnicity* (New York: Harper Collins, 1994), p. 78.

4.   Quoted in Rosanna Hertz, *More Equal Than Others: Women and Men in Dual-Career Marriages* (Berkeley and Los Angeles: University of California Press, 1986), p. 69.

5.   Quoted in Rubin, *Families on the Fault Line,* p. 82.

6.   Quoted in Hertz, *More Equal Than Others,* pp. 93–94.

7.   Ibid., p. 97.

8.   Comparable percentages of working-class wives earned more than their husbands up to 1980, but—in a now familiar pattern—these women made no further gains in the 1980s and 1990s.

9.   Lawrence Mishel, Jared Bernstein, and John Schmitt, *The State of Working America, 1998–99* (Ithaca, N.Y.: Cornell University Press, 1999), pp. 169–172. Nevertheless, both black and white college educated women trailed their male coun-

terparts in absolute wages. In 1997 white college educated women earned an average of $16.09 an hour compared to college educated white males' average of $21.45. Black college educated women earned an average of $14.66 an hour, compared to black college educated males' $16.53 an hour. White women, while making remarkable gains, still trailed white males significantly.

10.   Quoted in Rubin, *Families on the Fault Line*, p. 74.

11.   Ibid., p. 103.

12.   Quoted in Hertz, *More Equal Than Others*, pp. 68–69.

13.   Jean L. Potuchek. *Who Supports the Family? Gender and Breadwinning in Dual-Earner Marriages* (Stanford, Calif.: Stanford University Press, 1997), pp. 118–119.

14.   John G. Richardson, "Wife Occupational Superiority and Marital Troubles: An Examination of the Hypothesis," *Journal of Marriage and the Family* 41 (February 1979): 63–72.

15.   Hertz, *More Equal Than Others*, p. 72.

16.   Ibid., p. 72.

17.   Mishel et al., *The State of Working America 1998–99*, p. 171. The declines in average wages for white, black, Latino, and Asian men were 4.1, 3.8, 6.1, and 8.8 percent, respectively.

18.   See chapter 7, note 10, for a description of this study.

CHAPTER 7. HUSBANDS AND HOUSEWORK:
A STALLED REVOLUTION?

1.   Arlie Russell Hochschild, *The Time Bind: When Work Becomes Home and Home Becomes Work* (New York: Henry Holt, 1997).

2.   John P. Robinson, *How Americans Use Time: A Social Psychological Analysis of Everyday Behavior* (New York: Praeger, 1977).

3.   The two earliest national representative data sets employed were "The Panel Study of Income Dynamics," a longitudinal study of over five thousand families conducted by the Survey Research Center at the University of Michigan, and the National Longitudinal Survey cohort file of mature American women, funded by the labor department and collected at Ohio State University.

4.   The principal methods used to obtain information on household work are direct questions answered orally or in writing and time diaries. In the case of the latter approach, individuals are asked to keep a diary of time expended on a series of activities in a given day. Marini and Shelton suggest that comparisons with information obtained from diaries indicate that answers to direct questions tend to overestimate time spent. See Margaret Mooney Marini and Beth Anne Shelton, "Measuring Household Work: Recent Experience in the United States," *Social Science Research* 22 (1993): 361–382, and John P. Robinson, "The Va-

lidity and Reliability of Diaries versus Alternative Time Use Methods," pp. 33–62 in F. Thomas Juster and Frank Stafford, eds., *Time, Goods and Well-Being* (Ann Arbor: Survey Research Center, Institute for Social Research, University of Michigan, 1985).

5.   Shelley Coverman and Joseph F. Sheley, "Change in Men's Housework and Child-Care Time, 1965–1975," *Journal of Marriage and the Family* 48 (May 1986): 413–422.

6.   Shelley Coverman, "Gender, Domestic Labor Time, and Wage Inequality," *American Sociological Review* 48 (October 1983): 623–637.

7.   Donna Hodgkins Berardo, Constance L. Shehan, and Gerald R. Leslie, "A Residue of Traditions: Jobs, Careers, and Spouses' Time in Housework," *Journal of Marriage and the Family* 49 (May 1987): 388.

8.   Shelley Coverman and Joseph F. Sheley, "Change in Men's Housework and Child-Care Time."

9.   Elizabeth Maret and Barbara Finlay, "The Distribution of Household Labor among Women in Dual-earner Families," *Journal of Marriage and the Family* 46 (May 1984): 357–364.

10.   Ibid.

11.   For chapter 6, I used the two waves of the National Survey of Families and Households (1987–1988 and 1991–1994) collected under the direction of Larry Bumpass and James Sweet at the University of Wisconsin's Center for Demography and Ecology. The first wave consisted of a national representative sample of 13,017 households. For the second wave 10,008 households from the original survey were reinterviewed. For a complete description of the first wave see James Sweet, Larry Bumpass, and Vaughn Call, "The Design and Content of the National Survey of Families and Households," NSFH Working Paper No. 1, Center for Demography and Ecology, University of Wisconsin, Madison, 1988. While researchers have used many small samples over the years to estimate the level and changes in household work performed by husbands and wives, these two surveys collected the most comprehensive and representative data to date. They therefore offer the best opportunity to estimate changes in the household roles of husbands today.

12.   That is, the survey included a larger number of blacks than their actual proportion in the population. This technique is used to yield a subsample of blacks that is large enough to allow meaningful analysis.

13.   Isik A. Aytac and Jay D. Teachman, "Occupational Sex Stratification, Marital Power, and Household Division of Labor," unpublished paper; Elizabeth Bergen, "The Multidimensional Nature of Domestic Labor: An Investigation of Husbands' Participation," paper presented at the annual meeting of the National Council of Family Relations, Seattle, Wash., November 1990; Sampson Lee Blair and Daniel T. Lichter, "Measuring the Division of Household Labor: Gender Seg-

regation of Housework among American Couples," *Journal of Family Issues* 12, no. 1 (March 1991): 91–113.

14.   Elizabeth Bergen, "The Multidimensional Nature of Domestic Labor."

15.   Blair and Lichter, "Measuring the Division of Household Labor." This study includes all 3,190 married or cohabiting couples in the sample. Both employed and unemployed wives are also included.

16.   Ibid. Another 28.9 percent of the couples were classified as moderately gender segregated.

17.   Mary Clare Lennon and Sarah Rosenfield, "Relative Fairness and the Division of Housework: The Importance of Options," *American Journal of Sociology* 100, no. 2 (September 1994): 506–531.

18.   To conform to most studies of housework using NSFH1, driving was excluded in the following calculations.

19.   See M. Fishbein and I. Ajzen, *Beliefs, Attitude, Intention, and Behavior: An Introduction to Theory and Research* (Reading: Mass.: Addison-Wesley, 1975).

20.   See Beth Anne Shelton, "The Distribution of Household Tasks: Does Wife's Employment Status Make a Difference?" *Journal of Family Issues* 11, no. 2 (June 1990): 115–135. The question is whether husbands increase their absolute hours of housework when wives are employed. Some researchers have attempted to answer this question by comparing relative hours of housework. Since employed wives reduce their hours of housework, however, absolute increases in husbands' hours are in question, not relative increases. See also J. H. Pleck, "Husbands' Paid Work and Family Roles: Current Research Issues," pp. 251–333 in H. Z. Lopata and J. H. Pleck, eds., *Research in the Interweave of Social Roles and Family Jobs* (Greenwich, Conn.: JAI Press, 1983); and David M. Almeida, Jennifer L. Maggs, and Nancy L. Galambos, "Wives' Employment Hours and Spousal Participation in Family Work," *Journal of Family Psychology* 7, no. 2 (1993): 233–244.

21.   Rubin, *Families on the Fault Line: America's Working Class Speaks about the Family, the Economy, Race and Ethnicity* (New York: Harper Collins, 1994), p. 92.

22.   Wives' employment also received greater support among black than white working-class husbands and wives. Among blacks, 77.0 percent of husbands and 86.4 percent of wives agreed that both husbands and wives should contribute to family income; among whites, 49.2 percent of husbands and 52.3 percent of wives.

23.   On this issue 49.1 and 54.3 percent of black middle-class husbands and wives, respectively, supported the mother's employment, compared with 35.8 and 44.8 percent, respectively, of white middle-class husbands and wives. The figures were lower in the working class: 40.1 and 48.3 percent of black husbands and wives, respectively, and 26.2 and 33.0 percent of white husbands and wives, respectively.

CONCLUSION: THE FUTURE OF DUAL-WORKER
FAMILIES

1.   Arlie Russell Hochschild, *The Time Bind: When Work Becomes Home and Home Becomes Work* (New York: Henry Holt, 1997).

2.   Rosalind C. Barnett and Caryl Rivers, *She Works, He Works: How Two-Income Families Are Happy, Healthy, and Thriving* (Cambridge, Mass.: Harvard University Press, 1998), p. 1.

3.   Richard Morin and Megan Rosenfeld, "With More Equity, More Sweat: Poll Shows Sexes Agree on Pros and Cons of New Roles," *Washington Post*, March 22, 1998, p. A1.

4.   Ibid.

5.   Rubin, *Families on the Fault Line*, p. 86.

6.   Morin and Rosenfeld, ibid., p. A17.

7.   Andrew J. Cherlin, "By the Numbers," *New York Times Magazine*, April 5, 1998, p. 39.

8.   Jane Smiley, "Mothers Should," *New York Times Magazine*, April 5, 1998, p. 37.

9.   Jill Zuckman, "Senate Overrides Bush on Family Leave Act," *Congressional Quarterly Weekly Report*, September 26, 1992, 50, no. 38, p. 2941.

10.   Ibid.

11.   Stephen Alfred, "An Overview of the Family and Medical Leave Act of 1993," *Public Personnel Management* 24 (Spring 1995): 67–73.

12.   Michele Cohen Marill, "Will Motherhood Cost You Your Job?" *Redbook*, May 1993, pp. 84–87.

13.   The U.S. Family and Medical Leave Act allows for the exemption by employers of the highest paid 10 percent of employees.

14.   Eileen Trzcinski and William T. Alpert, "Pregnancy and Parental Leave Benefits in the United States and Canada: Judicial Decisions and Legislation," *Journal of Human Resources* 29 (1994): 538.

15.   Ibid, pp. 538–539.

16.   Ibid., p. 540.

17.   Ibid., p. 547. Italics added.

18.   Ibid.

19.   Ibid., p. 548.

20.   See also Hillary Rodham Clinton, *It Takes a Village, and Other Lessons Children Teach Us* (New York: Simon & Schuster, 1996).

21.   Yvonne Hirdman, "State Policy and Gender Contracts: The Swedish Experience," pp. 36–46 in Eileen Drew, Ruth Emerek, and Evelyn Mahon, eds., *Women, Work and the Family in Europe* (New York: Routledge, 1998), p. 43.

22.   Jeanne Fagnani, "Recent Changes in Family Policy in France: Political Trade-

offs and Economic Constraints," pp. 58–65 in Drew, Emerek, and Mahon, *Women, Work and the Family in Europe.*

23.   Lynne M. Casper, "What Does it Cost to Mind Our Preschoolers?" Current Population Report, Washington, D.C.: Bureau of the Census, 1995.

24.   Children's Defense Fund, "Facts About Child Care in America," www.childrensdefense.org/cc_facts.html.

25.   Katherine Boo, "Most D. C. Day-Care Centers Have Expired Licenses; Safety Concerns Threaten a Linchpin of Welfare Law's Success," *Washington Post,* October 6, 1997, p. AO1. Sara Rimer, "Children of Working Poor Are Day Care's Forgotten," *New York Times,* November 25, 1997, p. A1.

26.   Gina Adams, Karen Schulman, and Nancy Ebb, *Locked Doors: States Struggling to Meet the Child Care Needs of Low-Income Working Families* (Washington, D.C.: Children's Defense Fund, 1998); Robin Epstein and Brooke Richie, "Day Carelessness," *City Limits* 22 (August 1997): 12–13.

27.   Adams, et. al, "Locked Doors."

28.   Rubin, *Families on the Fault Line,* p. 94.

29.   Ibid., p. 96.

30.   Barbara Fitzsimmons, "The One-Wage Trial Balloon," *San Diego Union-Tribune,* August 29, 1998, p. E1.

31.   Ibid.

32.   Ellen E. Kisker, *Profie of Child Care Settings: Early Education and Care in 1990,* vols. 1–2 (Washington, D.C.: U.S. Department of Education, 1991).

33.   University of Colorado, Denver, "Cost, Quality and Child Outcomes in Child Care Centers," (1995).

34.   The Families and Work Institute, "Study of Children in Family Child Care and Relative Care" (1994).

35.   Marjorie Whigham-Desir, "Business and Child Care: Corporate America is Finally Listening to its Employees' Requests to Help Solve the Day-Care Dilemma," *Black Enterprise,* December 1993, pp. 86–92.

36.   Andrew Skolnick, "Health and Safety Standards Being Developed for Child-Care Programs," *Journal of the American Medical Association* 262 (December 22, 1989).

37.   Ibid.

38.   Ibid.

39.   NCAA Legislative Updates, "The White House Conference on Child Care a Spotlight on Our Future," www.careguide.net/careguide.cgi/ncca.

40.   Diane Harris, "Big Business Takes on Child Care," *Working Woman,* June 1993, p. 50.

41.   Rana Dogar, "Corporate Relief for Desperate Parents," *Working Woman,* March 1995, pp. 15–16.

42.   "Changing the Corporate Culture to Support Work and Family Programs,"

The BNA Special Report Series on Work and Family, Special Report 42 (Washington, D.C.: Bureau of National Affairs, 1991).

43.   "Corporate Work and Family Programs for the 1990s: Five Case Studies." *The BNA Special Report Series on Work and Family,* Special Report 13 (Washington, D.C.: Bureau of National Affairs, 1989), p. 1.

44.   Ibid.

45.   Harris, "Big Business Takes on Child Care," p. 51.

46.   Sharon Nelton, "Adjusting Benefits for Family Needs," *Nation's Business,* August 1995, p. 46.

47.   Ibid., p. 52.

48.   Lynn S. Dumas, "Teaming up for Child Care," *Working Mother,* April 1994, pp. 29–36.

49.   Ibid.

50.   Ibid.

51.   Jennifer Lenhart, "Keeping an Electronic Eye on the Kids: Day-Care Cameras Let Parents View Children Via the Internet," *Washington Post,* May 29, 1998, p. A1. However, the *Post* article reports that some civil liberties groups have questioned the invasion of child-care workers' privacy that results. Other day care providers suggest that this may lull some parents into a false sense of security, and that the best way to insure quality day care is by making unannounced visits and by developing a personal relationship with the provider.

52.   Kirstin Downey Grimsley, "Baby on Board: On-the-Job Day Care, Other Specialized Benefits Replace Wage Increases," *Washington Post,* September 14, 1997, p. H1.

53.   Kirstin Downey Grimsley, "A Little Baby Powder on the Bottom Line: Corporate Child Care Can Help Boost Profits," *Washington Post,* July 17, 1998, p. F1.

54.   Grimsley, "Baby on Board."

55.   Ibid.

56.   Harris, "Big Business Takes on Child Care," p. 56.

57.   Grimsley, "A Little Baby Powder on the Bottom Line."

58.   State support for day care varies considerably in the EU with the northwestern countries, especially those in Scandanavia, being the most generous.

59.   Bruce Bower, "Infant Daycare: Nothing Beats Quality," *Science News,* August 14, 1991, p. 118.

60.   Arnlaug Leira, "The Modernisation of Motherhood," in Drew et al., *Women, Work and the Family in Europe,* p. 165.

61.   Bower, "Infant Daycare."

62.   Ibid.

63.   Ellen Galinsky and Deborah Phillips, "The Day-Care Debate," *Parents' Magazine,* November 1988, p. 112.

64.   Ibid.

65.   Fagnani, "Recent Changes in Family Policy in France."

66.   Leira, "The Modernization of Motherhood," pp. 64–65.

67.   T. R. Reid, "Norway Pays a Price for Family Values: Parents Receive Stipends to Stay Home with Children," *Washington Post,* November 1, 1998, p. A26.

68.   Mike Meyers, "Taking Pregnancy Leaves," *Star-Tribune Newspaper of the Twin Cities,* February 6, 1995, p. 1D.

69.   "Families and Employers in a Changing Economy," www.dol.gov/dol /esa/public/regs/compliance/whd/fmla/summary.htm.

70.   Two national random sample surveys of employers and employees were conducted in 1995 for the Bureau of Labor Statistics by Westat, Inc. and the Institute for Social Research, Survey Research Center, University of Michigan.

71.   Darcy Olsen, "The Advancing Nanny State: Why the Government Should Stay Out of Child Care," Cato Policy Analysis No. 285, *The Cato Institute,* October 23, 1997, www.cato.org/pubs/pas/pa-285.html.

72.   Richard Morin and Megan Rosenfeld, "Full-Time Moms Earn Respect, Poll Says," *Washington Post,* March 22, 1998.

73.   Hochschild, *Time Bind,* p. 128.

74.   Ibid., p. 129.

75.   Ibid., pp. 199–200.

76.   Nancy Folbre, "Should Corporate America Be in the Baby-Sitting Business?" *Working Woman,* February 1995, p. 16.

77.   Grimsley, "On-the-Job Day Care," p. H1.

78.   Grimsley, "On-the-Job Day Care," p. H1.

79.   Grimsley, "Baby on Board."

80.   Janet G. Hunt and Larry L. Hunt, "The Dualities of Careers and Families: New Integrations or New Polarizations?" *Social Problems* 29, no. 5 (June 1982): 499–510.

81.   Lorraine Dusky, "Mommy Tracks that Lead Somewhere Good," *Working Woman,* November 1989, pp. 132–134.

82.   Nancy Folbre, *Who Pays for the Kids? Gender and the Structures of Constraint* (London: Routledge, 1994).

83.   Michele Cohen Marill, "Will Motherhood Cost You Your Job?" *Redbook,* May 93, pp. 84–88.

84.   Grimsley, "A Little Baby Powder on the Bottom Line."

85.   Marill, "Will Motherhood Cost You Your Job?" p. 88.

APPENDIX A. STATISTICS ON FAMILY HOUSEHOLDS

1.   Because these data for the later years are taken from the annual March Current Population Survey (CPS), a national sample of only about fifty thousand

households, there is considerable sampling variability. To minimize this variability I have adopted the common practice of averaging several years together.

2.   These figures do not include single mothers or fathers living with their parents or some other family. Such family groups in which the single parents are not heads of their own households are termed "subfamilies" by the Census Bureau. In 1994, according to the census, 22.7 and 21.5 percent, respectively, of white and black female "heads" were subfamilies. See Steve Rawlings and Arlene Saluter, *Household and Family Characteristics: March 1994* (U.S. Department of Commerce, Bureau of the Census, September 1995, P20–483, table 11).

Bibliography

Ackerman, F. and Zimbalist, A. (1986). The distribution of income and wealth. In R. C. Edwards, M. Reich, and T. E. Weisskopf (eds.), *The capitalist system*, 3rd ed., Englewood Cliffs, N.J.: Prentice Hall.

Adams, G., Schulman, K., and Ebb, N. (1998). Locked doors: States struggling to meet the child care needs of low-income working families. Washington, D.C.: Children's Defense Fund.

Alfred, S. (1995). An overview of the Family and Medical Leave Act of 1993. *Public Personnel Management* 24, no. 1 (Spring): 67–73.

Almeida, D. M., Maggs, J. L., and Galambos, N. L. (1993). Wives' employment hours and spousal participation in family work. *Journal of Family Psychology* 7 (2): 233–244.

Anderson, E. A. and Leslie, L. A. (1991). Coping with employment and family stress: Employment arrangement and gender differences. *Sex Roles* 24 (3/4): 223–37.

Axelson, L. J. (1970). The working wife: Differences in perception among Negro and white males. *Journal of Marriage and the Family* 32, no. 3 (August): 457–464.

Aytac, I. A. and Teachman, J. D. (n.d.) Occupational sex stratification, marital power, and household division of labor. Unpublished paper.

Barnett, R. C. and Rivers, C. (1998). *She works, he works: How two-income families are happy, healthy, and thriving.* Cambridge, Mass.: Harvard University Press.

Baron, A. S. (1987). Working parents: Shifting traditional roles. *Business and Human Resources,* January–March, 36–37.

———. (1987). Working partners: Career-committed mothers and their husbands. *Business Horizons,* September–October, 45–50.

Basow, S. A. (1992). *Gender stereotypes and roles.* 3rd ed. Pacific Grove, Calif.: Brooks/Cole Publishing.

Bell, D. (1974). Why participation rates of black and white wives differ. *Journal of Human Resources* 9, no. 4 (Fall): 465–479.

Berardo, D. H., Shehan, C. L., and Leslie, G. R. (1987). A residue of traditions: Jobs, careers, and spouses' time in housework. *Journal of Marriage and the Family* 49 (2): 381–390.

Berg, B. (1978). *The remembered gate.* New York: Oxford University Press.

Bergen, E. (1990). The multidimensional nature of domestic labor: An investigation of husbands' participation. Paper presented at the annual meeting of the National Council of Family Relations, Seattle.

Bernard, J. (1981). The good-provider role: Its rise and fall. *American Psychologist* 36 (1): 1–15.

Billingsley, A. (1968). *Black Families in White America.* Englewood Cliffs, N.J.: Prentice-Hall.

———. (1992). *Climbing Jacob's ladder.* New York: Touchstone.

Bird, C. (1979). *The two-paycheck family.* New York: Rawson, Wade.

Bird, G. W. and Bird, G. A. (1986). Strategies for reducing role strain among dual-career couples. *International Journal of Sociology of the Family* 16 (1): 83–94.

Blair, S. L. and Lichter, D. T. (1991). Measuring the division of household labor: Gender segregation of housework among American couples. *Journal of Family Issues* 12 (1): 91–113.

Blassingame, J. W. (1973). *Black New Orleans: 1860–1880.* Chicago: University of Chicago Press.

Blau, F. D. and Ferber, M. A. (1992). *The economics of women, men, and work,* 2nd ed. Englewood Cliffs, N.J.: Prentice-Hall.

Blood, R. O., Jr., and Wolfe, D. M. (1960). *Husbands and wives: the dynamics of married living.* Glencoe, Ill.: Free Press.

Blumin, S. M. (1989). *The emergence of the middle class: Social experience in the American city, 1760–1900.* New York: Cambridge University Press.

Boo, K. (1997). Most D.C. day-care centers have expired licenses: Safety concerns threaten a linchpin of welfare law's success. *Washington Post,* October 6, p. AO1.

Bowen, W. G. and Finegan, T. A. (1969). *The economics of labor force participation.* Princeton, N.J.: Princeton University Press.

Bower, B. (1991). Infant daycare: Nothing beats quality. *Science News* 140, no. 8 (August 14): 118.

Brady, M. D. (1994). Kansas federation of colored women's clubs, 1900–1930. In N. F. Cott, *Women together: Organizational life.* History of women in the United States, vol. 16. New Providence, R.I.: K. G. Saur.

Brown, E. B. Womanist consciousness: Maggie Lena Walker and the Independent Order of St. Luke. *Journal of Women in Culture and Society* 14 (3): 610–633.

Bryson, R. B., et al. (1976). The professional pair: Husband and wife psychologists. *American Psychologist* 3, no. 1 (January): 10–16.

Bureau of National Affairs, Inc. (1989). Corporate work and family programs for the 1990s: Five case studies. *The BNA Special Report Series on Work and Family,* Special Report No. 13. Washington, D.C.: Bureau of National Affairs.

Burley, K. A. (1991). Family-work spillover in dual-career couples: A comparison of two time perspectives. *Psychology Reports* 68: 471–489.

Cain, G. C. (1966). *Married women in the labor force: An economic analysis.* Chicago: University of Chicago Press.

Caplow, T., et al. (1982). *Middletown families: Fifty years of change and continuity.* Minneapolis: University of Minnesota Press.

Carby, H. V. (1987). *Reconstructing womanhood: The emergence of the Afro-American woman novelist.* New York: Oxford University Press.

Carlson, S. J. (1992). Black ideals of womanhood in the late Victorian era. *Journal of Negro History* 77, no. 2 (Spring): 61–73.

Casper, L. M. (1995). What does it cost to mind our preschoolers? *Current Population Reports.* Washington, D.C.: U.S. Bureau of the Census, pp. 70–52.

Cherlin, A. J. (1998). By the numbers. *New York Times Magazine,* April 5, p. 39.

Children's Defense Fund. 1999. Facts about child care in America. www.childrensdefense.org/cc_facts.html.

Clark, H. H. 1968. *The law of domestic relations in the United States.* St. Paul: West.

Clinton, H. R. (1996). *It takes a village, and other lessons children teach us.* New York: Simon & Schuster.

Connelly, J. (1990). How dual-income couples cope. *Fortune,* September 24, 129–136.

Coontz, S. (1992). *The way we never were: American families and the nostalgia trap.* New York: Basic Books.

Corey, L. (1935). *The crisis of the middle class.* New York: Covici, Friede.

Cornish, E. (1989). The future of the family. In A. S. Skolnick and J. H. Skolnick, eds., *Family in transition,* 6th ed. Boston: Scott, Foresman.

Coverman, S. (1983). Gender, domestic labor time, and wage inequality. *American Sociological Review* 48 (5): 623–637.

Coverman, S. and Sheley, J. F. (1986). Change in men's housework and child-care time, 1965–1975. *Journal of Marriage and the Family* 48 (2): 413–422.

Crovitz, E. and Steinman, A. (1980). A decade later: Black-white attitudes toward women's familial role. *Psychology of Women Quarterly* 5 (2): 170–176.

Danziger, S. and Gottschalk, P. (1995). *America unequal.* New York: Russell Sage
Foundation.

de Beauvoir, S. (1957). *The second sex.* New York: Alfred A. Knopf.

Dogar, Rana. (1995). Corporate relief for desperate parents. *Working Woman*
March, 15–16.

Domhoff, G. W. (1983). *Who rules America now?: A view for the '80s.* Englewood
Cliffs, N.J.: Prentice-Hall.

Dowd, N. E. (1997). *In defense of single-parent families.* New York: New York University Press.

Dumas, L. S. (1994). Teaming up for child care. *Working Mother,* April, 29–36.

Dusky, L. (1989). Mommy tracks that lead somewhere good. *Working Woman,*
November, 132–134.

Easton, B. (1976). Industrialization and femininity: A case study of nineteenth
century New England. *Social Problems* 23 (4): 389–401.

Elman, M. R. and Gilbert, L. A. (1984). Coping strategies for role conflict in married professional women with children. *Family Relations* 33: 317–327.

Epenshade, T. J. (1991). Current population reports, population characteristics:
Marital status and living arrangements. Series P-20, 461.

Epstein, C. F. (1971). Law partners and marital partners: Strains and solutions
in the dual-career family enterprise. *Human Relations* 24 (6): 549–563.

Epstein, R. and Richie, B. (1997). Day carelessness. *City Limits* 22 (7): 12–13.

Etzioni, A. (1977). The family: Is it obsolete? *Journal of Current Social Issues* 14
(1): 4–9.

Fagnani, J. (1998). "Recent changes in family policy in France: Political trade-
offs and economic constraints." In E. Drew, R. Emerek,and E. Mahon, eds.,
Women, work and the family in Europe. New York: Routledge.

The Families and Work Institute. (1994). *Study of children in family child care and
relative care.*

Felson, M. and Knoke, D. (1974). Social status and the married woman. *Journal
of Marriage and the Family* 36 (3): 516–521.

Ferree, M. M. (1987). Family and job for working-class women: Gender and
class systems seen from below. In N. Gerstel and H. E. Gross, eds., *Families
and work.* Philadelphia: Temple University Press.

Fishbein, M. and Ajzen, I. (1975). *Beliefs, attitude, intention, and behavior: An introduction to theory and research.* Reading, Mass.: Addison-Wesley.

Fishel, L. H. and Quarles, B. (1967). *The Negro American: A documentary history.*
Glenview, Ill.: Scott, Foresman and William Morrow.

Fitchter, J. H. (n.d.). *Graduates of predominantly Negro colleges: Class of 1964,* Public Health Service Publication No. 1571. Washington, D.C.: U.S. Government
Printing Office.

Fitzsimmons, B. (1998). The one-wage trial balloon. *San Diego Union-Tribune*, August 29, p. E1.

Flexner, E. (1975). *Century of struggle: The women's rights movement in the United States*. Cambridge, Mass.: Harvard University Press.

Folbre, N. (1994). Should corporate America be in the baby-sitting business? *Working Woman*, February, p. 16.

———. (1994). *Who pays for the kids? Gender and the structures of constraint*. London: Routledge.

Forderhase, N. (1992). "Limited only by earth and sky": The Louisville Woman's Club and progressive reform, 1900–1910. In N. F. Cott, *Women together: Organizational life*. History of women in the United States, vol. 16. New Providence, R.I.: K. G. Saur.

Fowlkes, M. R. (1987). The myth of merit and male professional careers: The role of wives. In N. Gerstel and H. E. Gross, eds., *Families and work*. Philadelphia: Temple University Press.

Fox, M. F. and Hesse-Biber, S. (1984). *Women at work*. Palo Alto, Calif.: Mayfield.

Frazier, E. F. (1966). *The Negro family in the United States*. Rev. and abridged ed. Chicago: University of Chicago Press.

Freedman, E. (1994). Separatism as strategy: Female institution building and American feminism, 1870–1930. In N. F. Cott, *Women together: Organizational life*. History of women in the United States, vol. 16. New Providence, R.I.: K. G. Saur.

Friedan, B. (1963). *The feminine mystique*. New York: Dell.

Furstenberg, F. F., Jr., Hershberg, T., and Modell, J. (1975). The origin of the female-headed black family: The impact of the urban experience. *Journal of Interdisciplinary History* 6: 211–233.

Gaines, K. K. (1996). *Uplifting the race: Black leadership, politics, and culture in the twentieth century*. Chapel Hill: University of North Carolina Press.

Galinsky, E. and Phillips, D. (1988). The day-care debate. *Parents' Magazine* November, p. 112.

Giddings, P. (1985). *When and where I enter: The impact of black women on race and sex in America*. New York: Bantam Books.

Gillespie, D. L. (1971). Who has the power? The marital struggle. *Journal of Marriage and the Family* 33: 445–458.

Glenn, E. N. and Feldberg, R. L. (1989). Clerical work: The female occupation. In J. Freeman, ed., *Women: A feminist perspective*. 4th ed. Mountain View, Calif.: Mayfield.

Goldin, C. D. (1977). Female labor force participation: The origin of black and white differences, 1870 and 1980. *Journal of Economic History* 37, no. 1 (March): 109–112.

Goode, W. (1963). *World revolution and family patterns*. New York: Free Press.

Gordon, L. (1991). Black and white visions of welfare: Women's welfare activism, 1890–1945. *Journal of American History* 78: 559–590.

Grimsley, K. D. (1997). Baby on board: On-the-job day care, other specialized benefits replace wage increases. *Washington Post,* September 14, H1.

———. (1998). A little baby powder on the bottom line: Corporate child care can help boost profits. *Washington Post,* July 17, F1.

Guelzow, M. G., Bird, G. W., and Koball, E. H. (1991). An exploratory path analysis of the stress process for dual-career men and women. *Journal of Marriage and the Family* 53 (1): 151–64.

Gutman, H. G. (1976). *The black family in slavery and freedom, 1750–1925.* New York: Random House.

———. (1978). Persistent myths about the Afro-American family. In M. Gordon, ed. *The American family in social-historical perspective.* New York: St. Martin's Press.

Hall, F. S. and Hall, D. T. (1979). *The two-career couple.* Reading, Mass.: Addison-Wesley.

Hareven, T. K. (1982). *Family time and industrial time: The relationship between the family and work in a New England industrial community.* New York: Cambridge University Press.

———. (1989). American families in transition: Historical perspectives on change. In A. S. Skolnick and J. Skolnick, eds., *Family in transition,* 6th ed. Boston: Scott, Foresman.

Harley, S. (1983). Black women in a southern city: Washington, DC, 1880–1920. In J. F. Hawks and S. L. Skemp, eds., *Sex, race, and the role of women in the South.* Jackson: University Press of Mississippi.

Harris, B. J. (1978). *Beyond her sphere: Women and the professions in American history.* Westport, Conn.: Greenwood Press.

Harris, D. (1993). Big business takes on child care. *Working Woman,* June, p. 50.

Henri, F. (1976). *Black migration: Movement north, 1900–1920.* New York: Doubleday.

Herskovits, M. J. (1958). *Myth of the Negro past.* Gloucester, Mass.: P. Smith.

Hertz, R. (1986). *More equal than others: Women and men in dual-career marriages.* Berkeley: University of California Press.

———. (1991). Dual-career couples and the American dream: Self-sufficiency and achievement. *Journal of Comparative Family Studies* 22 (2): 247–263.

Higginbotham, E. B. (1993). *Righteous discontent: The women's movement in the Black Baptist church, 1880–1920.* Cambridge, Mass.: Harvard University Press.

Higgins, C. A., Duxbury, L. E., and Irving, R. H. (1992). Work-family conflict in the dual-career family. *Organizational Behavior and Human Decision Processes* 51: 51–75.

Hill, R. (1971). *Strengths of black families*. New York: Emerson Hall.

———. (1997). *The strengths of African American families: Twenty-five years later.* Washington, D.C.: R & B Publishers.

Hiller, D. V. and Dyehouse, J. (1987). A case for banishing "dual-career marriages" from the research literature. *Journal of Marriage and the Family* 49 (4): 787–796.

Hine, D. C. (1994). *Hine sight: Black women and the re-construction of American history.* Brooklyn: Carlson Publishing.

Hirdman, Y. (1998). "State policy and gender contracts: The Swedish experience." In E. Drew, R. Emerek,and E. Mahon, eds., *Women, work and the family in Europe.* New York: Routledge.

Hochschild, A. R. (1997). *The time bind: When work becomes home and home becomes work.* New York: Henry Holt.

Holmstrom, L. L. (1972). *The two-career family.* Cambridge, Mass.: Schenkman.

Hunt, J. G. and L. L. Hunt. (1982). The dualities of careers and families: New integrations or new polarizations? *Social Problems* 29: 499–510.

Hunt, M. (1984). The future of marriage. In John F. Crosby, ed., *Reply to myth: Perspectives on intimacy.* New York: John Wiley.

Jacobs, H. (1911). *Incidents in the life of a slave girl.* In L. B. Child, ed. Paperback reprint. New York: Harcourt Brace Jovanovich, paperback reprint.

Jones, J. (1985). *Labor of love, labor of sorrow: Black women, work and the family, from slavery to the present.* New York: Vintage Books.

Katzman, D. M. (1973). *Before the ghetto: Black Detroit in the nineteenth century.* Urbana: University of Illinois Press.

Keller, S. (1983). Does the family have a future? In Skolnick, A. S. and Skolnick, J. H., eds., *Family in transition*, 4th ed. Boston: Scott, Foresman.

Kessler-Harris, A. (1973). Stratifying by sex: Understanding the history of working women. In R. C. Edwards et al., eds., *Labor market segmentation.* Lexington, Mass.: D. C. Heath.

Kinnier, R. T., Katz, E. C., and Berry, M. A. (1991). Successful resolutions to the career-versus-family conflict. *Journal of Counseling and Development* 69: 439–444.

Kisker, E. E. *Profile of child care settings: Early education and care in 1990.* Vols 1–2. Washington, D.C.: U.S. Department of Education.

Kleinberg, S. J. (1989). *The shadow of the mills: Working-class families in Pittsburgh, 1870–1907.* Pittsburgh: University of Pittsburgh Press.

Krasnow, I. (1999). It's time to end the "mommy wars." *Washington Post,* May 7, p. C5.

Kuhn, T. S. (1962). *The structure of scientific revolutions.* Chicago: University of Chicago Press.

Kusmer, K. L. (1976). *A ghetto takes shape: Black Cleveland, 1870–1930.* Urbana: University of Illinois Press.

Lammermeier, P. J. (1973). The urban black family of the nineteenth century: A study of black family structure in the Ohio Valley, 1850–1880. *Journal of Marriage and the Family* 35, no. 3 (August): 440–456.

Landry, B. (1987). *The new black middle class.* Berkeley: University of California Press.

Landry, B. and Jendrek, M. P. (1978). The employment of wives in middle-class black families. *Journal of Marriage and the Family* 40 (4): 787–798.

Leira, A. (1998). The modernisation of motherhood. In E. Drew, R. Emerek, and E. Mahon, eds., *Women, work and the family in Europe.* New York: Routledge.

Lenhart, J. (1998). Keeping an electronic eye on the kids: Day-care cameras let parents view children via the internet. *Washington Post,* May 29, p. A01.

Lennon, M. C. and Rosenfield, S. (1994). Relative fairness and the division of housework: The importance of options. *American Journal of Sociology* 100 (2): 506–531.

Lerner, G. (1974). Early community work of black club women. *Journal of Negro History,* 59 (2): 161.

Levy, F. (1987). *Dollars and dreams: The changing American income distribution.* New York: Russell Sage Foundation.

Maret, E. and Finlay, B. (1984). The distribution of household labor among women in dual-earner families. *Journal of Marriage and the Family* 46, no. 2 (May): 357–364.

Marill, M. C. (1993). "Will motherhood cost you your job?" *Redbook,* May, 84–88.

Marini, M. M. and Shelton, B. A. (1993). Measuring household work: Recent experience in the United States. *Social Science Research* 22 (4): 361–382.

Martin, T. P. (1987). The sound of our own voices: Women's study clubs, 1860–1910. Boston: Beacon Press.

May, M. (1987). The historical problem of the family wage: The Ford Motor Company and the five dollar day. In Gerstel, N. and Gross, H. E., eds., *Families and work.* Philadelphia: Temple University Press.

McAdoo, H. (1997). *Black families.* Thousand Oaks, Calif.: Sage.

McDaniel, A. (1990). The power of culture: A review of the idea of Africa's influence on family structure in antebellum America. *Journal of Family History* 15, (2): 225–238.

———. (1994). Historical racial differences in living arrangements of children. *Journal of Family History,* 19 (1): 57–77.

Meyers, M. (n.d.). Families and employers in a changing economy. www.dol. gov/dol/esa/ public/regs/compliance/whd/fmla/summary.htm.

———. (1995). Taking pregnancy leaves. *Star-Tribune Newspaper of the Twin Cities*, February 6, p. 1D.

Mills, C. W. (1951). *White collar: The American middle classes.* New York: Oxford University Press.

Mishel, L., Bernstein, J., and Schmitt, J. (1999). *The state of working America, 1998–1999.* Ithaca: Cornell University Press.

Morgan, S. P., et al. (1993). Racial differences in household and family structure at the turn of the century. *American Journal of Sociology* 98 (4): 799.

Morin, R. and Rosenfeld, M. (1998). Full-time moms earn respect, poll says. *Washington Post*, March 22, p. A16.

———. (1998). With more equity, more sweat: Poll shows sexes agree on pros and cons of new roles. *Washington Post*, March 22, Section A, p. A16.

Moynihan, D. P., et al. (1965). *The Negro family: The case for national action.* Washington, D.C.: Office of Policy Planning and Research, U.S. Department of Labor.

NCAA Legislative Updates. (199x). "The White House Conference on Child Care: A spotlight on our future." www.careguide.net/careguide.cgi/ncca.

Nelton, S. (1995). Adjusting benefits for family needs. *Nation's Business* 83, no. 8 (August): 27.

Neverdon-Morton, C. (1982). Self-help programs as educative activities of black women in the south, 1985–1925: Focus on four key areas. *Journal of Negro Education*, 51 (3): 207–221.

Nilson, L. B. (1976). "The social standing of a married woman," *Social Problems* 23 (5): 581–592.

Oakes, J. (1985). *Keeping track: How schools structure inequality.* New Haven: Yale University Press.

Olsen, D. (1997). The advancing nanny state: Why the government should stay out of child care. Cato Policy Analysis No. 285. *The Cato Institute.* October 23. www.cato.org/pubs/pas/pa-285.html.

Pagnini, D. L. and Morgan, S. P. (1996). Racial differences in marriage and child-bearing: Oral history evidence from the South in the early twentieth century. *American Journal of Sociology* 101 (6): 1,694.

Painter, N. (1996). *Sojourner Truth: A life, a symbol.* New York: W. W. Norton.

Papanek, H. (1973). Men, women, and work: Reflections on the two-person career. *American Journal of Sociology* 78: 852–871.

Parker, M., Peltier, S., and Wolleat, P. (1981). Understanding dual career couples. *Personnel and Guidance Journal* 60, no. 1 (September): 14–18.

Pendleton, B. F., Poloma, M. M., and Garland, T. N. (1982). An approach to quantifying the needs of dual-career families. *Human Relations* 35 (1): 69–82.

Peplau, L. A. and Campbell, S. M. (1989). The balance of power in dating and marriage. In J. Freeman, ed., *Women: A feminist perspective,* 4th ed. Mountain View, Calif.: Mayfield.

Pleck, E. H. (1978). A mother's wages: Income earning among married Italian and black women, 1896–1911. In Michael Gordon, ed., *The American family in social-historical perspective,* 2nd ed. New York: St. Martin's Press.

Pleck, J., Staines, G., and Lang, L. (1980). Conflicts between work and family life. *Monthly Labor Review,* March, 129–136.

Pleck, J. H. (1983). Husbands' paid work and family roles: Current research issues. In H. Z. Lopata and J. H. Pleck, eds., *Research in the interweave of social roles and family jobs.* Greenwich, Conn.: JAI Press.

Poloma, M. M. and Garland, T. N. (1971). The married professional woman: A study in the tolerance of domestication. *Journal of Marriage and the Family* 33: 531–540.

Porter, G. (1992). *The rise of big business, 1860–1920.* Wheeling, Ill.: Harlan, Davidson.

Potuchek, J. L. (1997). *Who supports the family? Gender and breadwinning in dual-earner marriages.* Stanford, Calif.: Stanford University Press.

Preston, S. H., Lim, S., and Morgan, S. P. African-American marriage in 1910: Beneath the surface of census data. *Demography* 29, no. 1 (February): 1–15.

Quarles, B. (1969). *The Negro in the making of America.* New York: Macmillan.

Rapoport, R. N. and Rapoport, R. (1971). *Dual-career families.* Harmondsworth, Middlesex, England: Penguin.

———. (1971). Further considerations on the dual career family. *Human Relations,* 24: 519–533.

Rawlings, S. and Saluter, A. (1995). *Household and family characteristics: March 1994.* U.S. Department of Commerce, Bureau of the Census, September, P20–483.

Reich, M. (1986). The proletarianization of the labor force. In R. C. Edwards, M. Reich, and T. E. Weisskopf, eds, *The capitalist system.* 3rd ed. Englewood Cliffs, N.J.: Prentice-Hall.

Reich, R. B. (1991). The work of nations: Preparing ourselves for the twenty-first century capitalism. New York: Random House.

Reid, T. R. (1998). Norway pays a price for family values: Parents receive stipends to stay home with children. *Washington Post,* November 1, A26.

Richardson, J. G. (1979). Wife occupational superiority and marital troubles: An examination of the hypothesis. *Journal of Marriage and the Family* 41, no. 1 (February): 63–72.

Riegel, R. E. (1968). *American feminists.* Lawrence: University Press of Kansas.

Rimer, S. (1997). "Children of working poor are day care's forgotten." *New York Times,* November 25, A1.

Robinson, J. P. (1977). *How Americans use time: A social psychological analysis of everyday behavior.* New York: Praeger.

———. (1985). The validity and reliability of diaries versus alternative time use methods. In F. T. Juster and F. Stafford, eds., *Time, goods and well-being.* Ann Arbor: Survey Research Center, Institute for Social Research, University of Michigan.

Rousmaniere, J. P. (1970). Cultural hybrid in the slums: The college woman and the settlement house, 1889–1984. *American Quarterly* 22 (1): 45–66.

Rubin, L. B. (1994). *Families on the fault line: America's working class speaks about the family, the economy, race and ethnicity.* New York: Harper Collins.

Ruggles, S. (1994). The origins of African-American family structure. *American Sociological Review* 59, no. 1 (February): 136.

Ryan, M. P. (1975). *Womanhood in America: From colonial times to the present.* New York: New Viewpoints.

———. (1981). *Cradle of the middle class: The family in Oneida County, New York, 1790–1865.* New York: Cambridge University Press.

Safilios-Rothschild, C. (1969). Family sociology or wives' family sociology? A cross-cultural examination of decision-making. *Journal of Marriage and the Family* 31 (2): 290–301.

Scanzoni, J. H. (1971). *The black family in modern society: Patterns of stability and security.* Chicago: University of Chicago Press.

Schwartz, M. A. and Scott, B. M. (1994). *Marriage and families: Diversity and change.* Englewood Cliffs, N.J.: Prentice-Hall.

Sekaran, U. (1982). An investigation of the career salience of men and women in dual-career families. *Journal of Vocational Behavior* 20: 111–119.

———. (1983). How husbands and wives in dual-career families perceive their family and work worlds. *Journal of Vocational Behavior* 22: 288–302.

Shaw, S. J. (1996). *What a woman ought to be and to do: Black professional women workers during the Jim Crow era.* Chicago: University of Chicago Press.

Shelton, B. A. (1990). The distribution of household tasks: Does wife's employment status make a difference? *Journal of Family Issues* 11 (2): 115–135.

Skinner, D. A. (1980). Dual-career family stress and coping: A literature review. *Family Relations* 29 (October): 473–481.

Skolnick, A. (1989). "Health and safety standards being developed for child-care programs." *Journal of the American Medical Association,* Dec. 22, 262 (24).

Smiley, J. (1998). "Mothers should." *New York Times Magazine,* April 5, p. 37.

Smith, A. W. and Reid, W. J. (1986). Role expectations and attitudes in dual-earner families. *Social Casework: The Journal of Contemporary Social Work* 67 (7): 394–402.

Spear, A. H. (1967). *Black Chicago: The making of a Negro ghetto, 1890–1920.* Chicago: University of Chicago Press.

St. John-Parsons, D. (1978). Continuous dual-career families: A case study. *Psychology of Women Quarterly* 3 (1): 30–42.

Staples, R. (1991). *The black family: Essays and studies.* Belmont, Calif.: Wadsworth.

Steinberg, S. (1981). *The ethnic myth: Race, ethnicity, and class in America.* Boston: Beacon Press.

———. (1989). *The ethnic myth: Race, ethnicity, and class in America.* 2nd ed. Boston: Beacon Press.

Sterling, D. (1980). Terrell, Mary Eliza Church. In B. Sicherman et al., eds., *Notable American women: The modern period.* Cambridge, Mass.: Harvard University Press.

Stetson, E. (1983). Black feminism in Indiana, 1893–1933. *Phylon* 44 (4): 292–298.

Sussman, M. B. (1985). The Family Today. In L. Cargan, ed., *Marriage and family: Coping with change.* Belmont, Calif.: Wadsworth.

Sutherland, D. E. (1989). *The expansion of everyday life, 1860–1876.* New York: Harper and Row.

Sweet, J., Bumpass, L., and Call, V. (1988). The design and content of the national survey of families. NSFH Working Paper No. 1. Center for Demography and Ecology, University of Wisconsin, Madison.

Terborg-Penn, R. (1983). Discontented black feminists: Prelude and postscript to the passage of the nineteenth amendment. In L. Scharf and J. M. Jensen, eds., *Decades of discontent: The woman's movement, 1920–1940.* Westport, Conn.: Greenwood Press.

———. (1998). *American women in the struggle for the vote, 1850–1920.* Bloomington: Indiana University Press.

Tilly, L. A., Scott, J. W., and Cohen, M. (1978). Women's work and European fertility patterns. In M. Gordon, ed., *The American family in socio-historical perspective.* 2nd ed. New York: St. Martin's Press.

Trzcinski, E. and Alpert, W. T. (1994). Pregnancy and parental leave benefits in the United States and Canada: Judicial decisions and legislation. *Journal of Human Resources* 29 (Spring): 535–554.

U.S. Bureau of the Census. (1992). *Current population reports.* Series P-20, nos. 461 and 467.

University of Colorado, Denver. (1995). *Cost, quality and child outcomes in child care centers.*

Vobejda, B. (1998). Unwed pairs make up 4 million households: Number has grown eightfold since 1970, *Washington Post,* July 27, p. A10–11.

Weiner, L. Y. (1985). *From working girl to working mother: The female labor force in the United States, 1820–1890.* Chapel Hill: University of North Carolina Press.

Weitzman, L. J. and Dixon, R. B. (1986). The transformation of legal marriage through no-fault divorce. In A. S. Skolnick and J. H. Skolnick, eds., *Family in transition,* 5th ed. Boston: Little Brown.

Welter, B. (1966). The cult of true womanhood, 1820–1860. *American Quarterly* 18, no. 2 (Summer): 151–174.

Whigham-Desir, M. (1993). Business and child care: Corporate America is finally listening to its employees' requests to help solve the day-care dilemma. *Black Enterprise* 24, no. 5 (December): 86–92.

White, D. G. (1999). *Too heavy a load: Black women in defense of themselves, 1894–1994.* New York: W. W. Norton.

Willie, C. V. (1981). *A new look at black families,* 2nd ed. Bayside, N.Y.: General Halls.

Zuckman, J. (1992). "Senate overrides Bush on family leave act." *Congressional Quarterly Weekly Report,* September 26, 50 (38): p. 2,941.

Index

Abbott, Grace, 66
accounts, individual and joint, 142
activism, 61, 67, 69, 72
Adams, Jane, 66
Afro-American Council, 71
Alcott, William, 22
Alten Brooks, Allen and Dixon et al. v. Canada Safeway Ltd., 170
Amerco, 114, 115, 164, 188
American Academy of Pediatrics (AAP), 175
American Public Health Association (APHA), 175
American Women Suffrage Association, 65
Americanization, 28, 29, 51, 52
anti-slavery societies, 25, 61

Barnett, Rosalind C., 164
Baron, Alma S., 129
Basow, Susan, 100
Bernard, Jessie, 21
Bethune, Mary McLeod, 75
Bird, Gerald, 130
Bird, Gloria, 130
black families, xii, 1, 12, 15–17, 31, 32–54, 73, 80, 83, 85, 86, 95, 117, 132, 135, 140, 154,

156, 159, 162; post-emancipation, 32, 36–40; in slavery, 33–36; two-parent, 7–9, 38; working-class, 46–48
black males, 33, 35, 47–48, 50, 52, 77, 131–132; support for black women's activism, 71–72
black wives: employment of, 30, 45; employment of as catalyst for family change, 5; as pioneers of family change, 6; upper-middle-class wives, pioneers of the American family revolution, 6, 17, 90–91; working-class, 48–55, 53–55
black womanhood, 31, 57, 74, 75, 80; combining public and private spheres, 57, 70–75; as competing ideology, 80; definition of, 75–79; and threefold commitment, 75–76
black women: activism, 61, 69, 72; and equal rights for women, 61; expansion of roles beyond domestic sphere, 71; participation in anti-slavery societies, 61; rejection of the cult of domesticity, 74; and rejection of public/private dichotomy, 70; sexual exploitation following emancipation, 37–40, 57, 58, 59; and social service, 62–63
Blackwell, Antoinette Brown, 66

255

Text:	10/14 Palatino
Display:	Snell Roundhand Script and Bauer Bodoni
Composition:	G&S Typesetters
Printing and binding:	Sheridan Books